GOD
CREATION
HISTORY
&FAITH

*A personal journey through
the history of religious belief*

PETER J A HEYDEN

GOD

CREATION

HISTORY

&FAITH

*A personal journey through
the history of religious belief*

MEMOIRS

Cirencester

Published by Memoirs

MEMOIRS
PUBLISHING

25 Market Place, Cirencester, Gloucestershire, GL7 2NX
info@memoirsbooks.co.uk www.memoirspublishing.com

Copyright ©Peter J A Heyden, October 2012

First published in England, October 2012

Book jacket design Ray Lipscombe

ISBN 978-1-909304-41-3

Printed in England

CONTENTS

INTRODUCTION

INTRODUCTION

As a young boy I became aware of the existence of God through my parents and my schooling. I was christened in the Church of England and was confirmed at the age of 14. I went to a church youth club and became a server at the eight o'clock communion service. I occasionally went to evening service with my father and grandmother. Interestingly, both my father and grandmother were baptised and confirmed after my confirmation.

In my mid twenties I got married and started a family. I still went to church about once a month with the family, but it was more a case of feeling I should go than wanting to go.

In 1968 my marriage faltered. My wife and I separated and I was left with a young family. My parents, both in their mid sixties, came to live with me to help look after my children. About 18 months later my mother was diagnosed with cancer and died within a short period of time.

At this time whatever faith I had was tested most severely, and I often sought God's help. Fortunately for me and my family most of my prayers were answered, and once the divorce was finalised and custody was settled, life took on new dimensions. In the latter part of my divorce proceedings I had met my second wife to be, and although this was a very happy period my relationship with my God suffered again. I could not come to terms with the fact that my second marriage could not take place in my church, such were the rules then of the Church of England. As an innocent party in the divorce I could not see the logic of this. This tended to isolate me somewhat from the Church, but not from my belief in God.

Fortunately it did not affect my second marriage, which has prospered now for over forty years and is still going strong. However it did start me thinking about the Church and religion in general, and I started to read the occasional book on the various origins and aspects of religion and Freemasonry. I had been a

Freemason for about five years. It was a great help, and taught me to accept people of all races and creeds, and that brotherly love has no bounds; in fact brotherly love, relief and truth are the principles on which the order was founded.

Since the end of the Second World War many archaeological finds have been made and much has been learned, particularly from the Dead Sea Scrolls and the Nag Hammadi texts. Many early documents have come to light which were buried to avoid the destruction of all kinds of early religious beliefs and practices ordered by the 'orthodox' Church. As a result a host of scholars, archaeologists, theologians and fiction writers have since written hundreds of books on the subject matter, which had been hidden for nearly 1800 years.

OVER THE PAST TEN YEARS I HAVE READ OVER TWO HUNDRED BOOKS, PAMPHLETS AND PAGES FROM NUMEROUS WEBSITES. I HAVE READ THEM ALL WITH INTEREST, BUT MORE IMPORTANTLY WITH AN OPEN MIND, WHATEVER THE PERSUASION OF THE WRITER AND WHATEVER ANGLE OR MESSAGE THEY HAVE BEEN TRYING TO CONVEY.

This book has been put together by amalgamating many of the thoughts, ideas and claims written in these books, interspersed with my own thoughts and ideas. The aim is to provide for me, and I stress for ME, an explanation of what may have happened historically, and how that has affected my thinking. We do not have sufficient information to state categorically what did happen most of the time, but I have tried to sort out from my own study of the literature what is feasible, or to be precise, what may possibly have happened. It is not meant to be cast in stone; it is for my own satisfaction to try to gauge the course of the history of creation and religion through to the establishment of the early Christian Church, and of course in so doing studying other religions as well.

At this point it is probably wise to put into words my definition of Christian.

From my earliest recollections, living a good Christian life was what I was brought up and expected to do and it entailed three main principles – love your neighbour, be kind and charitable to all people and always tell the truth. For me this was my first conception of being a Christian, and I understood that if I fulfilled these principles I could call myself one. To me now it is no coincidence that these are the principles of Freemasonry as well.

One thing is certain: you will not agree with all of my observations and thoughts or with some of the quotations I have taken from other sources. Indeed you may not agree with any of it, but please remember that I am not doing this for you to convince or convert you to my way of thinking, I am doing it for my own peace of mind and satisfaction. This is the problem with having an enquiring mind.

In the following pages I have set out a sortie into history, an attempt to explain to myself certain beliefs, certain events, certain teachings and certain thoughts which have formed part of the history and development of mankind. This is a kind of framework of possibility, which I hope you will find interesting. I have found it challenging, but then it is my quest and so it should have been.

What quickly became apparent in my study was just how many learned people through the ages had tried to find out for themselves exactly what I have been trying to find out, and how they have carried out exhaustive research to try to prove their belief from whatever angle they have approached the subject from.

My study of the history of religion has revealed that human beings are spiritual animals. Indeed, there is a case for arguing that Homo sapiens is also Homo religiosus. Men and women started to worship gods as soon as they became recognisably human; they created religions at the same time as they created works of art. This was not simply because they wanted to propitiate powerful forces. These early faiths expressed the wonder and mystery that seems always to have been an essential component of the human experience of this beautiful world. Like art, religion has been an attempt to find meaning and value in life, despite the suffering that flesh is heir to. Like any other human activity, religion can be abused, but it seems to have been something that we have always practised, some spark within us that can be ignited when we consider with awe and wonder the natural beauty of our planet.

The first books I read which started me thinking were Who Moved the Stone, by Frank Morrison and Jonathan Livingstone Seagull, by J S Bach. Both these books set me thinking. They started my real quest to try to discover why I believed in God.

My thanks go to all the authors whose books I have read, which you will find listed at the end. I have unashamedly used transcripts from many of them and in many cases adjusted some of their ideas and thoughts to add to my own.

Finally I owe a debt of gratitude to certain members of the clergy of the Church of England who helped me on my way and encouraged me to complete the project. I thank one in particular whose theological knowledge, enthusiasm, help and support has ensured that the quest has been completed.

Last and not least, my thanks go to my dear wife, who has put up with many rantings and ravings, typed numerous drafts and amendments and been a constant source of encouragement.

All the quotations from the Bible are taken from the Peshitta Bible translated from the Aramaic, except where specially mentioned, as this, for me, is the closest translation to the meaning of the original language used at the time much of it was originally written.

CHAPTER 1

※

Origins

It seems logical to begin my serious quest by looking at arguments against Jesus and Christianity, to consider the evidence as to why some scholars are convinced He never existed and that Christianity is an amalgam of old Pagan stories which used a mythical man to propagate a new cult within the Roman Empire, inflicted on humanity by force and oppression.

My starting point was a book called *The Christ Conspiracy, the Greatest Story Ever Sold*, by one Acharya S, a female author. One of the reviews of the book reads as follows:

'In this highly explosive book archaeologist, historian, mythologist and linguist Acharya S marshals an enormous amount of startling evidence to demonstrate that Christianity and the story of Jesus Christ were created by members of various secret societies, mystery schools and religions in order to unify the Roman Empire under one State Religion. In making such a fabrication this multinational cabal drew upon a multitude of myths and rituals that already existed long before the Christian Era and reworded them for centuries into the story and religion passed down today.'

This one review encapsulates all the doubts in one's mind. All the contradictions, all the historical mistakes, all the invented material in the Bible, all the false claims made over the years by

1

the Church in order to convince its 'believers' that they are not listening to an enclave of men bent on protecting their own position but to the voice of God.

The book itself is packed full of information, providing a detailed synopsis of many other books written by authors who have conducted much research into disproving the Christian belief from one angle or another. Some of the challenges it poses are undoubtedly correct, being based on fact or alternatively on information now available to disprove what has been accepted in the Bible and publicised by the Church as fact; quite simply because the Pope said so, it must be fact.

Where does this lead me? Well one thing is certain: it has led me to consider my quest even more thoroughly to try to sort the wheat from the chaff in my own mind, once and for all to put my mind at rest and provide me with some sort of acceptable path to follow, to find some sort of core belief or maybe non-belief. More important, the final product must be possible. In other words, whatever the conclusion reached from the path I have taken must satisfy my mind as being possible, feasible and above all acceptable as such to me.

SO WHERE DO WE START?

Scientists tell us that the Earth and the Universe were created from a 'big bang' and that the conditions on our planet that permit life come from that big bang and the combination of the elements that came together to form the Earth and the universe.

Mankind, as it has developed on our planet, has gradually become aware of the significance of the cosmos. In the scientific view of the universe, matter comes before the mind; mind is, if you like, an accident of matter, extraneous to matter. On the contrary, if one believes in a mind-before-matter universe the connection between mind and matter is a living thing. Everything in the universe is alive and to some degree conscious. In the mind-before-matter universe, not only was matter created by a supreme being, ie God, but it was created to provide conditions in which the human mind would be possible and would function and develop.

In this situation, as an idealist, you believe that the universe was created by an intelligence (ie a cosmic mind) for human minds.

The places of the sun, the moon, the planets and the stars are arranged in such a way that they affect our consciousness. Throughout mankind's history they have been an influence in our development, and especially of the mind.

What then tells more about the reality of being human? Is it the scientific approach or the esoteric one, encoded and developed and transferred in the ancient myths through generations? These stories preserve a memory of the experiences that transformed the human psyche over thousands of years.

The ancients believed that every single thing that happens on Earth was guided by the motions of the stars and the planets and controlled by gods. In their minds, mountains were the pedestals from which the gods viewed the handiwork of their creation. Occasionally these gods would descend from their lofty thrones to communicate with their human creations. These communications manifested themselves in various forms - fire and earthquake, thunder and lightning, wind and storm. The gods spoke with these thunderous voices that shook the earth, and were the essence of nature.

Sources and development of civilization, with the beginnings of religion as we know it

The major cultural advances in development of mankind discovered through archaeology

YEARS AGO	DEVELOPMENT
c 2,500,000	Use of small flints
c 1,700,000	Use of stone tools, 12 main types so far found
c 700,000	Use of fire
c 250,000	More advanced stone tools, 6 main types found
c 100,000	Ritual burials
c 40,000	Complex tools - ivory animal figurines, drilled necklace beads - musical instruments
c 28,000	Venus figurines - pottery
c 21,000	Cave painting
c 16,500	Advanced cave art - geometric patterns
c 11,000	Agriculture–stone buildings urbanisation - protowriting
c 6,000	City states
c 5,000	Pictographic writing

Many archaeologists and catastrophists now believe that a huge catastrophe occurred on our planet around 11,500 years ago, probably caused by the impact of a comet or asteroid in the ocean off the Carolina Coast in NW America, sending huge tsunami waves around the world causing wholesale destruction and chaos. It would seem that mountain-inhabiting peoples survived and in the 6th and 5th millennia BC they began to migrate to the lower lands.

AS IT WAS IN THE BEGINNING - THE CREATION STORY

Most traditional cultures of the world honour their stories of the creation of the Earth and mankind through myth, story-telling and ritual oration. The early people kept the creation stories alive in their hearts for a long time and without the need or ability to write them down as 'hidden' tribes and peoples do in underdeveloped areas to this very day. The stories are told by ritual play-acting combining poetry, gesture, movement and chant. As the first accounts were written they only included the bare essentials of the story, as it was still being orally developed and expanded.

The Hebrew language of Genesis lends itself to multiple translations and interpretations in much the same way, and allows the people to openly discuss meanings and interpretations among themselves. There is a psychological power in reciting, singing, reading poetry and chanting together in a group which is not found in individual renderings.

The earliest peoples in the Middle East laid great emphasis on their creation stories. Every story from the Epic of Gilgamesh to the many different stories of the Egyptian gods and goddesses either contained or assumed a particular version of the origin of life. Without knowing how things began one could not know where one was in the very moment, or might be in the future.

Nowadays in the modern western world, scientists have reopened the mysteries of our origins by admitting that they actually do not know (despite the Big Bang Theory) what happened in the first instant in the creation of the universe. If there was a big bang, what preceded it?

Much of what the earliest cultures preserved as myth or mysticism was simply their intuition or vision of the way things actually were. Their visions guided their lives and gave them a sense of awe and reverence for their environment, which included the farthest reach of the stars and the sky that they could see.

In the Middle East the ancient people told, chanted and enacted creation stories in the form of rituals at important moments in their lives and those of the community; for instance the birth of a child, the beginning of a new agricultural year and so on. The creation story was as important as it was ongoing. The birth of the cosmos ('the world or universe as an orderly or systematic whole as opposed to chaos'-Chambers' Dictionary) was continually before them. They did not consider the creation of the cosmos or the first human being as objective historical facts. The idea of an objective history outside of 'sacred time' had not yet arisen. The creation stories simply reaffirmed ongoing living realities and beliefs.

The phrase 'in the beginning' in Hebrew reminded people that at one sacred moment, which included now, creation is happening.

According to Jewish tradition the prophet Moses, the liberator of the Jewish people from Egypt, received the Genesis creation stories, as well as the whole Torah, direct from God. God also gave Moses the mysteries of creation as a spiritual practice and alchemy. Another Jewish mystical tradition relates that the knowledge of how to recreate creation was given to Abraham and then passed on by oral tradition.

Nowadays Jewish scholars have widely-differing views on the sources of the tradition incorporating the Garden of Eden theory and creation from a watery chaos. Some place it as late as the tenth century BC, during the United Kingdom of David and Solomon, while others go back to 6000 years or more BC. The various strands handed down through Genesis and Proverbs point to much earlier oral traditions.

The Genesis account of Abraham and his immediate descendants may indicate that there were three main waves of the early Hebrew settlement in Canaan, the modern Israel. One was associated with Abraham and Hebron and took place in about 1850 BC. A second wave of immigration was linked with Abraham's grandson Jacob, who was renamed Israel ('May God show his strength!'); he settled in Sheeham, which is now the Arab town of Nablus on the West Bank. The Bible tells us that Jacob's sons, who became the ancestors of the twelve tribes of Israel, emigrated to Egypt during a severe famine in Canaan. The third wave of Hebrew settlement occurred in about 1200 BC when tribes who claimed to be descendants of Abraham arrived in Canaan from Egypt. They said that they had been enslaved by the Egyptians but had been liberated by a deity called Yahweh, who was the god of their leader Moses. After they had forced their way into Canaan, they allied themselves with the Hebrews there and became known as the people of Israel. The Bible makes it clear that the people we know as the ancient Israelites were a confederation of various ethnic groups, bound together principally by their loyalty to Yahweh, the God of Moses.

Jesus in his teaching continued the telling of the living creation story. Matthew 22.31-3: 'But concerning the resurrection of the dead have you not read what was told unto you by God, saying 'I am the God of Abraham and the God of Isaac and the God of Jacob and yet God is not the God of the dead but of the living.' And when the people heard it they were amazed at this teaching.'

Here Jesus connects to the ancient tradition of living

beginnings. Abraham, Isaac and Jacob were not dead. Their divine image and breath lived on, moving ahead in the procession of divine life. The resurrection was to do with uniting with the source of one's own divine image, which God created at creation and which has never died.

In the Gospel of Thomas, Logo 18, Jesus acts as an embodiment of Holy Wisdom and counsels his disciples toward experiences of knowing the self and experiencing Creation as one's own story:

> *The disciples said to Jesus 'Tell us how our end will come*
> *Jesus said 'Have you found the beginning then*
> *That you are looking for the end.*
> *The end will be what the beginning is*
> *Congratulations to the one who stands at the beginning*
> *That one will know the end and will not taste death.*

In John 3 Jesus advises Nicodemus to be born again, a phrase which has generated enormous theological discussion. However the Peshitta Bible's strict Aramaic translation means to be regenerated from the first beginning, and so to Aramaic ears it would be as follows:

> *Unless you are reborn*
> *From the first beginning*
> *The first beginning moment of the cosmos*
> *You will not be able*
> *To understand the realm of God*

Now in John ch. 1 v 1 we find the famous prologue from which some Christian interpretations enshrine Jesus as the 'Son' of God.

The King James version relates: 'In the beginning was the Word and the word was with God and the word was God'. The Peshitta uses Aramaic expressions that can be rendered as follows:

Aramaic

In the very beginningness
Was, and is and will be existing
The word-Wisdom of the One.
The ongoing Word and sound
The message and conversation
That has not stopped
And has never started
Because it is now.

Peshitta

The world was in the
beginning and that
very word was with God
And God was that word

The Aramaic here conveys the message that the creation is a continuing process in which anyone can participate: a distinct message of the unique understanding Jesus had of creation, and of the fact that it was ongoing, hence the use of the present tense.

When we consider and begin to understand the community that produced the Peshitta Syriac Aramaic version of Jesus' words and sayings, we cannot be surprised that the rendering of Jesus' words in their original form led the Eastern (Christians) to ignore the councils and creeds of the Roman Church after Constantine.

This difference remains in the Assyrian Church to this day. Some of these interpretations undermine quite a bit of Western Christian theology, but they are the spiritual experiences of Jesus, to whom they are attributed using as a background the actual spiritual practices and cosmology of the time. Many Western interpretations arose from a non-Semitic rendering of Jesus' words and a total disregard for the understanding and view of the Universe that he and his contemporaries held.

All this would not have been so bad if these later interpretations had not caused the forces of power using them to justify turning their backs on and refuting his primary emphases by ignoring his belief in Creation and ongoing love for one's friends, enemies, neighbours and self. They are all embodied in the first two commandments. Thus in Western culture the inability to understand the creation story as a spiritual experience and practice, together with centralised political power as introduced by the old Roman Empire, produced incalculable consequences.

Jesus spoke of the 'I am', the self, the inner person within us all. When we look at our lives, what do we see, where we have been or where are we going?

Imagine that each day on awaking you remember those who have gone before you and feel your connection with them. As you go through each day you have the comfort and support of knowing that those ahead of you have faced similar situations, but none exactly the same as those you are facing. They succeeded and failed, or maybe part succeeded, but life carried on. They went ahead, sometimes changing their whole direction - nothing is written in stone. You are also conscious of what you are leaving for those who come after you, the memories you leave behind and the effect you may have had, the changes you may have made. The focus should be on today, not on what might happen tomorrow because that may spoil what you have done and achieved today.

In the earliest stages of human development, when far fewer humans inhabited the planet, people gathered together for safety, comfort and a desire for companionship. Communities were formed out of physical and emotional necessity, and nature was stronger than any individual being.

The practice of living the creation story was handed down from generation to generation. The view of the creation story as an actual spiritual practice takes centre stage in both Jewish and Islamic mysticism (Kabbalah and Sufism) respectively. What has happened since is that the Western world has lost this living spiritual practice.

Today, after a few centuries of trying to control nature, we need to rediscover the sense of community spirit again, if only out of physical and emotional necessity. We have neglected the link to nature which was there at creation and the links to other humans who are not of our tribe. Vast sums of money are spent on creativity, worldly possessions, weapons and travel, but these efforts focus on acquiring something outside ourselves rather than trying to recover what was ours in the beginning. As Jesus repeatedly says, we must divest ourselves of these worldly possessions and habits if we are to find the kingdom of God, which is within ourselves and has been there since creation (as it was in the beginning!)

AS IT WAS IN THE BEGINNING - THE OLD TESTAMENT OF THE BIBLE

The Bible is recognised as the world's greatest work of epic literature, not only for its scope (spanning hundreds of generations) but also in its vivid portrayal of humanity as seen through the eyes of one 'chosen' people-the Children of Yahweh. But the Old Testament, in so many respects, does not glorify these people in the way other documents of the ancient world do their kings and champions. The heroes of the Bible are humans with frailties and flaws. Their successes and failures are measured against their allegiance to one God - the God of the Israelites, who, through time, was known by many names: Eya/Enki, El/El-Shaddai, Yahweh, Adonai and simply Ya. This God Yahweh is both redeemer and executioner, a miracle-worker and yet a jealous deity who puts his chosen people through terrible trials and tribulations whenever they stray from his path, which they constantly do. Even Yahweh's heroes, such as Moses, Joshua and David, are sanctioned to commit what we today would regard as crimes against humanity. Life in the ancient world was bloody and cruel as different groups of humans vied to control the Earth's limited resources.

But is any of it true? For many years, leading archaeologists in the field had come to the conclusion that most biblical stories are not supported by the archaeological and textual evidence. These scholars are not anti-Bible - they simply looked at the remains from the past and saw no correlation. In a sense they have been courageous to point out and highlight the problems which have come to the fore over the last century and a half of research. One by one the biblical eras came under scrutiny and were found wanting.

So this is the uncomfortable position a reader of the Old Testament finds himself in today. Either you accept the biblical story as unerringly true through blind faith or you have to face up to the archaeological reality that most of this extraordinary book is fiction.

However, a new and revolutionary approach to the synthesis of Bible and archaeology is now on offer in the form of a new Chronology.

Professor David Rohl holds a degree in ancient history and Egyptology from University College London. He has been involved in many projects and excavations and is Field Director of the Eastern Desert Survey in Egypt. His books, including *The Lost Testament, A Test of Time* and *Legend*, have been responsible for proposing a new chronology which involves the adjustment of the archaeological timeline downwards by several centuries. This has the effect of placing events in the Bible in their proper historical position and context.

In the New Chronology the whole narrative of the Children of Yahweh comes to historical life. The people of the Bible did not live in an archaeological and historical vacuum. They existed and interacted with many ancient Near Eastern civilisations and their renowned leaders. As with Galileo, Professor Rohl's findings will take a long time to be fully recognised.

The New Chronology is able to explain and illuminate many of the events by setting them in an historical world reconstructed from the archaeological remains of our ancestral past. It is a world which is tangible, giving the biblical narrative a credible background to which to set the lives of its people.

What was 'the beginning'?

According to Genesis Chapter 1.v.1, 'God created the Heavens and the Earth in the very beginning'. Genesis is a Greek word meaning origins. The first book of the Hebrew Bible is headed by the word Bereshit, which literally means in the beginning.

In the beginning… one particular valley in the Zagros range of mountains in Iran with a canopy of 'every kind of tree' became the setting-off point on the long march to civilisation. This was the place where humankind turned away from the Neolithic (late Stone Age) and headed first east, then south through the mountain passes towards the Copper Age and on into the early Bronze Age.

The tribal system, based on the extended family, was already in existence. It centred on a ruler-chieftain who was both king and high priest of his clan.

Genesis 2.8 continues: 'And the Lord planted a garden eastward in Eden and there He put the Man whom He had formed.' Eden has long been identified as a place from which four of the ancient world's great rivers flowed, namely the Tigris, Euphrates, Pishon and Gihon.

According to scripture Eden was the place that gave birth to civilisation as we know it. This was the womb of the great Earth goddess, the mother of the Neolithic revolution, when Stone Age man stopped his wandering hunter-gatherer style of life and settled in villages, when crops were raised and animals domesticated.

The author of Genesis tells us that the river of Eden parted into four streams, which he calls the 'heads' (ie sources). These headwaters became the four great rivers which flowed down from Eden to water the rest of the then-known primeval world.

In the creation myths of Mesopotamia, man was made in the likeness of the Gods by combining the clay of the earth with the blood of a sacrificed God. The area is full of red clay or earth taken from the Red Mountain overlooking the Garden of Eden. Excavations have shown that red ochre was used to decorate walls of houses as well as clay figures, and to cover the bones of the dead.

Adam appears on the scene at the end of the Neolithic Age (circa 5375 BC) when the archaeological record reveals the first signs of agriculture and the domestication of animals in the Middle East.

The strict and correct translation of Adam is 'red earth' or 'red earth man', Genesis 2.7. 'And the Lord formed Adam out of the soil of the earth and breathed into his nostrils the breath of life and Man became a living being.'

The people of Eden especially sanctified the places where the life-giving waters of the abyss burst forth upon the dry earth. This practice would continue in the Zagros Mountains for thousands of years, right down to Persian times, when it was clearly still manifest in the fire-temple rites of the Zoroastrians.

The holiest site of all for the red-earth people was the sacred well at the summit of the Mountain of the Chalice, for this was the source of the waters of the Garden and the high throne of the 'Lord of the Earth' and the other Gods.

The Bible tells us that Adam was brought into the garden by his God. Adam was the red man, the first chieftain of the garden tribe. Then God said 'let us make man in our image after our likeness, and let them have dominion over the fish and the sea, and over the fowl of all the air and over the cattle, and all over the wild beasts of the earth and over every creeping thing that creeps upon the earth' (Genesis 1.26)

'And the Lord God took the man and put him in the Garden of Eden to till it and to keep it' (Genesis 2.15.)

Who was Adam? He is a metaphor for the oldest ancestor in memory, the first historical man, the head of a genealogy, a spiritual and political leader in one. He is the representative of the first settled people, former hunter-gatherers, who through the Neolithic revolution learned to domesticate animals and plant crops. Religion is a function of settlement, of social organization, of hierarchy, and of needing a leader/shaman-priest who is in touch with the gods of nature. Adam, with Eve, probably represents an important marriage between two such settled tribes. They were the founding family of civilisation as we know it.

But you can 'find' these founding characters in different ancient legends. Eve in Genesis is described as 'the mother of all the living', the same epithet used for Ninhursag, the Sumerian 'Mistress of the Mountain'. In the Sumerian creation myth, Enki is cursed by Ninhursag for eating forbidden plants growing in paradise. Enki begins to fade away - his ribs pain him- but Ninhursag relents and creates a goddess called Ninti to cure him. Ninti means 'Lady of the Rib' but it also means 'Lady of Life'. It's a Sumerian pun. But the Genesis author took the first meaning. And so the story of Eve's creation from Adam's rib was born.

To the south beyond the mountain of God in Eden lay the land of Havilah, where the Huwawa tribe lived. The chieftain had a daughter, a priestess of the Goddess Ninhursag, the mistress of the mountain peaks and mother of all the living. The chieftain offered his daughter Eve (Hawwah in Hebrew) in marriage to Adam and so it follows that Eve was given the epithet 'Mother of all the living' and so became the great female ancestor of the Hebrew line. The annual sacred marriage union was performed, and 3000 years later it was still being performed in the chambers at the top of the great ziggurats of Mesopotamia. Its purpose was to secure an heir to the throne and ensure the fertility of the land at the birth of each New Year.

If the dates given in the Bible are correct this places Adam no earlier than 5400 BC. However science has long since demonstrated man's existence long before, so it is obvious that Adam was not the first physical human being on earth. He and two of his sons had wives from other tribes.

Adam was in fact the first of a dynasty. He was the original ancestor of oral tradition and the first recorded as communicating with and worshipping the God of the Hebrews.

A thousand years later, in the time of Enoch (the city builder), the earliest cities were founded in the southern marshes of Mesopotamia. The ancient text of this region then tells of a great flood and a hero who saves mankind by building a ship in which to ride out the mighty storm. The story is set in the late Ubaid period at around 3113 BC - the time of the flood at Ur.

The Bible does not tell us where the events leading up to this flood (ie the building of the ark) took place. What we do learn is that the ark came to rest on the 'mountains of Ararat' - that is to say the Zagros mountains in the region later known as Urartu, but which was earlier known as the kingdom of Aratta. Ancient historians state that the ark came to rest on the mountains of Kurdistan.

After the flood subsided the survivors returned to the lowlands and began to rebuild the ravaged world. The Bible story tells us of the saving of the pious man Noah by his God while all around perished. In reality thousands, perhaps millions, died, but those living in the high mountain passes of Zagros survived.

The descendants of Noah journeyed along the southern coast of the Arabian peninsula to reach the coast of Africa near the Red Sea. They came ashore in the land we know as Ethiopia, then known as Kush. Noah had three sons, and we are told they were the ancestors of many nations. The Israelites' line descended through Shem down ten generations to Abram of Ur, who became the great biblical patriarch.

There exist Sumerian myths that were concerned with the hero of the floods, and this written text affords the best link between the Bible and extra biblical sources.

The epic of Gilgamesh was first discovered at Nineveh in 1853. It is the tale of the legendary hero king of Uruk. In tablet XI of the Gilgamesh epic, Gilgamesh, the King of Uruk, seeks out and finds Utnapishtim, the legendary hero of the flood, who is supposedly immortal. Utnapishtim explains how the Gods brought the floods and how he was instructed to build a boat to rise out the storm and flood. As the storm subsided he released a dove, then a swallow and finally a raven to see if dry land could be reached, which of course it ultimately was.

After the deluge or great flood in around 3000 BC Meskiagasher (known as Cush), who was the son of Ham and grandson of Noah, was king of Eridu. He expanded his kingdom and begat a son, Nimrod. Genesis 10:9: 'He was a mighty hunter before the Lord wherefore it is said even as Nimrod was a mighty hunter before the Lord.'

Around 2830 BC a new wave of Mesopotamian colonizers began to arrive in Upper Egypt at the same time as Semitic-speaking tribes from the west. Towards the end of the Uruk period (c 2800 BC) the first known Ziggurat or tower-temple was erected at Eridu - the prototype upon which the legend of the biblical Tower of Babel is based. Eridu's sacred temple was built on an island of pure sand surrounded by water. The island was called Nun ki - the 'Mighty Place'. The builder of the tower temple was Enmer the Hunter (Sumarian Emmer-kar), the biblical Nimrod, 'a mighty hunter against Yahweh.' His generation and that of his ancestral predecessor, Meskiagkasher (biblical Cush), successfully colonised northern Mesopotamia, Canaan and the Nile valley to herald the historical age of the great Old World civilisations.

Through their religious beliefs and burial incantations, the Egyptians of later times remembered the place of their ancestral homeland on the Isle of Flame in the Waters of Nun. Even as late as the Ptolemaic period temple, reliefs recall the journey made by the 'Founders' who brought the secret knowledge of the primeval temple of the 'First Time' from Mesopotamia to the Nile valley.

The most dramatic evidence of Sumerian technology, both artistic and religious, in Egypt and in particular the Nile Valley was the introduction of niched façade architecture round about 3000 BC. Thus the Mesopotamian culture had spread to Egypt. This has been substantiated by finds of pottery and ceremonial weapons. They also buried their dead in a totally different way. It is hard to refute the evidence that a foreign élite did migrate into the Nile Valley and so these land and seafaring travellers helped initiate the Pharaonic state. The stepped pyramid at Sakkara built by Djoser closely resembles the Ziggurats of Mesopotamia and had the same purpose - to provide a stairway for a dead ruler to reach the Gods, and at the same time a means for the Gods to visit the earth.

The official history of Egypt starts with the reign of Menes in 2920 BC, and the time before this and before the pyramid builders is known as the Predynastic period. At this time there was a tremendous upsurge of building and the practice of astronomy, due to the imported knowledge of the migrating peoples.

The date 2920 BC is specific, thanks to the work of Manetho, an Egyptian priest (c 250 BC) who recorded for posterity a list of the Kings of Egypt from Menes onwards.

We then leap forward a thousand years to the end of the Early Bronze Age when Abraham (c 1855 BC) migrated down into Canaan from Harran across the Euphrates. He entered Egypt in the time of the Heracleopolitan 10th Dynasty as a guest of Pharaoh Nebkaure Khety 1V. Having been expelled from the eastern Delta for deceiving Pharaoh over his wife Sarah, Abraham settled in the hill country of Canaan at a time when the Amorite tribes were moving into the region from the north. Abraham himself was an Amorite chieftain and a part of this historically-recognized movement. He became embroiled in a major revolt against the great superpower of the time, the Third Dynasty of Ur. Amar-Sin (biblical Amraphel) of Ur sent a great army to crush the rebellion among the Cities of the Plain (south of the Dead Sea). Abraham's nephew, Lot, was taken captive but then rescued by his uncle. Lot returned to the Dead Sea region to witness the great cataclysm which overwhelmed Sodom and Gomorrah. The imprint of that disaster was manifest in the Arabah basin.

Abraham had children by his wife Sarah and by two concubines called Hagar and Keturar. Abraham's wife Sarah forced his sons from these two concubines to be banished, and so began the schism between two factions, who became lifelong enemies as the Arabs and the Jews.

After Abraham, the Israelites are said to have descended

through Isaac, born in the land of Israel, and then through their eponymous ancestor Jacob who was also known as Israel. Israel's sons took Canaanite wives, adopting Canaanite customs. The Bible also describes a time when the Israelites relocated to Egypt, and following the Exodus back from Egypt, a time when they conquered (sometimes exterminating and sometimes absorbing) the ethnic groups there, reclaiming the land God promised them.

The earliest Canaanite to be mentioned in the Bible is Melchizedek, who is clearly associated with Abraham, the acknowledged father of the Jewish nation.

The aristocracy and middle classes of coastal Canaan controlled a profitable international trade. These well-to-do seaside cities did not need a large labour force; they made their money abroad and imported all the goods they needed. They lost contact with their unemployable peasant stock, the Apiru and the demoralized Apiru became an underclass who travelled the countryside looking for employment and food. Some went to Egypt to work, so the story of Moses being a Hebrew (Apiru) could be based on the actions of a successful mercenary general in the Egyptian army. The account of the Hebrews' exodus from Egypt now makes sense, as they escaped eastwards and northwards in search of their own land promised to them by birth.

On their return these Apiru organized the underclass into a new social order led by the Judges. The Canaanite city kings worried when they saw the country dwellers demanding a better lot for themselves.

By now two strata of Canaanite society had developed: the city dwellers, typically Byblos and Tyre, and the rural unwashed. The urban people were better educated in science, philosophy and theology. They enjoyed culture and tradition, while the Apiru could boast only a jumble of old myths, but the Apiru organised their myths into our religious heritage of monotheism.

The Canaanite city dwellers, ruled by Melchizedek in Jerusalem and Hiram in Tyre, worshipped the Sun and Venus, understood astronomy and practised secret rituals for king-making. The Apiru followed a less complex peasant religion, where the God or his son died each season to be reborn next spring.

This Canaanite astral religion grew from a race of extremely successful seafarers and traders who worshipped a Goddess who manifested herself as the planet Venus. The original Canaanite settlements, with their traditions of astronomically-aligned temple building, fused with a new wave of invaders who sailed in from Western Europe.

There are many Megalithic sites across Western Europe dating from 5000–4000 BC. They were built in such a way as to allow light from the sun, the moon and Venus to enter certain parts of their buildings on certain days of the year, particularly solstices and equinoxes. From the development of these buildings there emerged skilled craftsmen and priests who had superior knowledge as magi, and were fully acquainted with astronomy. They employed a standard unit of measurement, the megalithic yard, in building a wide range of structures, and this has close connections with the Sumerian foot and Pharaonic inch. Archaeologists have found that certain symbols used on buildings in Neolithic Western European settlements are also found in predynastic buildings in Egypt. There are striking similarities of procedure in the ancient Jewish text of the book of Enoch and the astronomically-aligned sites of Neolithic Britain and Western Europe.

Some two hundred years later in 1666 BC, a young man named Joseph became vizier in the court of Pharaoh Amenembat III - the most powerful king of the 12th Dynasty. He saved Egypt from the worst of a terrible famine by diverting the waters from a series of massive Nile floods into the Faiyum basin via what was later to be known as the Bahr Yussef ('waterway of Joseph'). His reward was to be given his own private estate in the eastern delta region of Goshen, where he settled his Hebrew brethren (including his father Jacob). Their extended sojourn in Egypt was marked by the cultural phase known as Middle Bronze (c 1800-1440BC). When Joseph died he was buried in a pyramid tomb furnished with its own cult-statue. The empty tomb, with its (subsequently) smashed statue, has been unearthed at tell ed-Daba within the earliest strata of the ancient city of Avaris.

Moses was born in the middle years of the 13th Dynasty (c1530BC) and adopted by the Queen of Pharaoh Khanefere Sobekhotep IV, the greatest King of that dynasty. Moses Prince of Egypt, of Hebrew parentage, fought a war on Kush on behalf of his Egyptian father-in-law, but dynastic rivalries and intrigue forced him to flee into exile. He remained for several decades with a community of nomadic Midianites wandering the Negreb and Sinai wilderness, marrying the daughter of Jethro, Priest of Yahweh.

Through his Midianite kin, Moses learned of the common heritage between the 'sons of Abraham' (through Ishmael and Isaac). The Israelite slaves in Egypt had forgotten their ancestral history and the God of the patriarchs, but the descendants of Abraham dwelling in the desert had retained their knowledge of the past through oral tradition. Moses, as an educated prince with language skills, was able to read cuneiform tablets which were circulating in the Middle East thanks to their wide publication during the reign of Hammurabi of Babylon (1565 -1523 BC). These tablets contained the great epic poetry of the early Mesopotamian period, including the stories of Creation, Paradise, the Flood and the Tower of Babel, all of which involved Enki/Eya - the God who was 'the friend of Man'. Eya was the same as Ya (Hebrew Yah), the ancestral deity worshipped by the Midianites and dwelled upon Mount Horeb at the heart of the black peaks in southern Sinai.

When Moses later compiled the Bible's own legendary epic - the book of Genesis - these early Mesopotamian stories relating to Eya and his followers were incorporated into the work to become one of the finest pieces of ancient literature.

Having returned from exile, Moses challenged the new pharaoh Dudimose to 'let his people go' out of Egypt and worship their God Ya in his Sinai abode. But Pharaoh refused to allow his slaves to abandon their servitude. In 1447 BC a terrible disaster struck the Egyptians, resulting in the deaths of thousands. The dead were cast into makeshift burial pits (now unearthed at Tell ed-Daba/Avaris.) The city of Avaris, in which a major part of the Israelite slave population dwelt was abandoned.

At Mount Horeb (probably Gebel Musa), Moses employed the recently-invented Proto-Sinaitic script (Egyptian hieroglyphic signs used to represent the Semitic alphabet) to record the Laws of Yahweh. These oldest tablets of the Hebrew script were placed in a golden box known as the Ark of the Covenant and carried at the head of the army on its conquest of the Promised Land.

The Middle Bronze Age cities of Jericho, Ai and Hazor were destroyed and 'sown with salt' by Joshua and the Israelite tribes. All the cities sacked by the Children of Yahweh in the biblical text were destroyed. The great covenant ceremony was then celebrated before a gleaming white monolith erected in front of the bronze age Migdol temple of Ball-Berith in Schechem. The Covenant Stone of Joshua still stands today in the same spot, at the heart of the modern city of Nablus. The Migdol temple was later destroyed by Abimelech during the late Bronze period, when this brutal Israelite king burned one thousand of his citizens alive in the sanctuary of Schechem.

The Judges period spans the last part of the Middle Bronze Age through to the end of the Late Bronze. Then we have the golden age of the United Monarchy period - the era of Saul, David and Solomon.

The el-Amarna letters (c 1020-1000 BC), found in Akhenaten's royal city, attest to Saul's 'Hebrew revolt' against the Philistine lords on the coastal plain. The kings of Gath and Megiddo wrote to Pharaoh, informing him of the death of Saul (here known by his birth name, Labaya - 'lion (of Yah)'), while other letters dealt with the aftermath of Saul's death on Mount Gilboa and the rise of David (here called by his Hurrian royal title, Tadua - 'beloved (of Yah)'. Involved in all the political turmoil of Amarna-period Syro-Palestine was a king of Amurru named Aziru, erstwhile enemy of King David of Jerusalem.

In Akhenaten's twelfth year the palace at Ugarit was partially destroyed by fire. Three thousand years later, a tiny clay tablet was recovered from the charred ruins of the palace archive. This tablet records a solar eclipse at Ugarit just as the sun was setting over the Mediterranean Sea. This extremely rare event (occurring once in every four thousand years or so) has been calculated (using an astronomy computer programme) to have taken place in 1012 BC -

nearly three hundred and thirty years later than the conventional date for Akhenaten's twelfth year, but exactly when the heretic pharaoh succeeded his father, Amenhotep III, in the New Chronology. This eclipse thus confirms Akhenaten's contemporaneity with Saul and David and the foundation of the Israelite monarchy. It was Akhenaten's flawed rule which created the political conditions for the dramatic birth of the kingdom of Israel.

David, an ambitious leader of the apiru, persuaded the Jebusite aristocracy of Jerusalem to hand over control of the city to him, but they did so only after insulting his kingly credentials. David immediately set about creating a shrine to the God he had inherited from Moses, and brought the Ark of the Covenant to Jerusalem. Hiram of Tyre was worried by these developments and instituted a two-pronged political solution. He made friends with David by building him a palace in Jerusalem, while also moving his city and its king-making temples to safety on an artificial island he had built in the sea.

There was a continuation of the Canaanite priesthood after David took the kingship for himself. So King David carried on the tradition which Abraham started with Melchzidek, of recognizing the validity of the Canaanite High Priest and King of Jerusalem. This began the Jewish belief in distinct kingly and priestly Messiahs.

In the late 1950s a French Archaeologist, Claude Schaeffer, excavated a magnificent late Bronze Age palace of King Nikmaddu of Ugarit (the ancient name of Ras Sharma) on the coast of Syria. The construction of their palace showed the use of courses of cedar beam construction as used by the Phoenicians, who introduced it to Israel and in particular to King Solomon's Temple. Nikmaddu was a contemporary of Akhenaten and therefore of David.

Also at Ugarit were found tablets now known as the Ras Sharma tablets, which contain a number of poems and rituals of religious importance from the 2nd millennium BC and have enormously enlarged our knowledge and understanding of early beliefs and practices in Canaan during that period. In particular they point to:

1. The existence of a priest king.
2. An organised body of people possessing the knowledge of the correct way to perform the rituals.
3. A myth enacted within the ritual, to convey a message. The knowledge was restricted to the priest/king.
5. A secret ritual involving the death of the God, conducted at the Autumn equinox.

Freemasons will recognize the ritualistic similarities. Masonic ritual drama ceremonies have been performed for around 350 years and the present form of ritual was stabilized in the early 19th Century. It is strange that these ceremonies bear such a resemblance to ancient practices, especially as the Ras Sharma tablets were not unearthed until the 1950s.

David was succeeded by Solomon, son-in-law of Pharaoh Harembeb. He built the magnificent palaces at Megiddo and Hazor and is portrayed on a beautiful ivory plaque originating from archaeological excavations of the Megiddo palace. The Phoenician building techniques of Late Bronze Age Megiddo are identical to those employed in the construction of Solomon's palaces and the Jerusalem temple (as described in the biblical text).

The copper mines at Timnah were being worked to their maximum during the Late Bronze Age when Solomon was casting his elaborate bronze furnishings for Yahweh's temple in the Israelite capital. The mines were abandoned during the 20th Dynasty when the divided monarchy of Israel was under increasing pressure from Aramaean raids and the Transjordanian states were rebelling against their once-powerful Israelite master. The fortunes of the Children of Yahweh were at their lowest ebb as the outlying tribes flocked for protection to the central hill, where they built refugee camps. The people living in the region were fellow Israelites from Galilee and Gilead, fleeing the Aramaean oppression of Ben-Hadad 911 and Hazaal (c 873-800 BC).

A new dynasty now arose. The Assyrians referred to it as Bit Humri, the 'House of Omri'. Kings Omri and Ahab established a new capital at Samaria and a winter palace at Jezreel. At both sites these Israelite rulers and their courts are represented by the Iron Age pottery found in the fills of buildings belonging to a later King, Jeroboam II, in whose time the Northern Kingdom of Israel was reinvigorated as a powerful and wealthy state. Jeroboam built the Iron Age casemate walls and six-chambered gates of Jeareel, Hazor, Gezer and Megiddo. But within twenty years of Jeroboam's death the kingdom of Israel had fallen to Sargon II and the royal capital at Samaria was in the hands of an Assyrian provincial governor.

A century later, Assyria too had succumbed to the new power in the region - the Babylonians. The kingdom of Judah had held out against the Assyrians, in spite of losing major cities such as Lachish to Sennacherib's mighty army. However, the Babylonians were another matter. Under the leadership of Nebuchadnezzar II the army of Babylon was simply too strong for the now isolated

Judaean hill country state. Jerusalem surrendered in 598 BC, its new king, Jehoiachin, taken off into exile. Ten years later Zedkiah, the last ruler of Jerusalem, rebelled against his Babylonian overlord and Nebuchadnezzar returned south to put an end, once and for all, to his troublesome vassal. The holy city of Yahweh fell in 587 BC and its remaining population was deported to Mesopotamia. Jerusalem and its magnificent temple were systematically dismantled by the Babylonian army and turned into mounds of rubble, fit only as the abodes of scavengers and wild animals.

AS IT WAS IN THE BEGINNING - EGYPT

The Egyptians were by no means the first people to acquire the prerequisites of civilisation, ie the art of farming and urban living. Egypt began its march to civilisation rather later than some areas of the Near East and indeed Western Europe. But once it had taken root it proved to be most durable, spanning more than 3000 years until the final eclipse of Egyptian culture in the early Christian era.

For most of its ancient history Egypt was ruled by kings or pharaohs. The seeds of Egyptian civilisation lay in a number of Neolithic cultures that emerged between 5000 and 4000 BC. Symbols and signs found in ancient British Neolithic sites, for example, have been found and identified in Egypt in the pyramids and temples.

The Pharaoh occupied a unique position at the top of the social and political hierarchy. In Egypt he was even more; he was a discrete and essential element in the cosmos alongside the Gods and the spirits of the deceased. This was necessary to maintain the divine order known as MA-AT. Without Pharaoh, Egyptians believed the cosmos would be in disarray and the world would be in chaos. The monarch was thus considered to be a living descendant of the Sun God and his title was SA-RE, son of Re.

The legendary first King of the earth was Osiris, the supreme deity who was born every morning as the sun rose and died every evening as it set. Pharaoh thus embodied continuous regeneration, as with Osiris. To Egyptians the sky was primarily the domain of the gods; they studied the sky and the stars and tried to recreate the sky on earth. Not only were pyramids designed to fit in with the path of the heavens, they were placed to replicate them. For example the Pyramids at Giza are arranged almost exactly to match the constellation of Orion.

CHAPTER 2

❧

The birth of monotheism

Egyptian cultures and religion remained remarkably uniform throughout most of the country's 3000 years of history, except for the two decades from 1353-1336 BC, when the Pharaoh Akhenaten promoted a view of the world that challenged the very foundation of Egyptian belief. One of the earliest known references occurred in Egypt when Pharaoh Akhenaten proclaimed Aten to be the One God. A hymn attributed to the Pharaoh himself begins 'O living Aten, creator of life!' It continues:

> O Sole God, beside whom there is none!
> You made the earth as you wished, you alone.
> All peoples, herds, and flocks;
> All upon earth that walk upon legs,
> All on high that fly on wings.
> You set every man in his place,
> You supply their needs;
> Everyone has his food,
> His lifetime is counted.
> Their tongues differ in speech,
> Their characters likewise;
> Their skins are distinct,
> For you distinguished the peoples.

For you made them for yourself
Lord of all lands
You are in my heart.

THE MISSION OF AKHENATEN AND
THE MESSAGE FROM EGYPT

Egypt, it very much seems, was 'made in the image of Heaven', incorporating in its unique geography and in the locations and alignments of its pyramids and temples the various astronomical cycles that were believed to be regulated by the cosmic order or Maat. What is more, by integrating the cosmic order into the very fabric of the religious mythology and rituals and into the social and legal systems, an ideal state was created. This state was itself regulated by the natural laws acknowledged by all. Eventually, however, the pure mechanism of the cosmic order was corrupted by the power-driven priesthood and the complex mythology and iconography they injected into it. It was left to Akhenaten to clean up the mess, to free the old natural religion from the yoke of the priesthood and to strip it of the confusing iconography and mythology by fixing it to a single God symbol; the disc of the Sun, representing the universal God. After trying for 17 years Akhenaten eventually failed, but he nonetheless managed to inject the fragile seed of monotheism that would influence the three great Semitic religions of our modern world.

In place of many natural elements and forces that Egyptians had always worshipped as their Gods Akhenaten recognised only one, the supreme force of light which came into the world and gave it life every day through the sun.

The very wise and observant priests of ancient Egypt taught not with dogmas and doctrines, nor did they threaten the populace with the fear of their God's wrath; rather they offered a clever and enlightened initiation that would open the mind and sharpen the senses, so that nature was seen as the manifestation of the divine principles. Man himself was not only an integral part of nature, but responsible for keeping it in harmony and balance. Ancient Egypt is not a science but an idea. For what is more important, the material legacy of ancient Egypt or its spiritual legacy? What is more important, the ancient stones of pyramids and temples or the ideas and aspirations they represent?

When dealing with ancient Egypt, you are dealing with a spiritual civilisation which believed emphatically in eternity and in an afterlife attained by an adherence to the cosmic order. It should be studied as such.

The change was short lived. After the death of Akhenaten the old ways were quickly restored by the priests, and attempts were made to remove every trace of Akhenaten from Egyptian history.

SOME EGYPTIAN ACHIEVEMENTS

Many people are unaware of the depth of the talents of the Egyptians. Here are a few of the things the Egyptians achieved, not all of which have been fully appreciated:

1. They built the Pyramids and were able to shift huge weights, even hundreds of tons. Quite how they achieved this still mystifies modern engineers.

2. They had batteries, as discovered by an examination in 1938 of a curious clay jar in the National Museum of Iraq. After the Second World War the General Electric Co., in a laboratory in Massachusetts, constructed an exact replica of the device - two volts of electricity were obtained. There is also evidence in the same museum of copper utensils being electroplated with silver. This was also replicated by using several batteries and connecting them.

3. In 1904 the British archaeologist Sir W M Flinders Petrie made a very important discovery in the Sinai desert. He discovered the ruin of an old Egyptian temple with inscriptions dating it to the time of the 4th Dynasty Pharaoh Sneferu, who reigned c 2600 BC. The discovery of this site received very little publicity, yet it is probably the most important biblical discovery ever made. The reason for this is that the Memorandum and Articles of the Egypt Exploration Fund, which sponsored the find, stated that surveys and excavations would only be approved if they upheld the Biblical Narrative, and this discovery did not! At least it did not uphold the Church's interpretation and teaching of the Narrative. Among many finds, the explorers found a metallurgist's crucible and a considerable amount of pure white powder. What Petrie had found was possibly the alchemical workshop of Akhenaten, which had laid buried for thousands of years untouched.

It has been suggested that the white powder can be formed by striking the metal (gold for example) under strictly controlled conditions for a precalculated time with a designated high temperature. The white powder resulting from this process amounts to only 56% of the weight of the metal from which it is transformed. Still further the remaining 56% (white powder) can be made to disappear completely from sight; turning itself into another dimension (The process can be wholly reversed). Not only does the invisible substance weigh less than nothing but the pan in which it was setting also registers less than its starting point weight. It is hardly surprising that the discovery has never been fully publicised.

It is interesting to note that Wikipedia (http://en. wikipedia.org/wiki/Flinders_Petrie), recording the achievements of Flinders Petrie, omits the years 1897-1920.

It is not difficult for us now to realize how advanced a civilisation the Egyptians were, with a great command of creation and the wonders of the cosmic universe.

MONOTHEISM

If there is only one god this necessitates an exclusive relationship; there are no logical alternatives. Thus Akhenaten, who is credited with the beginning of monotheism, did not insist that everyone worshipped Aten but that they who did should worship Aten alone. It is illogical to deal with a host of gods for all different purposes. One true god has unlimited scope and capacity and can deal with all things.

It is now widely accepted that the Old Testament was created around the sixth century BC, when wise men and scribes combed through the vast amount of oral traditions to form a single storyline back to the creation. This myth tells of a great transition from a period dominated by rural nomads through to a time of great cities and warrior princes. It seems to be trying to make sense of what folk memory preserved of the shift from the Old Stone Age culture of hunting and herding wanderers to the Bronze and Iron Ages, when more powerful weapons of warfare became available.

Could this story be an attempt to explain how the secrets of building and astronomy had been transmitted from the grooved Ware People to their own culture? We know from the evidence of the book of Enoch that Enoch was believed to have travelled north to be trained in these subjects, and the secret knowledge he brought back was written down in that book around 250 BC.

Belief in God affirms a reality beyond ourselves which we did not create. We experience our own lives, and human life, within this context - nature, the earth, the universe.

CHAPTER 3

❧

The Church of the East – the Peshitta Bible

In the first century AD Jesus and his earliest followers spoke Aramaic, which together with Hebrew had been equally spoken by the Jewish people. Aramaic was the language of the early Christian Church that spread east. This differed from the language of Palestine in much the same way as American English differs from British English. The Jews and early Christians used Syriac, the literary dialect of Aramaic, at the same time to spread their translations of the sacred texts.

The Patriarch of the Church of the East states that it (the Church) received the scriptures from the hands of the Blessed Apostles in the original Aramaic, the language spoken by Jesus himself. The Peshitta Bible is the text of the Church of the East, which has been handed down from biblical times pure and unsullied without any change or revision.

North of the Garden of Eden in the basin of the River Tigris is the mountain region of Kurdistan. An ancient people lived there who were descendants of the Assyrians, founders of the Great Assyrian Empire. They originated the alphabet and many of the sciences which contributed to their culture and from which the Bible ultimately sprang.

Some of these Assyrians and some of the ten tribes captured by them were some of the first converts to Christianity. Descendants of the Hebrew tribes still live in Iraq, Iran and Turkey and many still converse in Aramaic. The Assyrian Church is known as the Ancient Apostolic and Catholic Church of the East (in short, Church of the East). It reigned supreme until the 14th Century when it was overshadowed by the Church of Rome.

Eastern Christians still adhere to God's Commandments:

Deuteronomy 4:2: You shall not add to the commandment which I command, neither shall you take from it.

Revelation 22:19: And if any man shall take away from the words of the book of this prophecy, God shall take away his portion from the tree of life.

Discrepancies occur between different translations of the Bible mainly because of the use of different sources for the translation. For my purposes I have used quotations from the Peshitta Bible. In the main the differences are small, but I do consider that a translation direct from the Aramaic is likely to be more accurate.

The Peshitta Bible is an eastern book written primarily for the Israelites and then the Gentile world. For several centuries after the death of Jesus, himself a Jew, the Christian movement was directed and guided by Jews and all the Apostles and Evangelists were Jewish. The early Christians then were mostly Jews, men and women of Hebrew origin who had been looking for the coming of the Promised Messiah as directed by the Hebrew prophets.

Introduction to the Holy Bible from the ancient eastern text - George M Lamsa's translation from the Aramaic of the Peshitta into English.

This translation of the Old and New Testaments into English is based on Peshitta manuscripts which have comprised the accepted Bible of all of those Christians who have used Syriac as their language of prayer and worship for many centuries. It is appropriate that as we have translations based on the Greek Septuagint of the Old Testament and on the Latin Bible of Jerome, so also should there be available to the modern reader that form of the text which was translated in ancient times into a branch of the Aramaic language which has been used by Christians from earliest times.

In the long history of the Aramaic language, there are three periods of special interest. From the sixth to the fourth century before Christ, it was a language of empire, extending from the borders of Persia to Europe and down the Nile through the length of Egypt. It was in those days spoken and written by the Jewish people at least equally with Hebrew; and so we have parts of Ezra and Daniel and one verse in Jeremiah (10:11), that were composed in Aramaic and preserved in that ancient form of the language in the midst of the Hebrew Old Testament.

In the first century, Jesus and his earliest followers certainly spoke Aramaic for the most part, although they also knew Hebrew. Therefore the Gospel message was first preached in the Aramaic of the Jews of Palestine. Modern scholarship tells us that the originals of the Four Gospels and of other parts of the New Testament were written in Greek. This is disputed by the Church of the East and by some noted Western scholars. Regardless of which view one may accept, Aramaic speech is an underlying factor. It is unquestionably true that documents written in Aramaic were drawn on by writers of the New Testament, the basic inspired form of the Christian message.

Aramaic was the language of the Church that spread east,

almost from the beginning of Christianity, from Antioch and Jerusalem, beyond the confines of the Roman Empire. This differed from the language of Palestine in choice of words and grammatical forms rather more extensively than does American English from British English, and in written form these differences became regular and standardized. The Jews and Christians used the literary dialect of Aramaic that we call Syriac almost at the same time, to propagate their translation of the sacred books brought from Palestine and the West, reaching into Syria and Mesopotamia and the nearby mountains, quite early into India, and in the course of time into China.

Modern scholars believe that as in other parts of the Church, the earliest copies of the sacred books in Syriac were revised again and again to bring them closer to the standard of the Hebrew and Greek texts from which they were drawn. However this view is not accepted by the Church of the East. Under these conditions, by the fifth century AD the Peshitta version in its present form held the field, by universal acclaim.

The fixed stand of the Church of the East with respect to some of the points mentioned above can best be understood by reference to the following letter from the Patriarch and Head of that Church:

Patriarchate of the East, Modesto, California, April 5, 1957
With reference to your letter concerning Lamsa's translation of the Aramaic Bible, and the originality of the Peshitta text, as the Patriarch and Head of the Holy Apostolic and Catholic Church of the East we wish to state that the Church of the East received the scriptures from the hands of the blessed Apostles themselves in the Aramaic original, the

language spoken by our Lord Jesus Christ himself, and that the Peshitta is the text of the Church of the East which has come down from the Biblical times without any change or revision.

Mar Eshai Shimun
By Grace, Catholicos Patriarch of the East

From the Mediterranean east into India, the Peshitta is still the Bible of preference among Christians, though today nearly all who use it speak Arabic or one of the tongues of South India. West of the Euphrates, spoken Aramaic as a mother tongue survives today only in two mountain villages north west of Damascus, differing as much from the speech of Jesus' day as French from its parent Latin. East of the Euphrates, in the Kurdish mountains and near Lake Urmia, perhaps 100,000 people (Christian, Jew, and Muslim) speak another form of it, strangely mixed with borrowed words from the various languages of their polyglot neighbours, but still basically akin to the Aramaic (Syriac) of olden times.

George M Lamsa BA FRSA, the translator of this work, is uniquely fitted for the task to which he has devoted the major part of his life. He is an Assyrian and a native of ancient biblical lands, where he lived until World War I. Until that time, isolated from the rest of Christendom, his people retained biblical customs and Semitic culture which had perished everywhere else. This background, together with his knowledge of the Aramaic (Syriac) language, has enabled him to recover much of the meaning that has been lost in other translations of the Scriptures.

41

Extracts from the Introduction to the Peshitta Bible,
written by George M. Lamsa to accompany his translation

North of the Garden of Eden in the basin of the river Tigris, in the mountain fastnesses of what is known today as Kurdistan, there lived an ancient people, the descendants of the Assyrians, the founders of the great Assyrian empire and culture in Bible days, the originators of the alphabet and many sciences which contributed so generously to the Semitic culture from which sprang the Peshitta Bible. These people, the Assyrians, played an important part in the history of the Near East, of the Bible, and of religion in general.

When Nineveh was destroyed in 612 BC, many of the princes and noblemen of this once vast empire fled northward into inaccessible mountains, where they remained secluded and cut off until the dawn of the twentieth century.

Some descendents of the Assyrians and some of the descendants of the ten tribes who were taken captive by the Assyrian kings in 721 BC and settled in Assyria, Babylon, Persia and other places east of the river Euphrates were among the first converts to Christianity.

When Jesus sent seventy of his disciples to preach the gospel, he instructed them not to go in the way of the Gentiles or into any city of the Samaritans but to go to the lost sheep of the house of Israel, meaning the ten tribes who were lost from the house of Israel. Some of the descendants of these Hebrew tribes are still living in Iraq, Iran and Turkey, and most of them still converse in Aramaic. Jesus' command was carried out. The gospel was preached to the Jews first. 'Now those who had been dispersed by the persecution which occurred on account of Stephen travelled as far as Phoenicia and even to the land of Cyprus and to Antioch, preaching the word to none but the Jews only' Acts 11:19.

The Assyrian Church, or as it was known, the ancient Apostolic and Catholic Church of the East, was one of the strongest Christian churches in the world and was noted for its missions in the Middle East, India, and China. Its missionaries carried the Christian gospel as far as China and Mongolia, Indonesia, Japan and other parts of the world. It was the most powerful branch of Christendom in the near East, Palestine, Arabia, Lebanon, Iran, India and elsewhere.

All the literature of this church was written in literary Aramaic, the *lingua franca* or common language of that time.

The transition from Aramaic into Arabic, a sister tongue, took place after the conquest of the Near East by the Moslem armies in the 7th century AD. Nevertheless, Aramaic lingered for many centuries and still is spoken in Lebanon, Syria, Iraq, and north-western Iran, as well as among the Christian Arab tribes in northern Arabia. Its alphabet was borrowed by the Hebrews, Arabs, Iranians and Mongols. Aramaic and most of the ancient Biblical customs which were common to Semitic people have survived in northern Iraq until today. Aramaic is still spoken in Iraq and north-western Iran by remnants of the Assyrian people and the Jews of the exile, and the literary Aramaic remains the same today as it was of yore. Some of the Aramaic words which are still retained in all Bible versions are still used in the Aramaic language.

The Scriptures in the Church of the East, from the inception of Christianity to the present day, are in Aramaic and have never been tampered with or revised, as attested by the present Patriarch of the Church of the East. The Biblical manuscripts were carefully and zealously handed down from one generation to another and kept in the massive stone walls of the ancient churches and in caves. They were written on parchment and many of them survive to the present day. When these texts were copied by expert scribes, they were carefully examined for accuracy before they were dedicated and permitted to be read in churches. Even one missing letter would render the text void. Easterners still adhere to God's commandment not to add or omit a word from the Scriptures. The Holy Scripture condemns any addition or subtraction or modification of the Word of God.

'You shall not add to the commandment which I command you, neither shall you take from it, but you must keep the commandments of the Lord your God which I command you.' Deut. 4:2

'Everything that I command you, that you must be careful to do; you shall not add nor take from it.' Deut. 23:32.

'Do not add to his words; lest he reprove you, and be found a liar.' Prov. 20:6.

'And if any man shall take away from the words of the book of this prophecy, God shall take away his portion from the tree of life and from the holy city and from the things which are written in this book.' Rev. 22:19.

It is also true of the Jews and Moslems that they would not dare to alter a word of the Torah or Koran. Easterners are afraid that they may incur the curse if they make a change in the word of God.

Biblical Hebrew and Aramaic were very closely related, like American English and English spoken in England. Whether the Hebrew prophets wrote in Hebrew or Aramaic would make little difference. The difference would be like those between several Arabic dialects which are spoken in Arabia. Even though the vernacular speech differs because of the local colour and idioms, the norm of the written language remains the same. This is true today with written Arabic when compared with spoken Arabic.

The strongest points in ascertaining the originality of a text are the style of writing, the idioms, and the internal evidence. Words which make sense and are easily understood in one language, when translated literally into another tongue, may lose their meaning. One can offer many instances where scores of Aramaic words, some with several meanings and others with close resemblance to other words, were confused and thus mistranslated.

This is why in Jeremiah 4:10 we read in the King James:

'......Ah, Lord God! Surely thou hast greatly deceived this people...'

The Aramaic reads:

'......Ah, Lord God! I have greatly deceived this people...' The translator's confusion is due to the position of a dot, for the position of a dot frequently determines the meaning of a word.

In Isaiah 43:28, the King James version reads:

'Therefore, I have profaned the princes of the sanctuary...'
The Aramaic reads:
'...Your princes have profaned my sanctuary...' This error was caused by misunderstanding of a passive plural verb. The same error occurs in John 12:40, which in the Eastern Text reads:
'...Their eyes have become blind...' Instead of '...He hath blinded their eyes...'

The Israelites never wrote their sacred literature in any language but Aramaic and Hebrew, which are sister languages. The Septuagint was made in the 3rd century, BC, for the Alexandrian Jews. This version was never officially read by the Jews in Palestine, who spoke Aramaic and read Hebrew. Instead, the Jewish authorities condemned the work and declared a period of mourning because of the defects in the version. Evidently Jesus and his disciples used a text which came from an older Hebrew original. This is apparent because Jesus' quotations from the Old Testament agree with the Peshitta text but do not agree with the Greek text. For example, in John 12:40, the Peshitta Old Testament and New Testament agree. This is not all. Jesus and his disciples not only could not converse in Greek but probably they had never heard it spoken.

The teaching of Greek was forbidden by Jewish rabbis. It was said that it was better for a man to give his child meat of swine than to teach him the language of the Greeks.

When the King James translation of the Bible was made, western scholars had no access to the East as we have today. In the 16th century, A.D., the Turkish empire had extended its borders as far as Vienna. One European country after another was falling under the impact of the valiant Turkish army. Europe was almost conquered. This is not all. The reformations and controversies in the Western Church had destroyed Christian unity. Moreover, the Scriptures in Aramaic were unknown in Europe. The only recourse scholars had was to Latin and to a few portions of Greek manuscripts. This is clearly seen from the works of Erasmus. Besides, the knowledge of Greek was almost lost at this time and Christians were just emerging from the Dark Ages.

Many people have asked why the King James translators did not use the Peshitta text from Aramaic or the Scriptures used in the East. The answer is, there were no contacts between East and West until after the conquest of India by Great Britain and the rise of the imperial power of Britain in the Near East, Middle East, and the Far East.

Discrepancies between various translations have been the cause of contentions and divisions among sincere men and women who are earnestly seeking to understand the Word of God. At times, they do not know what to believe and what not to believe. They cannot understand why the Scriptures in one place says, 'Love your father and mother.' And in another place admonishes 'Hate your father and mother'. Moreover they are bewildered when told that Jesus on the cross cried out, 'My God, my God, why hast thou forsaken me?' The Peshitta text reads: 'My God, my God, for this I was spared!'

After all the Bible is an eastern Book, written primarily for the Israelites, and then for the Gentile world.

When we come to the New Testament, the new Covenant, we must not forget that Christianity grew out of Judaism. The Christian Gospel was another of God's messages, first to the Jewish people and then to the Gentile world. For several centuries, the Christian movement was directed and guided by the Jews. All the apostles and the evangelists were Jewish.

CHAPTER THREE

THE CONFUSION OF TRANSLATING WORDS
RESEMBLING ONE ANOTHER.

Aramaic is the richest and most expressive language of the Semitic group, but it has a small vocabulary when compared with Greek and Latin. This is because Aramaic is one of the world's most ancient languages. This limitation of words made necessary the use of the same words with various shades of meanings.

Translators are well aware of these grammatical difficulties, particularly in a language like Aramaic where a single dot above or under a letter radically changes the meaning of a word. These tiny dots are made by scribes, who are not authors but mere copyists, hired for the purpose by rich and learned men. But owing to the humidity of the climate and the nature of the ink, blots appear on the pages when pressed against each other. Because of exposure of a manuscript and careless handling, flies alight on the pages and leave marks. Furthermore, as the lines are crowded for lack of space, a dot placed above one letter may read as though it were placed under a letter in the previous line. For example, the only difference between the words for 'learned man' and 'stupid man' is a dot, over or under the word respectively.

Some Aramaic words are written and pronounced alike, but their meaning differs according to the context. In other cases the differences are indicated by dots which alter the pronunciation. In yet other instances, if the translator does not speak the language from which he translates, the meaning and usage of some words must be left to his knowledge and judgement.

Moreover, some Aramaic letters resemble one another, especially in manuscripts. For instance, Nun, Aey, Lamed and Yoth

48

are very close to one another when placed in certain positions. Nun and Yoth are hard to distinguish when in the middle of a word. Some of the most important mistranslations were due to the confusion of letters and words.

Owing to its great antiquity, the Peshitta is one of the most valuable documents in ascertaining the original text of the Bible. In fact, in point of age, the Peshitta takes precedence over every other Oriental version.

Over the page are some examples of the mistranslations caused by placement of dots and different meanings.

PESHITTA TEXT		KING JAMES VERSION
Jeremiah 4:10	*ataeth*	I have deceived
(the placement of a dot)	*ataih*	You have deceived)

10 Then I said, I beseech the, O Lord God Surely I have greatly deceived this people And Jerusalem: for I have said…

10 Then said I, Ah, Lord God! surely thou hast greatly deceived this people and Jerusalem, saying

Ezekial 32:5	*rimtha*	dust
(the placement of a dot)	*ramtha*	height

5 And I will scatter your flesh upon the mountains, and fill the valleys with your dust

5 And I will lay thy flesh upon the mountains, and fill the valleys with thy height

Obadiah 1:21	*preekey*	saved
(placement of 2 dots)	*parokey*	saviours

21 And those who are saved shall come up to Mount Zion to judge Mount Esau…

21 And saviours shall come up on Mount Zion to judge the Mount of Esau

Misah 1:12	*mirdah*	rebellious
(placement of 2 dots)	*maroth*	bitter

12 For the rebellious inhabitant is sick of waiting for good, for disaster is come down from the Lord to the gates of Jerusalem

12 For the inhabitant of Maroth waited carefully for good, but evil came down from the Lord unto the gates of Jerusalem

Habakkuk 3:4	*keritha*	town
(either 1 or 2 dots)	*karnatha*	horns

4 And his brightness was as the light: in the city which his hands had established shall he store his power.

4. And his brightness was as the light; he had horns coming out of his hand: And there was the hiding of his power.

St Matthew 19:24	*gamia*	rope
(same word having different contextual meaning)	*gamia*	camel

CHAPTER 4

❦

The connection between the Old and New Testaments

The Old Testament is concerned with the Society of Israel; the New Testament with the individual Jesus.

The New Testament writers then regard the Old Testament as a source of anticipations of the events in the life of Jesus. These are often explicitly alluded to and the source given, for example in the Crucifixion, the piercing of Jesus' hands and feet, the mockery of the passers-by, and the fact that his legs were not broken on the cross, are related to passages in Psalm 22. Jesus' great cry on the cross, 'My God, why hast thou forsaken me?' is a quotation from the first verse of this psalm. Sometimes the relationship is implicit only.

The thirty pieces of silver and the potter's field of the Judas story are found in Zechariah 11:12-13. A resurrection on the third day is mentioned in Hosea 5:2. The suffering servant of Isaiah 53 is close behind the account of the Passion, and the 'Emmanuel' prophecy earlier in Isaiah (7:14) is related to the Incarnation. Even in more doctrinal passages, Christian conceptions are presented not as new doctrines but as realizations of Old Testament conceptions. Thus Paul's central axiom 'The just shall live by faith' (Romans 1:17) is a quotation from Habbakuk 2:4.

There is a very large number of these references to the Old Testament in the New: they extend over every book in the New Testament. Some New Testament books, notably Revelation and the Epistle to the Hebrews, are a dense mass of such allusions, often with direct or oblique quotations. The New Testament, in short, claims to be, among other things, the key to the Old Testament, the explanation of what the Old Testament really means. Jesus' disciples could not understand even the Resurrection until Jesus had explained its relation to Old Testament prophecy (Luke 24:44).

The central figure of the New Testament is called 'Messiah', a word which means 'anointed one' and of which the Greek equivalent is 'Christ'. In the Old Testament the word 'Messiah' means only a legitimate ruler, whose right to rule has been symbolised by an anointing ceremony, real or assumed. The word is applied to the rejected King Saul and, once, to someone outside the Israelite community altogether, Cyrus of Persia (Isaiah 45:1). But by the time of Jesus, with the successful rebellion of the Maccabees fresh in the Jewish mind, there was a good deal of discussion about a figure called 'the' Messiah, a figure concerned with not merely restoring Israel's power but with bringing about an end to what we have known as history. It is fairly common knowledge that the identification of 'the' Messiah with Jesus of Nazareth is the issue that divides Christians from Jews.

The Bible records only two periods of relative independence and prosperity for Israel, and the reason was the same in both cases: one world empire had declined and its successor had not yet risen. The period of David and Solomon came between the decline of Egypt and the rise of Assyria. This is the period following the Maccabean wars, between the decline of Syria and the rise of Rome.

The general principle of interpretation is traditionally given as 'In the Old Testament the New Testament is concealed; in the New Testament the Old Testament is revealed.

THE NEW TESTAMENT

The most widely-accepted historical understanding of how the Synoptic gospels developed is known as the two-source hypothesis. This theory holds that Mark is the oldest gospel. Matthew and Luke are believed to come later, and draw on Mark and also on a source that is now believed to be lost, called the Q document, or just 'Q'.

Traditional views assume that the bulk of New Testament texts date to the period between AD45 and AD100, with the Pauline epistles among the earliest texts. Other views may pre-date or post-date the individual books by several decades. The earliest preserved fragment for each text is included as well.

Book	Scholarly opinions	Generally accepted earliest preserved fragment
Gospel of Matthew	AD 70-100	(AD 150 - 200)
Gospel of Mark	AD 63-85	(AD 350)
Gospel of Luke	AD 70-100	(AD 175 - 250)
Gospel of John	AD 90-110	(AD 125 - 160)
Acts	AD 80-100	(AD 250)
Romans	AD 57–58	(late 2nd century or 3rd century AD)
Corinthians	AD 57	(late 2nd century or 3rd century AD)
Galatians	AD 45-55	(late 2nd century or 3rd century AD)
Ephisians	AD 65	(late 2nd century or 3rd century AD)
Philippians	AD 57–62	(late 2nd century or 3rd century AD)

Colossians	AD 60+	(late 2nd century or 3rd century AD)
1 Thessalonians	AD 50	(late 2nd century or 3rd century AD)
2 Thessalonians	AD 50	(AD 300)
Timothy	AD 60-100	(AD 350)
Titus	AD 60-100	(AD 200)
Philemon	AD 56	(3rd century AD)
Hebrews	AD 80-90	(late 2nd century or 3rd century AD)
James	AD 50-200	(early 3rd century AD)
First Peter	AD 60-96	(3rd / 4th century AD)
Second Peter	AD 60-130	(3rd / 4th century AD)
Epistles of John	AD 90-100	(3rd / 4th century AD)
Jude	AD 66-90	(3rd / 4th century AD)
Revelation	AD 68-100	(AD 150 - 200)

PRE-EXISTING LEGENDS AND THE GOSPELS

The Roman dogma is a mixture of historical and pre-existing themes. Mithraism, a religion derived from Zoroastrism, was very popular in Rome at the time Christianity was spreading. Mithras was believed to be the son of the sun, sent to Earth to rescue humankind. Two centuries before the appearance of Jesus, the myth of Mithras held that Mithras was born of a virgin on December 25th in a cave, and his birth was attended by shepherds. Mithras sacrificed himself and on the last day had a supper with twelve of his followers. At that supper Mithras invited his followers to eat his body and drink his blood. He was buried in a tomb and after three days rose again. Mithras' festival coincided with the Christian Easter. This legend dates from at least one century before Jesus. It was absorbed in the Roman dogma.

The Egyptian god Osiris was also born on the 25th of December, died on a Friday and resurrected after spending three days in the underworld.

The Roman god Dionysus was hailed as 'The Saviour of Mankind' and 'The Son of God'. He was born (again on December 25th) when Zeus visited Persephone. Therefore, his father is God and his mother is a mortal virgin. Announced by a star, he is born in a cowshed and visited by three Magis. He turns water into wine and raises people from the dead. He is followed by twelve apostles. Dionysus' resurrection was a popular myth throughout the Roman Empire, although his name was different in each country. The rituals in honour of Dionysus included a meal of bread and wine, symbolising his body and blood.

The early Christians revered Dionysus's birthday as Jesus' birthday (Christmas) and the three-day spring festival of Dionysus roughly coincides with Easter. Jews had their own version of this festival (Theapeutae) since at least the year 10 (it is reported by Philo of Alexandria), 23 years before the crucifixion of Jesus (Armenians still celebrate the birthday of Jesus on January 6th).

The most credible theory of why the Christians of the third century chose the 25th of December as Jesus' birthday instead of the 1st of January is that the 25th December was already a major holiday, a festival called 'Dies Natalis Solis Invicti' instituted before 220AD.

CHAPTER FOUR

Pre-Christian universal myths and their comparison to the Jesus story

THE MAJOR PLAYERS

Attis of Phrygia

The story of Attis, the crucified and resurrected Phrygian son of God, predates the Christian saviour by centuries. As in the gospel tale, Attis shares the following characteristics with Jesus:

- Attis was born on December 25th of the Virgin Nana.
- He was considered the saviour who was slain for the salvation of mankind.
- His body was eaten as bread by his worshippers.
- His priests were 'eunuchs for the Kingdom of Heaven.'
- He was both the Divine Son and the Father.
- On 'Black Friday' he was crucified on a tree, from which his holy blood ran down to redeem the earth.
- He descended into the underworld.
- After three days Attis was resurrected, on March 25th (as tradition held of Jesus) as the 'Most High God'

The Buddha character has the following in common with the Christ figure:

Buddha

- Buddha was born on December 25th of the Virgin Maya, and his birth was attended by a 'Star of Announcement,' wise men and angels singing heavenly songs.
- At his birth, he was pronounced ruler of the world and presented with costly jewels and precious substances.

- His life was threatened by a king 'who was advisee to destroy the child, as he was liable to overthrow him'.
- Buddha was of royal lineage.
- He taught in the temple at 12.
- He crushed a serpent's head (as was traditionally said of Jesus) and was tempted by Mars, the 'Evil One,' when fasting.
- He was baptised in water, with the 'Spirit of God' or 'Holy Ghost' present.
- He performed miracles and wonders, healed the sick, fed 500 men from a 'small basket of cakes' and walked on water.
- Buddha abolished idolatry, was a 'sower of the word,' and preached 'the establishment of a kingdom of righteousness.'
- His followers were obliged to take vows of poverty and to renounce the world.
- He was transfigured on a mount, when it was said that his face shines as the brightness of the sun and moon.
- In some traditions he died on a cross.
- He was resurrected, as his coverings were unrolled from his body and his tomb was opened by supernatural powers.
- Buddha ascended bodily to Nirvana or heaven.
- He was called 'Lord', 'Father of the World' Almighty and All-knowing Ruler' 'Redeemer of all,' 'Holy One,' the 'Author of Happiness,' 'Possessor of All,' the 'Author of Happiness,' 'the Omnipotent', the 'Supreme Being' and 'the Eternal One'.
- He was considered the 'Sin Bearer', the 'Good Shepherd', the 'Carpenter', the 'Infinite and Everlasting' and the 'Alpha and Omega'.
- He came to fulfil, not destroy, the law.
- He is to return 'in the latter days' to restore order and to judge the dead

DIONYSUS/BACCHUS

Dionysus or Bacchus is thought of as being Greek, but he is a remake of the Egyptian god Osiris, whose cult extended throughout a large part of the ancient world for thousands of years. Dionysus' religion was well-developed in Thrace, northeast of Greece, and Phrygia, which became Galatia, where Attis also later reigned. Although Dionysus is best remembered for the rowdy celebrations in his name, Latinized as Bacchus, he had many other functions and contributed several aspects to the Jesus character:

- Dionysus was born of a virgin on December 25th and, as the Holy Child, was placed in a manger.
- He was a travelling teacher who performed miracles.
- He 'rode in a triumphal procession on an ass'. He was a sacred king killed and eaten in an Eucharistic ritual for fecundity and purification.
- Dionysus rose from the dead on March 25th.
- He was the God of the Vine, and turned water into wine.
- He was called 'King of Kings' and 'God of Gods'.
- He was considered the 'Only Begotten Son,' 'Saviour', Redeemer', 'Sin Bearer', 'Anointed One' and the 'Alpha and Omega'.
- He was identified with the Ram or Lamb.
- His sacrificial title of 'Dendrites' or 'Young Man of the Tree' intimates that he was hung on a tree or crucified.

CHAPTER FOUR

OSIRIS/HORUS

Osiris was also the god of the vine and a great travelling teacher who civilised the world. He was the ruler and judge of the dead. In his passion, Osiris was plotted against and killed by Set and 'the 72.' Like that of Jesus, Osiris' resurrection served to provide hope to all that they may do likewise and become eternal.

Osiris' 'son' or renewed incarnation, Horus, shares the following in common with Jesus:

- Horus was born of the virgin Isis-Meri on December 25th in a cave/manger with his birth being announced by a star in the East and attended by three wise men.
- His earthly father was named Seb (Joseph).
- He was of royal descent.
- At age 12, he was a child teacher in the Temple, and at 30 he was baptised, having disappeared for 18 years.
- Horus was baptised in the river Eridanus or Iarutana (Jordan) by Anup the Baptiser (John the Baptist), who was decapitated.
- He had 12 disciples, two of whom were his 'witnesses' and were named Anup and Aan (the two Johns).
- He performed miracles, exorcised demons and raised El-Azarus (El-Osiris) from the dead.
- Horus walked on water.
- His personal epithet was Iusa, the 'ever-becoming son' of Ptah, the Father. He was thus called Holy Child.
- He delivered a 'Sermon on the Mount' and his followers recounted the 'Sayings of Iusa.'
- Horus was transfigured on the Mount.

- He was crucified between two thieves, buried for three days in a tomb and resurrected.
- He was also the 'Way, the Truth, the Light', 'Messiah', 'God's Anointed Son', the 'Son of Man', the 'Good Shepherd', the 'lamb of God', the 'Word of Truth', etc.
- He was 'the Fisher' and was associated with the Fish ('Ichthys'), Lamb and Lion.
- He came to fulfil the Law.
- He was called 'the KRST,' or 'Anointed One.'

Furthermore, inscribed about 3500 years ago on the walls of the Temple at Luxor were images of the Annunciation, Immaculate Conception, Birth and Adoration of Horus, the 'Holy Ghost', impregnating the virgin and with the infant being attended by three kings, or magi, bearing gifts. In the catacombs at Rome are pictures of the baby Horus being held by the virgin mother Isis - the original Madonna and Child.

KRISHNA OF INDIA

The similarities between the Christian character and the Indian messiah Krishna number in hundreds, particularly when the early Christian texts now considered apocryphal are factored in. It should be noted that a common earlier English spelling of Krishna was 'Christna,' which reveals its relation to 'Christ.' Also, in Bengali, Krishna is reputedly 'Christos,' which is the same as the Greek for 'Christ' and which the soldiers of Alexander the Great called Krishna. It should be further noted that, as with Jesus, Buddha and Osiris, many people have believed and continue to believe in a historical Krishna. The following is a partial list of the correspondences between Jesus and Krishna:

- Krishna was born of the Virgin Devaki ('Divine One') on December 25th.
- His earthly father was a carpenter, who was off in the city paying tax while Krishna was born.
- His birth was signalled by a star in the east and attended by angels and shepherds, at which time he was presented with spices.
- The heavenly hosts danced and sang at his birth.
- He was persecuted by a tyrant who ordered the slaughter of thousands of infants.
- Krishna was anointed on the head with oil by a woman whom he healed.
- He is depicted as having his foot on the head of a serpent.
- He worked miracles and wonders, raising the dead and helping lepers, the deaf and the blind.
- Krishna used parables to teach people about charity and love, and he 'lived poor and he loved the poor.'
- He castigated the clergy, charging them with ambition and hypocrisy. Tradition says he 'fell victim to their vengeance'.
- Krishna's 'beloved disciple' was Arjuna or Ar-jouan (John).
- He was transfigured in front of his disciples.
- He gave his disciples the ability to work miracles.
- His path was 'strewn with branches.'
- In some traditions he died on a tree or was crucified between two thieves.

- Krishna was killed around the age of 30, and the sun darkened at his death.

- He rose from the dead and ascended to heaven 'in the sight of all men.'

- He was depicted on a cross with nail-holes in his feet, as well as having a heart emblem on his clothing.

- Krishna is the 'lion of the tribe of Saki.'

- He was called the 'Shepherd God,' and considered the 'Redeemer.' 'Firstborn', 'Sin-Bearer', 'Liberator', 'Universal Word'.

- He was deemed the 'Son of God' and ' our Lord and saviour' who came to earth to die for man's salvation.

- He was the second person of the Trinity.

- His disciples purportedly bestowed upon him the title 'Jezeus' or 'Jeseus', meaning 'pure essence.'

- Krishna is to return to judge the dead, riding on a white horse, to do battle with the 'Prince of Evil,' who will desolate the earth.

MITHRA OF PERSIA

Mithra/Mitra is a very ancient god found both in Persia and India and predating the Christian saviour by several thousand years. In fact, the cult of Mithra was shortly before the Christian era 'the most popular and widely spread 'Pagan' religion of the times.'

- Mithra was born of a virgin on December 25th in a cave, and his birth was attended by shepherds bearing gifts.

- He was considered a great travelling teacher and master.

- He had 12 companions or disciples.
- Mithra's followers were promised immortality.
- He performed miracles.
- As the 'great bull of the Sun', Mithra sacrificed himself for world peace.
- He was buried in a tomb and after three days rose again.
- His resurrection was celebrated every year.
- He was called 'The Good Shepherd' and is identified with both the Lamb and the Lion.
- He was considered the 'Way, the Truth and the Light' and the 'Logos', 'Redeemer', 'Saviour' and 'Messiah'.
- His sacred day was Sunday, the Lord's Day, hundreds of years before the appearance of Christ.
- Mithra had his principal festival on what was later to become Easter.
- His religion had a eucharist or 'Lord's Supper' at which Mithra said, 'He who shall not eat of my body nor drink of my blood so that he may be one with me and I with him, shall not be saved'.
- His annual sacrifice is the Passover of the Magi, a symbolic atonement or pledge of moral and physical regeneration.

Furthermore, the Vatican itself is built upon the papacy of Mithra, and the Christian hierarchy is nearly identical to the Mithras version it replaced.

The cave of the Vatican belonged to Mithra until 376 AD, when a city prefect suppressed the cult of the rival Saviour and seized the shrine in the name of Christ on the very birthday of the pagan god, December 25th.

THE MESSIAH

Messiah is a Hebrew word meaning anointed; it was originally used to initiate rulers who were actually appointed to their office. It was also used in connection with priests and sometimes prophets. The Greeks used their own word for the anointed, Christos. By the beginning of the AD era expectations of the coming of a Messiah were widespread and figured in all the Gospels. Here however we seem to have radically different images of the Messiah. Some seem to anticipate the coming of a priestly Messiah, while others expect a Royal or Kingly Messiah.

It is interesting that the Essenes taught of two Messiahs. The Kingly Messiah is 'The shoot of David and pre eminently the Messiah of Israel who will bring death to the ungodly and establish the kingdom of his people'. The Priestly Messiah is the Messiah of Aaron who will 'teach righteousness at the end of days'. The point of interest here is that the gospel writers managed to utilise such different traditions and create such divergent images of Jesus, while agreeing that he was the Messiah.

A Messiah is not a God. A Messiah is a person who prepares a way for a God.

Micah 5. (2): And you Bethlehem Ephratah though you are little among the thousands of towns of Judah yet out of you will come forth a ruler to govern Israel whose goings forth have been predicted from of old from eternity.

Micah 5. (6) …thus shall he deliver us from the Assyrians.

This was a messianic prophecy based on Bethlehem, from whence the warrior King would come.

Jesus could not have been the Messiah referred to in the prophecy as it was not fulfilled. He came anyway from Nazareth and went to Bethlehem, according to some of the Gospels, only for the census. In any case Jesus was not a warrior who could achieve success in battles.

Of the two main usages of the title Messiah, high priestly function is plainly not applicable to the Jesus of the Synoptics as he was not a hereditary Jewish priest. This leaves us with the image of the royal figure, the traditional anointed King of Israel. Clearly at some later stage clumsy attempts were made, especially by Matthew in his 'infancy' story, to create a Davidic pedigree for Jesus, but the main Synoptic tradition includes little support for it. Contrary to the general context, the portrait of Jesus in the Synoptics and in the rest of the New Testament shows that he was not a pretender to the throne of David or a would-be leader of a revolt against Rome.

The accusation that Jesus sought to become king of the Jews, or royal Messiah, first surfaces in the Gospels on the day of his crucifixion, or more precisely, at the moment of the transfer of his case from Jewish to Roman jurisdiction. Thereafter Pilate is always cited as referring to Jesus as the King of the Jews. The Roman charge or *titulus*, written on the cross, also read 'The King of the Jews' (Mark 15:26; Matt.27:37). The explicit indictment of disloyalty to the Emperor is probably Luke's creation. 'We found this man misleading our people, and forbidding us to pay the head tax to Caesar, and he says, concerning that He is a King' (Luke23:2). The charge is refuted by the only relevant reference to the payment of tax preserved in the Gospels, where Jesus is recorded as declaring, 'Give therefore to Caesar what is Caesar's'

(Matt.22:21). In fact, when under pressure from Pilate to substantiate their accusation, in even Luke's version the chief priests become rather vague: 'He has stirred up people, teaching throughout Judaea, and beginning from Galilee even to this place'(Luke 23:5). All in all, the whole political charge against Jesus sounds hollow.

Ideas about the coming of the Messiah developed over the last centuries BC; different groups were speculating, creating contradictory stories of where He would come from and what He would do. Would He be from the 'Davidic line' and would He fulfil the prophecies on His birthplace? More fundamentally, the Messiah was emphatically never expected to be anything like the Christ of Christianity, as first proposed by Paul. He was supposed to be a King like David, with a divine mandate, but still a King. Some expected him to have the power to work miracles like prophets and other holy men, but then people have always expected such powers of even their secular rulers.

The Messiah was not only expected to drive the foreign oppressors out of the sacred land, but also to restore the Kingdom of Israel to its original state. This necessarily involved the rather difficult task of gathering the twelve tribes back together.

CHAPTER 5

The god of the early Jews

Jews at the time of Jesus did not learn theology by studying it philosophically, proving it in the context of academic debate or by going to university or a seminary. Instead, in the same way that modern children learn to value freedom and human rights, Jesus learned Judaism from his father and mother and his extended family and his community. The first thing he learned came to him in the form of a sacred creed that was known as much by living it out as by thinking one's way through it. Theology is more caught than taught. It is an old ethnic identity, Land, Torah and Temple. That story is a theology, and that theology is caught in the web of daily recitation of a Creed.

THE SHEMA

As a young child Jesus would have been taught by his father and mother to begin and end his day by reciting (aloud) the sacred Shema:

Hear, Israel: the Lord is our God, the Lord is our one God; and you must love the Lord your God with all your heart and with all your soul and with all your strength.

These commandments which I give you this day are to be remembered and taken to heart; repeat them to your children, and speak of them both indoors and out of door, when you lie down and when you get up. Bind them as a sign on your hand and wear them as a pendant on your forehead; write them on the doorposts of your houses and on your gates.

This is the shape of Israel's 'theology': there is only one God; his name is Yahweh; Israel is to love him with every part of its being - heart, soul and strength.

GOD AS FATHER

Jesus learned about God and about Israel and his own relationship to God and Israel through the Shema, and the key word in the Shema is to 'love' God. Like any teacher of his day, Jesus carried on this tradition about God and developed it in his own way. God, whose personal name is Yhwh (Yahweh) for Jews, Jesus often calls Abba, which is the Aramaic word for 'father'. For him, God is to be called and to be related to as Abba. And this is the language of the home and the community.

God is a word we learn in our earliest childhood, and even very young children can use it with a certain level of competence. Seven-year-olds can discuss whether God is a being who lives in heaven, a kind of presence spread throughout the Universe, or an idea 'inside you'. In these simple ideas they show an ability to deal with the concepts of theism - God as a being separate from and superior to the Universe.

The classical concept of God is beyond space and time, infinite and eternal. God is the all-powerful Creator, who created all things out of nothing simply by a command. God cannot be influenced by any external factor. But God is not simply all-powerful. God is supremely good, and God's purpose in creating the world was to bring about the maximum possible distribution of goodness and happiness. In creating, God did not simply act upon impulse. God is all-knowing.

THE EARLY HISTORY OF THE JEWS

Jesus was a Jew, not a Christian. This single historical fact opens the door to understanding Jesus as he really was in his own time and place. It is a door that many have never thought to enter. Jesus was circumcised, observed the Passover, read the Bible in Hebrew and kept Saturday as the Sabbath day. Two thousand years of relatively hostile separation and alienation between Judaism and Christianity has tended to obscure the fact that Jesus grew up in a religious and cultural world that has been almost entirely lost to the subsequent developments of Christianity.

The origins of Judaism are at least as mysterious and controversial as those of Christianity, and need only be summarised here. The sacred texts of the people of Israel - to Christians, the Old Testament - were put together in the sixth century BC, and though obviously based on more ancient sources they were heavily edited and adapted, making it impossible to judge their accuracy.

The legendary history - undoubtedly containing nuggets of truth, although opinions differ as to just how much - goes back to the time when Yahweh made a covenant with the patriarch Abraham that if he and his descendants worshipped Him as the one true God, he would make them into a mighty people and present them with Canaan as their homeland. Abraham's grandson, Jacob - whom God renamed Israel - was, through his sons, the legendary proprietor of the twelve tribes of the nation.

According to the story, the sons settled in Egypt, where their descendants were enslaved. Generations later Moses led the Israelites out of Egypt to the promised land of Canaan, which was divided between the twelve tribes, around the thirteenth century BC.

However, many historians and archaeologists, including Jewish ones, now believe that the Israelites were a mix of immigrants from Egypt and the already established Canaanites.

Similarly the evidence reveals that the Jews' early religion was by no means as uncompromisingly monotheistic as the sixth-century BC reformers pretended. Although Yahweh reigned supreme, other deities, particularly his spouse, the Canaanite goddess Asherah, sat with him in the Temple. The first commandment, 'You shall have no other gods before (or besides) me', implies that other gods existed.

Monotheism today is taken to mean a belief in one God and one only. In the ancient world many - probably most - religions believed in a single supreme creator - God, who existed before, and created, all the other gods and goddesses.

For about three hundred years the Israelites were a loose confederacy of tribes under the dominant Ephraim, which produced Moses' successor Joshua, conqueror of the promised land, and also had the honour of protecting the Hebrews' most sacred object, the Ark of the Covenant. It was only in c 1000 BC that the Israelites were unified into one kingdom of Israel under David, who moved the Ark to Jerusalem, triggering the age-old rivalry between the tribes of Judah and Ephraim that endured until Jesus' day in the form of antagonism between Jews and Samaritans (previously Jerusalem was sacred to the Canaanite god Shalim, from which the name is derived, and not, as is often claimed, from the Hebrew shalom, peace - this can be seen in an Egyptian text of the nineteenth century BC in which the city appears as Urusalim, 'the foundation of Shalim').

David's son and successor Solomon, famed for his wisdom, had the great Temple built in Jerusalem as the focus for the worship of Yahweh.

However, after Solomon the kingdom split into two. Ten tribes in the north, led by Ephraim, formed the kingdom of Israel, while the two in the south - centred on Jerusalem - became the kingdom of Judah (after the largest of the two tribes, the other tribe being Benjamin, although the two became virtually indistinguishable because of intermarriage). Two centuries afterwards, the northern kingdom was invaded by the Assyrian Empire, leaving Judah predominant. As a result, Judah gave its name to the religion and the people itself (although they would always think of their land and religious community as 'Israel').

But in 607BC it was Judah's turn to be invaded, by the Babylonians under Nebuchadnezzar. Solomon's Temple was utterly destroyed and the people carried off into captivity in several traumatic waves of deportation. Seventy years later the Babylonians were defeated by the Persians and the exiled Hebrews - almost all of whom, having been born in captivity, and had never seen Jerusalem - returned to their homeland, where, although it remained under Persian control, they were permitted to practise their religion.

The catalogue of conquest continued. In 313BC Alexander the Great drove the Persians out and Israel was absorbed into the Hellenistic world. After his death it fell under the control of the Selucids, a dynasty of Hellenised Syrians. In 167 BC the Selucid king, Antiochus Epephanes, concerned by the number of his subjects converting to Judaism, began a concerted massacre. The religion was banned, women and their circumcised male babies were executed, the Temple was plundered and - an act of deliberate blasphemy- a statue of Zeus set up over the high altar. It was this that sparked off the Maccabean Revolt, led by Judas Maccabaeus ('the Hammer'), son of the high priest. After a lengthy struggle the Maccabees drove out the Selucids and established themselves as both secular and spiritual rulers of Jerusalem, founding the Hasmonean dynasty (after Hasmon, a venerable Maccabean ancestor).

Now it was the Jews' turn to be conquerors. Under the Hasmoneans there was a forty-year period of expansion and conquest of neighbouring regions: Sumaria, Idumea (the biblical Edom) to the south, and later Galilee to the far north, beyond Samaria. One result was the destruction of the Samaritan's own temple on the sacred mountain of Gerizim - a rival to the one in Jerusalem- which did nothing to endear the Jews to them.

In 63 BC the Roman general Pompey was invited to intervene in an internal power struggle: an unwise move as, somewhat predictably, he claimed the land for Rome instead. After various struggles a distinguished Idumean general named Herod 'the Great' was appointed King of the Jews, and ruled from 37 to 4 BC.

When Herod died in 4 BC, his lands were divided among his three sons. Later a deputation of Jews and Samaritans went to Rome to complain about his successor, his eldest son, Herod

Archelaus. The emperor Augustus banished him to Gaul, giving over his lands to a Roman prefect, or governor. The most infamous prefect, Pontius Pilate, was appointed in 26 AD. Although the prefect had overall control in Judaea, the council of the Sanhedrin had authority over certain civil matters - mainly the practice of the religion, subject to oversight by the Romans.

So the Palestine into which Jesus emerged was complicated and fraught with division and tension, most obviously between the people and their Roman overlords, although the degree to which the Jews actively opposed their rule varied. There were militant nationalist groups, such as Zealots, who regarded the presence of Romans in their holy city as blasphemy pure and simple and aimed to kick them out. Others were more philosophical, convinced that nothing could be done. And there were even those who thought that since nothing could happen without God's approval, he must have wanted Rome to rule over Israel. Paul suggested that the emperor could only have power if God ordained it, therefore Christians should not oppose him. But then Paul was related to Herod and Agrippa and ironically the emperor Paul was referring to was Nero. The Roman presence was a fact of Jewish life in first-century Palestine. Any would-be religious preacher would have been expected to make his views on the issue known, including of course Jesus.

A startling example of this multiculturalism surfaced in 1990, with the discovery in the southern suburbs of Jerusalem of a group of ossuaries belonging to the family of Caiaphas, High Priest from 18 to 36 AD, whom the Gospels describe as responsible for the plot that killed Jesus. One of the ossuaries contained his bones and another those of his son Jehosaf. But the biggest surprise is that one member of this family, a woman named Miriam, had been buried according to pagan customs, as a coin (dated 42-3 AD) was found in her mouth. The practice of Hellenised Jews or even non-Jews marrying into Jewish families was by no means unknown in Jerusalem, but a member of the High Priest's own family being blatantly buried as a pagan! If such a thing was acceptable so far up the hierarchy, Jerusalem really must have been multicultural.

Although we can regard Jesus as entirely and fundamentally Jewish, he was living and operating in a dual culture.

THE RELATIONSHIP OF JESUS THE JEW WITH GOD AND GOD'S KINGDOM

Much biblical scholarship of the last decades (especially since the second Vatican Council absolved the Jews from the nineteen-centuries-old charge of deicide) has rediscovered the 'Jewishness' of Jesus.

So the question arises - just how Jewish was Jesus, and given the varieties of Judaism in his time, what kind of Jew was he? One tendency among scholars of the last century, now largely discarded, was the attempt to strip him and his message of Jewish contexts. The idea was that Jesus, though born a Jew, realised the deficiencies of his obsolete ancestral faith and moved beyond it into a type of 'universalism'. Jesus, according to this view, proclaimed the Fatherhood of God and the brotherhood of humankind with a set of universal ethics that superseded the legalistic ways of Judaism. We now understand that such views have no historical basis and in fact are subtle manifestations of Christian anti-Semitism. Yet they have become deeply etched into our Western cultural consciousness.

To be a Jew in 1st century Roman-occupied Palestine had as

much to do with national and ethnic identity as with abstract religious beliefs. To put it another way, for many Jews it was impossible to separate the social and political realities of military occupation and economic oppression from Jewish piety and faith. The Jewish belief that the people of Israel had been chosen by God to become a 'model nation' that would exemplify justice and righteousness to the entire world was fundamental. The Hebrew Prophets had predicted that in the last days all nations would go up to Jerusalem to learn about the one true Creator God, drawn by Israel's moral example of peace and piety.

Not all Jews accepted such an idealistic vision but enough did that John the Baptizer, Jesus and his brother James were able to spark a movement that threatened the highest levels of the political and religious establishment.

Jesus' family, like all Galilean Jews, would have made the pilgrimage trek south to Jerusalem as required by the Torah three times a year, every year, in the spring at Passover, in the early summer for the feast of Pentecost and in the fall for the feast of Tabernacles.

Judaism can be summed up under four rubrics: God, Torah, Land, and Chosen People.

As a Jew, Jesus would have affirmed his belief in the one Creator God Yahweh above all the other Gods or spiritual entities: the divine revelation of the Torah as a blueprint for social, moral, and religious life; the holiness of the Land of Israel as a perpetual birthright to the nation; and the notion that the people of Israel, descendants of Abraham, Isaac and Jacob, had been chosen by God to enlighten all nations. Their historic mission was to draw humanity to the one God and his Torah revelations.

As a Jew, Jesus was circumcised at the Jewish temple in

Jerusalem at eight days old. He observed the Sabbath as a weekly day of rest. He avoided eating certain forbidden animals or consuming blood. He celebrated the required pilgrim festivals, and he practised ritual purity as commanded in the Torah. As a Jewish male Jesus wore the fringed tassels (tzitzit) on his outer garment, which would indicate his strict observance of the mitzvoth, or commandments of the Torah or Jewish Law. What he did not accept, as we shall see, were certain oral traditions and interpretations that some rabbinic teachers had added to the biblical commandments. He would have been horrified to see similar additions made to the original Gospels.

There is a sense in which Judaism is both exclusive and universal. These 'marks' of being Jewish can be seen as social 'separators', and they were well known in Roman society. We find Roman writers who attack the Jews and hold them in contempt, but also those who admire them and even adopt some of their ways. There is substantial evidence that significant numbers of non-Jews were attracted to Judaism and even attended synagogues throughout the Roman world. To do this it was not required that one should formally convert and become Jewish, although that could be done. Gentiles who turned from 'idols' to the 'true and living God' and observed the prohibitions against stealing, murder, and sexual immorality were considered 'righteous Gentiles' or 'God fearers'. Various Jewish groups differed radically in attitudes toward non-Jews, ranging from exclusion and separation to welcoming accommodation.

Jesus always stressed the importance of his relationship with God, but in Jewish First Century terms the expression Son of God did not have a literal meaning but it meant specifically having a special relationship with God. Giza Vermes is one of the worlds leading Jewish scholars, the first professor of Jewish studies at Oxford. He says in his book, the Authentic Gospel of Jesus, under the heading 'The Religion of Jesus and Christianity': 'In the light of all that has been said how can the religion of Jesus be summarized? His religion is a particular response to a specific situation by an extraordinary man. Christianity on the other hand is the general development of the religion of Jesus by practical people planning for the future in an ordinary time setting. The two are definitely connected yet they are also radically different.'

For Jesus the stage was soon to be set. The situation arose from the political turmoil generated by Roman rule in Palestine, first established in 63 BC. The unrest was clearly manifest in rebellious acts following the death of Herod the Great in 4 BC, which were violently suppressed by the Romans, and in the bitter resentment caused by the census or Roman tax registration imposed on Judaea by Quirinius, governor of Syria, in AD 6.

The political unrest stirred up and nurtured a feverish longing for an impending divine intervention, especially in the wake of the widely influential ministry of John the Baptist in the late twenties. Jesus was to address and respond to this feverish expectation. The Kingdom of God was believed to be at hand. The Kingdom was a wholly Jewish issue, involving Jews alone and requiring an exclusively Jewish solution. The non-Jewish world played no active part in it.

Jesus had a particular way of promoting the cause of the Kingdom that stemmed from his total conviction of the necessity of the task for which he was commissioned. In consequence he demanded unfettered trust in God from his disciples. Owing to the final solution nature of their task, its pursuit could not tolerate either slowness or procrastination and required absolute devotion, irrespective of the cost. The goal in view was a seat at the last banquet table prepared by God for those who responded to the invitation which Jesus conveyed to them with prophetic urgency. To follow his appeal and enter into the spirit of his fears for the death of Judaism, the disciples of Jesus were to leave behind uninspired religion, switch their sight to the highest ideals and steam ahead at top speed.

What makes this religion particularly distinctive is the relentless effort imposed by Jesus on himself and on his followers. He never showed signs of hesitation, nor did he suffer evasion on the part of his disciples. The belief that the Kingdom is near, is coming, has come, carried with it a permanent air of urgency.

Compared with the early dynamic religion of Jesus, fully-evolved Christianity seems to belong to another world. It is a mixture of the introduction of the triune God (three in one), a dying and risen only Son of God, embellished with sacramental symbolism, ecclesiastical discipline and a built-in anti-Judaism, it is hard to imagine how the two could have sprung from the same source.

Geza Vermes continues:

Yet 2000-year-old Christianity, which is responsible for the survival of the Gospel tradition, proudly considers Jesus as its founder. The historical Jesus believed in the coming of the Kingdom in his lifetime and this belief furnished the motivation of his action. However, this belief did not come true. Yet, one would imagine that detached observers familiar with the Roman world could easily have anticipated such a tragic outcome. It would seem that only when he let out the Aramaic cry, 'Eloi, Eloi, lama sabachthani' (My God, My God, why hast thou forsaken me'), did Jesus suddenly perceive that he would not be able to complete his task, a thought which previously had not even crossed his mind. What we know of his religious personality makes it unlikely that he died as a rebel against God. Indeed, it is easy to imagine that the further cry, mentioned by Mark and Matthew (Mark 15:37; Matt.27:50) and restored by Luke as 'O My Father, into thy hands I commit my spirit!' (Luke 23:46), was a sigh of final submission to God: 'Thy will be done' or 'Your will is done'.

For a twenty-first-century person with genuine spiritual insight, the absence of the literal fulfilment of Jesus' belief in the arrival of the Kingdom in his time does not count as a failure. Nor does it detract in any way from the fundamental truth that no religious attitude is real without an all-pervading sense of urgency which converts ideas into instant action. And death, which is never far distant from any human being, is a sufficient reason for anyone to feel constantly under pressure on account of the shortness of the allotted time.

It should be remembered that this extract comes from a very Jewish standpoint. It is none the less interesting, as we should of course consider the perspective from more than one direction if we are to obtain some idea of the background that prevailed in the first few centuries after Jesus' death.

CHAPTER 6

❧

The esoteric history behind the origins of Christianity

The initiate Kings of the Old Testament - Saul, David and Solomon - had kingdoms centred on Salem, or Jerusalem as we know it. The powerful neighbouring cultures of the time were also ruled by initiate Kings, for example in Egypt and Mesopotamia. These dynasties had ruled since the 'time of the Gods'. They were divine figures filled with divine power. According to the ancient Sumerian king list, the kingship descended from Heaven and the Man who held it or inherited it had to be initiated into the secrets of the Heavenly World. In Egypt, Sumeria, Babylon and Iran, the ceremony of coronation took place alongside the initiation. An insight into the Divine World was not for ordinary mortals. The King was the Solar Dignity, the Lord of the Cosmos, who ruled the Earth from the mountain of God.

The Israelite conception was however somewhat different. The King was an initiate and a priest, but could hardly be identified directly with Jahweh, the God of Abraham, and the invisible God who made all things but who was not present in any external form. In Israel the King was not worshipped as 'God on Earth'. Through this approach, and gradually through change in the surrounding cultures, democracy demanded a much wider access to the personal spiritual experience - why should it be limited to the few? Thus the religion of Israel began to look for the beginnings of spiritual awareness and values in individuals themselves. In the older parts of the Old Testament Yahweh manifested himself in storm and other natural forces, which to the seers of those days were revelations of spiritual energies.

Later on in the Old Testament, Yahweh speaks as a 'still small voice' within. The seer becomes a prophet, who is not an initiate but a man specially gifted by birth in spiritual matters. He hears the voice of Yahweh and proclaims to mankind what he hears.

The great myths by which man has lived his life gradually fade away and man now needs counselling or instructing on how to orientate himself in this world. In ancient Israel, humanity begins to walk along the long road that leads to our sense of freedom over desire for autonomy as spiritual agents in the world. Now the central idea of creation was formed. The old world did not believe the world was created but that it was more the birth of the cosmos, but the Israelites made creation one of the foundation stones of the religion of Israel.

One of the Nag Hammadi works is particularly interesting; it is called Dialogue of the Saviour. It presents ideas of an esoteric kind and is partly based around the mystical sequence of seeking, finding, wondering, reigning and resting, which is remarkably similar to the teachings of Jesus recorded in the Gospel of Thomas, in which the disciples ask questions of Jesus and are led from understanding (seeking and finding) to actual visions (wondering) and look forward to greater stages of attainment (reigning and rest).

THE SYNOPTIC GOSPELS: MATTHEW, MARK AND LUKE

Scholars over many years have noted the similarity of these three gospels from the common material in each. They are called Synoptic, which means 'seeing from the same point of view'.

THE 'I AM'

Jesus used the 'I am' statement often in his communication with his disciples, but what does it mean?

With the Aramaic subtext of Jesus 'I am' statements, we have to consider the approach to the problem of individuality. If everything is linked in communion with 'The One', why do we have individuality? The Aramaic use of the word 'I' means literally one to one, or one of one. It is a bridge to the consciousness of the One (the only individual). So by using the 'I am' Jesus is including and pointing beyond his personal awareness of cosmic unity. He is acting as the bridge for those who can attune to Him in this way. He points out that a deep unfolding sense of I guides all primal matter.

John 8:12: 'I am the light of the world, he who follows me shall not walk in darkness, but he shall find for himself the light of life.'

Time and again Jesus spells out in many different ways his messages to his disciples and to the world.

Gospel of Thomas Logo 1:
And he said
He who finds the inner meaning of these logia
will not taste death

This first logo sets the tone for all 114 sayings or parables attributed to Jesus in the Gospel of Thomas, so what is the message in those Logos?

We must keep searching for the true meaning of the parables, and when we can understand this inner meaning we will marvel.

We shall find that life is independent of the death of the body, a life everlasting. We are being directed to seek and realise the awareness of the spiritual truth which is within ourselves and is independent of time. It is now the ongoing Creation where we come from and where we will ultimately go. The secret is to understand the oneness of the beginning and the end.

JOHN Chapter 1 verse 1-4 (Peshitta Bible)

1. The Word was in the beginning and that very Word was with God and God was that Word

2. The same was in the beginning with God

3. Everything came to be by his hand and without Him not even one thing that was created came to be.

4. The life was in Him and the life is the light of men.

Thus life is unrelated to time and hence to death, and is therefore only an experience here and now and part of an ongoing creation.

In the Christian Church as it evolved in the West, it became more important to determine what Jesus represented as the Christian Messiah than to look at his sayings in the original Middle East sense. This was a type of spiritual translation or interpretation which uses the possible and difficult translation of the Hebrew words as a basis for contemplation, devotion and spiritual practice. This led to the earliest so-called Jesus movements to adopt a multiplicity of different practices and beliefs. The same was true for what we call Judaism, which did not begin to take the organised shape it has today until after the destruction of the Temple in AD70.

Jesus then may be seen not as an orthodox Christian of the first century AD nor even just as a Jew, but as a teacher influenced by the spirituality of the Middle East in general; he was after all a 'native' Middle East person. Quotations from Jesus were always given in Aramaic or possibly Hebrew, when quoting from scripture. An examination of Jesus' words in Aramaic and a translation straight from Aramaic to English reveals the spirituality of his teachings in the light of Middle East tradition. Aramaic had been spoken in the region of Palestine and indeed the whole Middle East since the 3rd century BC. It should be remembered that the people heard the stories and as they were repeated, oral tradition prevailed, depending on the telling of the story and circumstances surrounding the telling.

As an example of difference of translation, consider the following from John 8:58:

New International Bible:

'I tell you the truth before Abraham was born I am'

The Pershitta Bible

'Truly truly I say to you before Abraham was born I was.'

I am what I am

Or in Hebrew, *Ehyeh asher ehyeh*, the correct interpretation of which is 'I will be who I will be'.

In the early years following the death of Jesus there were many diverse ideas about what Jesus said and did by people who were in fact Jewish Christians or Christian Jews. As a result there were many 'Gospels' in the first three centuries after his death. As the remembered words were put into writing, their diversity began to diminish. The process by which an oral story turns into a written one involves selection, as many differences occur in oral tradition. Each group of people will make their own selection from their various oral recollections into one written form. Translations vary as to source used and the belief or persuasion of the translator.

REFLECTION AND THE PATERNOSTER (THE LORD'S PRAYER)

It is time to stop, to think, to consider. Why can't all God's people worship Him in their own particular way? Why must all creeds and religions other than the one we follow be wrong, and ours the only true path to God?

The vision of Jesus was one of total union with God, which is exemplified in the Pater Noster.

PATER NOSTER IN ARAMAIC

Avvon-d-bish-maiya, nith-quaddash ahimmukh.
Tih-the mal-kutukh. Nih-weh shiw-yanukh;
Ei-chana d'bish-maiya; ap b'ar-ah.
Haw lan lakh-ma d'soonqa-nan yoo-mana.
O'shwooq lan kho'bein;
Ei-chana d'ap kh'nan shwiq-qan l'khaya-ween.
Oo'la te-ellan l'niss-yoona;
Il-la pash-shan min beesha.
Mid-til de-di-lukh hai mal-kutha
OO kai-la oo tush-bookh-ta
L'alam al-mein. Aa-meen.

ENGLISH TRANSLATION FROM THE ARAMAIC

Our heavenly Father, hallowed is your name.
Your kingdom is come. Your will is done,
As in heaven so also on earth.
Give us the bread of our daily need.
And leave us serene,
Just as we allow others serenity.
And do not pass us through trial,
Except separate us from the evil one.
For yours is the kingdom.
The Power and the Glory
To the end of the Universe, of all the Universes. Amen.

The Paternoster has seven petitions modelled on the psalms. The first three are concerned with the Glory of God.

Our heavenly Father,

1. Hallowed is your name

2. Your Kingdom is come

3. Your will is done, as in heaven so also on earth.

You will notice that in the translation of the Aramaic version these three petitions are in the present tense. God's name is hallowed, his kingdom is come and his will is done. In the standard biblical versions, this segment is in the future - God's name be hallowed, his kingdom come, his will be done.

The emphasis on the present in the Aramaic version is of ritual importance, because it underlines Jesus' teaching of the paramount relevance of the Now in all petitions to God and all acts of will. Things must happen Now for Jesus, because Now implies the petition has already been granted. God's name is always hallowed, his kingdom always comes and his will is always done. Not in the future, but Now and always. This emphasis on the present is missing in the traditional versions of the Bible, diminishing significantly the power of prayer.

The remaining four petitions are requests for divine assistance to humanity:

4. Give us the bread for our daily need.

5. And leave us serene, just as we allow others serenity.

6. And do not pass us through trial,

7. Except separate us from the evil one.

The fifth petition is careful in reminding God that we have allowed serenity to others. This means we have forgiven others for their offences, granting them peace thereby. Therefore we are worthy to receive God's forgiveness for our own sins. That is why Jesus advises his disciples to forgive their debtors before they pray.

The prayer then closes with the doxology (a hymn or liturgical formula ascribing Glory to God), glorifying God:

For yours is the Kingdom, the Power and the Glory to the end of the Universe, of all Universes. Amen.

This remarkable hymn, in the original Aramaic, goes beyond 'forever and ever'. The person who wrote it professes a profound knowledge of cosmology, for he believes that there are other universes, something astrophysicists have only recently hypothesised.

The total union with God presumes that what is being asked of the Creator has already taken place, because the person reciting the prayer has complete faith, untainted by doubt that their request has been granted before the words have been uttered. That is implied in God's wisdom and understanding.

Our Heavenly Father, Hallowed is your name.

If Jesus had wanted to introduce a formula for the religion he taught, he had many opportunities to do so. In the Gospel of Mark, a scribe is reported as having asked Him which was the first of all the commandments. At this stage he could have answered in a way to involve himself, to promote himself, for example if he wished us to believe that he was part of a Holy Trinity on an equal footing with God and the Holy Spirit. Instead he reverted to his Jewish roots.

Mark 12:29/30

Hear Oh Israel The lord our God is one Lord. And you must love the Lord your God with all your heart and with all your soul and with all your mind and with all your might.
This is the first commandment.

If Jesus refers to God, as he does, as 'The Lord our God' and then as 'The Lord your God', how can we possibly refer to Jesus as Lord? There is only one Lord - The Lord our God.
In the Gloria in Excelsis, in the book of common worship for the Church of England, we say:

Lord Jesus Christ only Son of the Father
Lord God, Lamb of God
You take away the sin of the world

Have mercy on us
You are seated at the right hand of the Father
Receive our prayer
For you alone are the Holy one
You alone are the Lord.

How can this deliberate contradiction of Jesus' words be acceptable? Why say you alone are the Lord when Jesus himself is often quoted as referring to the Lord our God, and the Lord our God is one Lord?

It is very important to note that 'lord' is never linked in the Synoptic Gospels to the messianic function of Jesus. There is not a single instance in Mark, Matthew or Luke in which Jesus as 'Lord' is associated with anything to do with divinity. Only in John, and even there only once, are the two concepts formally linked by Doubting Thomas, saying 'Oh My Lord and my God' (John 20:28). It is therefore beyond doubt that this reverential title, in addition to being applicable to God, possesses a variety of other meanings, so its precise significance cannot be determined without a context any more than, for instance, that of the English 'Sir' can be identified as the title of a schoolmaster in a school or the form of address of a King in a royal palace.

CHAPTER 7

The recorded Jesus

Sometimes historical tradition is overturned by such revelatory archaeological finds, but all too often they are ignored because they conflict with preferred establishment dogma.

In this context the biblical scriptures are records of past events like any other, and are therefore defined as history. Whether they are accurate or wholly factual is another matter. The New Testament is a compilation of Christian documents, and scholars are in general agreement that these canonical gospels were written some decades after the events which they portray.

Since the gospels are of specifically Christian origin, it is evident that the Romans would not necessarily have written about Jesus and his apostles in a positive manner, as is made clear in The Annals of Imperial Rome, which describe Jesus' mission as a 'shameful practice'.

The Annals cement Jesus in history outside his Christian portrayal. In this manner the existence of Jesus Christ as a real figure of the era is confirmed by a parallel record from his enemies, whose perception of his character was entirely different from that of the gospel writers. His followers are described in the Roman annals as being 'notoriously depraved'; his beliefs are stated to have been a 'deadly superstition', and his sentence of execution by the governor of Judaea, Pontius Pilate, is documented in 1st-century Roman history as well as in the Christian gospels.

In the Jewish archive, we find that Jesus is also mentioned twice in the Antiquities of the Jews. Compiled in about AD 92, this chronicle relates that Jesus began his ministry during the reign of Tiberius Caesar, in the period AD 26-35 when Pilate was the Roman governor in Jerusalem. This locates Jesus firmly within the historical fabric of the era, but without any mention of his divinity. When discussing the early establishment of the Christian movement, the Hebrew narrative refers to 'James, the brother of Jesus who was called Christ'. This supports the Roman Annals, which also identify Jesus as being the Christ (from the Greek word *christos*, meaning 'king').

In another Antiquities entry, Jesus is referred to as 'a wise man and a teacher... who drew to him many of the Jews in addition to many of the Gentiles'. The chronicle further states that 'when Pilate, at the suggestion of the principal men among us, had him condemned to be crucified, those that had loved him from the first did not forsake him'.

Overall, there is firm documentary evidence, from both Roman and Jewish sources, as well as the Christian scriptures, that Jesus was present in Judaea during the reign of Emperor Tiberius; that he was a teacher with a significant following; and was sentenced to execution by Pontius Pilate.

For instance some perceived Jesus as the son of God, while to others he was an earthly Messiah, and many thought he was an intuitive prophet. Some factions upheld the notion of the virgin birth while others denied it absolutely, and there were constant disagreements concerning the extent to which the Judaism of Jesus should influence Christianity. If it can be said that the constitution of the Church of Rome achieved a unified end, then that achievement arose from confronting these disagreements in order to produce a doctrinal canon and a commonly regulated set of ground-rules for the Faith. Those bishops and leaders who did not agree with the decisions were either reluctantly brought into line or henceforth excluded from the self-styled orthodox movement.

In essence, what emerged was a religion based on the opinions of the most influential Church Fathers, along with a modicum of debated compromise. Into this were amalgamated various aspects of pagan belief in order to ease the conversion for hitherto non-Christians of the Empire. The resultant new Christianity was either good or bad news, depending on one's perspective. Either way, however, it was in many respects far removed from anything that Jesus himself might have recognised.

Jesus, we are told in the New Testament, began his ministry in the year AD 29 - 'the fifteenth year of the reign of Tiberius Caesar' as given in Luke 3:1 - and was sentenced to crucifixion in AD 33. The religious movement which sprang from his teachings acquired the name Christianity 11 years later in Antioch, Syria.

SO WHO WAS THE REAL JESUS?

So who was Jesus? He was a person in harmony with the mythic first human in Jewish cosmology, Adam, and with Holy Wisdom. He spoke about sacred unity in the form of spirit breath, holiness, spaciousness and Heaven and Earth in ways that a people raised with a Semitic view of the universe would understand. At the same time he challenged the conventional way in which these concepts were interpreted by the ruling powers of his time.

If we look at the overall content of his sayings and teachings as recorded in both the canonical Gospels and in early writings like the Gospel of Thomas, we can develop more of a feeling of what he was like and what he means to us. This is not a matter of what Jesus means in a factual or theological sense but what his aura, his name or teaching activates in each of us. Which aspect of his wisdom teachings can we embody in our everyday lives?

The western view of Jesus, his life and teachings, taught by the Roman Church, is one of a fixed interpretation, totally inflexible. There can only be one translation, one meaning, one way. The written word as recorded and copied by the Roman Church must be correct, because the Church has said so. Any other deviations are heretical and have had to be removed and destroyed by whatever means was necessary.

For example, in AD 591 Mary Magdalene suddenly became a fallen woman, a prostitute, thanks to Pope Gregory the Great, who confused her with the fallen woman in Chapter 7 of Luke's gospel. 1378 years later, in response to information contained in the Dead Sea Scrolls and the Nag Hammadi texts, which included the Gospel of Mary Magdalene, the Vatican finally rescinded that statement and confirmed Mary Magdalene as one of Jesus' followers and sponsors. Pope John Paul II bestowed on her the title of Apostle to the Apostles. Why today is she then still widely regarded as a prostitute? How much else did the early Church get wrong, either accidentally or deliberately?

Basically, everything Christians believe in today and have believed since the fourth century, all the rituals we observe, the Eucharist, the holy days - none of it was part of what the immediate followers of Jesus believed in. Most of the rituals and supernatural beliefs were imported from other religions, from the Resurrection and Easter to Christmas. They are not new and exclusive to Christians.

But the Church's founders did a great job. It's been a runaway bestseller for almost two thousand years. And every body or sect that did not toe the 'party line' were eradicated like the Ebionites, the Nasoreans, the Cathars, the Templars, and many more besides.

The early days of Christianity are just one big scholarly black spot when it comes to verifiable, documented facts. There isn't much we can definitely say did happen in the Holy Land almost two thousand years ago, but there is one thing we do know: none of the four Gospels that make up the New Testament was written by contemporaries of Jesus. This never fails to take followers of the faith by surprise. We do know that the man we know as Jesus lived and was crucified.

Rank-and-file Christians have been betrayed over the years and are still being kept in near-complete ignorance about the often cataclysmic flaws in the Gospel stories, and treated condescendingly by scholars and priests as if they were children unable to cope with the revelation that Santa does not exist. (Pope John Paul II's pronouncement that Christ was not actually born on 25 December upset a great many of his flock, and even greater revelations about the man believed to be God would have a traumatic effect on millions - but then whose fault is that? Who has led them to believe without question in the first place? And with whom do we still celebrate 25th December as his birthday?

One thing that has become startlingly clear, however, is the extent of the Church's cover-up of certain matters that are absolutely fundamental to the understanding of Christianity and Christ himself. And make no mistake, it continues to this day.

In trying to find the historical Jesus, let us draw a distinction between the Jesus of history and the Christ of faith. The former is an individual - maybe man, maybe God, perhaps a bit of both - who lived out his significant life in a specific geographical location in a certain period of history. Because he did so he is open to the same methods of historical inquiry as any other individual from the past. On the other hand, the Jesus Christ of pure faith is beyond the reach of historians, since they have no means of dealing with the transcendental and indescribable. What people claim to 'know' in their hearts and souls can never be weighed, measured or assessed by any of the usual academic methods.

Christianity, more than any other religion, demands that certain events really happened, in real locations and on specific dates. In most religions it is the revelation, not the circumstances in which it is given, that is important. Christianity, by contrast, is based on an event or sequence of events, through which salvation was made available to all: the Crucifixion and Resurrection of Jesus Christ. This opens up the 'revelation' of Christianity to historical inquiry, and poses a risk for the religion - if it could be shown, for example, that these events never happened, or happened in a way fundamentally different from the Gospel's description, Christianity has a major problem.

However Jesus and his core teachings would not be a problem. His teachings stand firm. His belief in God and his communion with God, which he tried through his teachings to help us achieve, stand clear and unchallenged. The answer is within each and every one of us. God is part of us now.

This makes it a top priority to establish the reliability of the writers who recorded the life of Jesus. Our major source of information about Him is a set of texts - the four New Testament Gospels - which can be examined according to the same criteria that may be applied to any historical document. And once their narrative is seen in the cold light of day, it becomes apparent that not only have the authors rewritten the story to suit their own personal agendas, but that what they produced was subsequently edited and changed, sometimes long after the event. It is a grave error to take anything the Gospels say about Jesus as fact simply because it is written there.

It is a fact of life that history is written by the victors. Pauline Christianity has been the victor; the original 'church' of Jesus, continued after his death by his brother and family, was the loser, along with many other forms of Judeo-Christianity in the first and second centuries AD.

The earliest of the four Gospels is the Gospel of Mark - or rather, the one we refer to as the Gospel of Mark. We don't even really know who wrote it, as it was common practice at that time to attribute written works to famous people - but it is thought to have been written at least forty years after Jesus' death. That's forty years without television, without videotaped interviews, without a Google search turning up scores of eyewitness reports from those who actually knew him. So at best, what we're talking about here are stories that were passed on by word of mouth. Over forty years, without any written record. If you were running an investigation, how accurate, would you consider such evidence? Forty years of primitive, uneducated, superstitious people telling stories around their campfires?

Far more troubling is the story of how these particular four Gospels actually came to be included in the New Testament. Over the two hundred years following the writing of the Gospel of Mark, we know that many other Gospels were written, with all kinds of tales about Jesus' life. As the early movement grew more popular and spread among the scattered communities, stories of Jesus' life took on local flavours that were influenced by the particular circumstances of each community. Dozens of different Gospels were floating around, often at odds with one another. We know this for a fact because, in December 1945, some Arab peasants were digging for fertilizer in the Jabal al-Tafif Mountains of Upper Egypt, close to the town of Nag Hammadi, when they discovered an earthenware jar almost six feet high. At first they hesitated to break it, fearful that a djinn - an evil spirit- could be trapped inside. When they did break into it, hoping to find gold, they made one of the most astonishing archaeological discoveries of all time. Inside the jar were thirteen papyrus books, bound in gazelle leather. The peasants, unfortunately, didn't realize the value of what they had found, and some of the books and the loose papyrus leaves went up in flames in the ovens of their homes. Other pages were lost as the documents found their way to the Coptic Museum in Cairo. What did survive, though, were 52 texts which are still the subject of great controversy among biblical scholars.

These writings are commonly referred to as the Gnostic Gospels. Gnostic, like the Cathars, refers to sayings and beliefs of Jesus that are at odds with those of the New Testament.

Among the texts found at Nag Hammadi was the Gospel of Thomas, which identifies itself as a secret Gospel and opens with the line: 'These are the secret words which the living Jesus spoke, and which the twin, Judas Thomas, wrote down'. The twin of Jesus?

And there are more. Bound in the same volume was the Gospel

of Philip, which openly describes Jesus' relationship with Mary Magdalene as an intimate one. Mary has her own text - The Gospel of Mary in which she is regarded as a disciple and a leader of a Christian group. There's also the Gospel of Peter, the Gospel of the Egyptians, the secret book of John. There's the Gospel of Truth, with its distinctly Buddhist undertones. The list goes on.

A common thread in all these gospels, apart from attributing acts and words to Jesus that are pretty different from those in the Gospels of the New Testament, is that they considered common Christian beliefs, like the virgin birth and the Resurrection, to be naïve delusions. Even worse, these writings were also uniformly Gnostic, because although they refer to Jesus and his disciples, the message they conveyed was that to know oneself at the deepest level was also to know God - that is, by looking within oneself to find the sources of joy and sorrow, love and hate, one would find God.

Thus their path to God is through oneself and within the reach of each and every one of us. It was this message that Jesus continually tried to get his disciples to understand.

In his book *The Hidden Gospel* (p19) Neil Douglas Klotz gives an insight into decoding the lost Gospels and quotes as follows: 'If we consider Jesus' words in Aramaic, we can then participate in an important Semitic language tradition: translation and interpretation as personal spiritual practices'.

The practices themselves have many layers and nuances. To begin with, a single word in Aramaic or Hebrew can often mean several seemingly different things. For instance, the Aramaic word 'shema' as well as its Semitic root ShM, or shem, can mean light, sound, name, or atmosphere. If we consider the counsel of Jesus To pray 'with or in my shem' (usually translated 'in my name'), which meaning is intended? According to Middle Eastern tradition, in the words of sacred scripture or the words of a prophet, all possible meanings may be present. One needs then to look at a given statement several different ways. In addition, Aramaic and Hebrew lend themselves to rich and poetic wordplay, like inner rhyming of vowels, repetition of consonant sounds and parallel phrasing. These devices further increase the possible translations and interpretations of a given statement.

When a root word like 'shem' becomes modified, its meanings may expand further. For instance, the first line of the prayer usually called The Lord's Prayer or 'Our Father' contains the word shem-aya, usually translated 'Heaven'. The ending added to shem implies that its effect extends without limit. In order to hear more of the possibilities of this first line, one needs to render the phrase from the Aramaic Gospels, Abwoon d'bashmaya, several different ways-something like this:

Oh Thou, the One from whom
Breath enters being in
all radiant forms.

O Parent of the Universe, from your
Deep interior comes the next wave
of shining life.

O fruitful, nurturing Life-giver!
Your sound rings everywhere
throughout the cosmos.
Father-Mother who births Unity,
You vibrate life into form
in each new instant.'

The King James version gives us 'Our Father which art in Heaven'. Three hundred years later, the New Jerusalem Bible improved this only by shortening it slightly to 'Our Father in Heaven'. In both, the additional nuances and suggestions of the Aramaic, which would have been heard by the Semitic listener, are missing. It's not that these English translations are wrong; they are simply very limited. They can't hold the spiritual possibilities of the original Aramaic - and there are many others, even for this one line of the prayer. Metaphorically, they are like fruit juice that has been strained through a very fine filter and heated, leaving all the valuable vitamins, minerals, trace elements, and pulp behind.

Each stanza of the poetic translation above is itself incomplete, yet points toward a unity that is only expressed in the Aramaic words themselves: Abwoon d'bashmaya. Likewise, when read aloud, one line may be heard more clearly than another by a particular person, depending upon her or his life experience. According to the Middle Eastern tradition of spiritual interpretation, this would be the translation of the moment for that person.

In this tradition of translation and interpretation, the words of a prophet or mystic stories, prayers, and visionary statements challenge listeners to understand them according to their own life experience. These traditions propose that we can only fix the meaning of a sacred text at a particular time and place in relation to our own life experience. This type of translation-interpretation not only bridges languages but connects that which can be said in language and that which remains a wordless experience. It is a translation 'between our outer and inner lives, as well as between our lives as individuals and as members of a community; as we look at the major themes in Yeshua's teaching, we need to remember that the search we are engaged in is for our own souls, rather than for some so-called objective notion of who Jesus was.'

The mistake is to treat as 'Gospel' anything that has been said or indeed has been reported as having been said. We have heard Barack Obama's inauguration speech to the world. It was recorded by all available means for posterity. It can be referred back to at any point in the future. Imagine now in two hundred years time that you want to preach about its aims and ambitions to people who never saw or heard Obama and certainly had never met him. Without the modern aids all you would have is a verbal recollection, handed down from generation to generation, possibly just orally, maybe in song, maybe in the re-enactment of a ritual drama. How near the truth would you get?

From the information handed down, not by Obama's family but by anyone who wanted to recount the speech, you would have to try to ascertain for yourself what was the truth; an impossible challenge. To have any chance of doing so you would need to study his life and his background, the language he spoke, his aim, the political climate at the time, the state of the land and indeed the state of the world. Or perhaps you would just rely solely on the works of black and white Democrats who believed he was the Messiah.

So who was Jesus? It's all down to each individual's personal choice. The hard facts are few but the stories are endless, and so varied as to be totally unreliable. The choice is yours; and of course mine.

CHAPTER 8

The teachings of Jesus by the use of
parables - the Son of God

Jesus often used spiritually-significant stories called 'parables' to illustrate his teaching. A parable is a metaphor or simile drawn from nature or common life that stimulates the imagination of the listener to examine and interpret its meaning. As a teaching method it draws parallels with surroundings familiar to the listener, thus making profound truths easier to understand.

Parables do not appear in the Hebrew Bible except in the works of Solomon, who is credited with inventing them. The Hebrew word for parable is *mashal*. The word has many meanings, including 'proverb', 'riddle' and 'sayings of the wise'. The rabbis, by employing a series of complicated wordplays, portrayed Solomon as the inventor of parables. Solomon wrote many of them, and since proverbs and parables are defined by the word mashal, they are deemed one and the same.

The rabbis interpreted Ecclesiastes 12:9 as referring to Solomon: 'Besides being wise, the Teacher 'also taught the people knowledge, weighing and studying and arranging many proverbs (parables)'. The teacher in this quotation is Solomon, but Jesus, also a teacher, used the mashal to teach people knowledge, as Solomon had done centuries earlier.

Parables are a very Jewish way of storytelling. They have no real parallel in any other literature. They are not even common in early Christian writings or in Greek literature, but they are abundant in the rabbinical tradition. In the times of Jesus they were a very common way of explaining the sacred texts and the Torah.

Jesus used parables to explain the nature of the Kingdom of God and how it could be gained. There are many quoted in the Gospels, each filled with a wealth of similes and allegories.

Jesus said: 'There was a good man who owned a vineyard. He leased it to tenant farmers so that they might work it and he might collect the produce from them. He sent his servant so that the tenants might give him the produce of the vineyard. They seized his servant and beat him, all but killing him. The servant went back and told his master. The master said 'Perhaps (they) did not recognise (him)'. He sent another servant. The tenants beat this one as well. Then the owner sent his son and said, 'Perhaps they will show respect to my son'. Because the tenants knew that he was the heir to the vineyard, they seized him and killed him. Let him who has ears hear...'

The meaning of this parable is quite unmistakable. The vineyard is God's Earth, and the tenant farmers mankind. The servants are the Old Testament *nabi'im*, or prophets, some of whom were indeed badly treated in their time. But quite distinct from these, and suffering a far worse fate, is the individual described as 'the son'. Jesus could scarcely have more succinctly or more prophetically explained his own role in a parable drama that he would enact in his own life. And he could hardly have more plainly spelled out that his relationship with God was distinctive and special.

But exactly how special? A Jewish historian such as Dr Geza Vermes will quite happily acknowledge Jesus as a 'son of God' in the Jewish sense of one having a special relationship with God. Even as devout a Hindu as Mahatma Gandhi expressed his preparedness to recognise Jesus in similar terms:

'To me he was one of the greatest teachers humanity has ever had. To his believers he was God's only begotten son. Could the fact that I do or do not accept this belief have any more or less influence in my life? Is all the grandeur of his teaching and his doctrine to be forbidden to me? I cannot believe so… My interpretation… is that in Jesus' own life is the key to his nearness to God; that he expressed, as no other could, the spirit and will of God. It is in this sense that I see and recognise him as the son of God, but not the only Son of God.'

Following on from Ghandi's acceptance of 'The Son of God', the Christian, the Nicene Christian at least, will demand much more, starting off the theological merry-go-round all over again. Whether he or Gandhi is right is a matter of faith. But there is an uncanny aspect to the parable of the wicked husbandmen that is relevant here: its author, a human Jew of the first century AD, essentially outlined his own excruciating path of death just as calmly and clearly as if he were seeing it through a window. Was Jesus so completely a vessel of God, the living, breathing word of God, that to all intent and purpose God was speaking through Him, and was Him? There is only one way of finally resolving this great dilemma: a preparedness on the part of all to recognise that in the case of Jesus, perhaps uniquely, there is no formula, no one view of Him that can adequately explain or encompass Him.

Everybody will have their own path to God; for many it will be through Jesus.

If we take 'Son of God' as being compatible with being made in God's image then perhaps we can all be considered as 'sons' of God.

CHAPTER 9

※

Contemporaries of Jesus

JOHN THE BAPTIST

John the Baptist was a mission preacher and a major religious figure who led a movement of Baptism in the River Jordan in expectation of a divine apocalypse that would restore occupied Israel. John followed the example of previous Hebrew prophets, living austerely, challenging sinful rulers, calling for repentance and promising God's justice.

Some scholars maintain that he was influenced by the Essenes. John's baptism was a purification rite for repentant sinners, performed in 'living water' (in this case a running river) in accord with Jewish custom. John anticipated a messianic figure who would be greater than John himself. Jesus was among those whom John baptised and was apparently a follower of John. Jesus' own ministry followed John's and some of Jesus' early followers had previously been followers of John. John, like Jesus, preached at a time of political, social, and religious conflict. John, who was active a short time before Jesus, warned of the approaching Day of Judgement and of the bitter fate in store for whose who would not repent of their deeds and renounce their evil ways. He had many followers and the authorities feared that his preaching would incite popular unrest. Herod Antipas, ruler of Galilee and Perea, whom John had condemned for marrying his brother's wife, Herodias, had him beheaded (Matthew 14).

Accounts of John in the New Testament are not incompatible with the written accounts of Josephus, the Jewish historian. Josephus recalled that Jesus was the one whose coming John foretold. The Christian Church commonly refer to John as the precursor or forerunner of Jesus, since in the Gospels, John announces Jesus' coming. He is also identified with the prophet Elijah, and is described s a relative of Jesus.

Muslims also regard John as a prophet, as do Bahais and Mandaeans.

The lives of Jesus and John are thought to have been similar. John is thought of as the last prophet by the Church and Jesus as the Messiah. The problem that arose from Jesus' baptism by John is that Jesus was later considered to be without sin yet received John's baptism which was for the forgiveness of sins.

EASTERN ORTHODOX VIEW OF JOHN

The Eastern Orthodox believe that John was the last of the Old Testament prophets, thus serving as a bridge between that period of revelation and the New Covenant. They also teach that, following his death, John descended into Hades and there once more preached that Jesus the Messiah was coming, so he was the Forerunner of Christ in death as he had been in life. According to Sacred Tradition, John the Baptist appears at the time of death to those who have not heard the Gospel of Christ, and preaches the Good News to them, that all may have the opportunity to be saved. Orthodox churches will often have an icon of St John the Baptist in a place of honour on the screen separating the nave from the sanctuary, and he is frequently mentioned during the Divine Services. Every Tuesday throughout the year is dedicated to his memory.

ISLAMIC VIEW

John the Baptist is known as 'Yahya' in Arabic and in the Koran. The Koran, in the Sura Maryam, identifies John as the son of Zachariah and maternal cousin of Jesus. It relates an account similar to that of the Gospel of Luke, including the barrenness of Zachariah's unnamed wife and his doubts, though Zachariah is not described as actually mute, it is only said that the sign of the coming of John was that he would not speak for three nights. John, whose tidings are foretold by the angels, is exhorted to hold fast to the Scripture and was given wisdom by God while still a child. He is described as 'pure', 'devout', 'dutiful towards his parents' and 'not arrogant or rebellious', and is called 'a Prophet of the Righteous' coming 'to confirm a word from Allah'.

MANDAEAN VIEW

John the Baptist plays a large part in some Mandaean writings, especially those dating from the Islamic period. Mandaeans highly revere him and may possibly have some remote connection with his original disciples. They believe John the Baptist, called Yahya in the Book of John, was the latest and greatest of the prophets.

While Mandaeans agree that he baptized Jesus (Yeshu), they reject Jesus as either a saviour or prophet. They view John as the only true Messiah.

MARY MAGDALENE - THE MYTH

In AD 591, Pope Gregory I was working on a homily and needed a model to represent Christianity's forgiving and transformative nature. He recalled the image of the promiscuous woman who, because she had 'loved much' (a phrase often interpreted literally), had wiped Jesus' feet with her unbound hair in violation of Jewish rabbinical norms of behaviour. In homily number 33, Pope Gregory I merged the repentant Mary Magdalene with the woman who had the alabaster jar. The Gospel of Luke dubbed her the 'sinful woman', while only the Gospel of John referred to her as Mary of Bethany. In linking these two portraits, Pope Gregory I ensured the composite image would stick to Mary Magdalene for a long time.

He whom Luke calls the sinful woman, whom John calls Mary, we believe to be the Mary from whom seven devils were ejected according to Mark. And what did these seven devils signify, if not all the vices? It is clear, brothers, that the woman previously used the unguent to perfume her flesh acts.
Gregory I: Homily XXX111

What was Pope Gregory thinking? Was he being clever, careless, or just short-sighted? Was he emphasising what others already believed? Did he view women as highly impressionable, perhaps foolish and morally and spiritually inferior to men? We can only speculate. Various scholars have asserted that the making of the myth was intentional and that it served the Pope's purpose.

Is this treatment of Mary Magdalene in particular due merely to a basic misogyny on the part of a man writing for a predominantly male audience, or is there something else going on, some kind of cover up?

Paul's Letters make it clear that women held prominent and respected positions in Christian communities in his day - when the Gospels were taking shape - so there was no obvious reason to suppress the fact that they also enjoyed high status in Jesus' original following. Famously, however, the situation is very different when we turn to the Gnostic sources, in which Jesus' female disciples figure prominently, particularly Mary Magdalene. Even more famously - or notoriously, depending on one's point of view - those sources attribute an intimate personal relationship to her and Jesus.

Because the majority of the Gnostic gospels are known only from fourth-century Coptic copies, many commentators reject the image they paint of Mary Magdalene and the other female disciples as a much later invention by Christian sects who had their own axes to grind and no access to authentic sources. But that is manifestly not the case.

Mary Magdalene, along with Salome, appears as a key figure in the Gospel of Thomas, which is at least contemporary with, if not earlier than, the canonical Gospels. So she was already, at that early date, considered a prominent member of Jesus' following: whatever the historical reality, this was not a fourth-century invention.

It has taken two millennia, but Mary Magdalene's reputation and role as an important (perhaps pre-eminent) disciple are being revisited, revised, and repaired. Although the Vatican has reversed its position that Mary was ever a prostitute and revised its missal to reflect that fact, and even though Pope John Paul II proclaimed her the Apostle to the Apostles, many modern people still think of her as the repentant, sinful prostitute. Perhaps because of centuries of interpretations by the fathers of the Church (not to mention the innumerable revisions and translations) or perhaps because of her inaccurate representations in art, Mary Magdalene was written off and written out of the Gospels. Now, in the twenty-first century, that is changing. Efforts of modern scholars, feminist, theologians, historians, writers, and Christians who believe Mary Magdalene has been unfairly treated for far too long are working to give this woman of spirit a higher profile.

In his novel the Da Vinci Code, Dan Brown took the character of Mary Magdalene, a follower of Jesus, traditionally portrayed by the Church as a prostitute, and put her alongside him at the centre of the story. In Brown's retelling, Mary Magdalene is Jesus' wife and equal, royal in her own right. She is the one commissioned by Jesus to lead his Church. When he is crucified, she is pregnant with their child and flees to France, where the child, a daughter, is born. The subsequent history of Christianity is described in terms of a massive cover-up by a male-dominated Church, desperate to suppress this feminine aspect of God's revelation.

This of course is a best-selling story line, but the fact remains that at the time that Jesus lived a Jew, and particularly a Rabbi, would have been expected to be married.

But now take a pragmatic view of all of the above. If she had been a prostitute, if Jesus was married to her or if he had fifteen children by five wives, how would it change his teaching to 1st century Jews? Indeed how would it change his message to us today?

Let us not lose sight of Yeshua's teaching. We should remember that the search we are engaged in is for our own souls, rather than some so-called objective notion of who Jesus was.

THE PHARISEES

The Pharisees were God-fearing, Torah-observing, nation-loving Jews. It was the Pharisees who most often went toe-to-toe with Jesus and, because the story is usually told by Christians, their reputation got stuck in reverse. Each of the two, the Pharisees and Jesus, lost confidence in each other as a result of their constant toe-tapping over what God expected of his people, with Jesus saying one thing and the Pharisees something else.

Pharisees might best be seen as persons thoroughly committed to the Torah and its obedience. Because of their commitment, they were just as committed to 'interpreting' that Torah in such a manner that it could reasonably practised by all who cared to follow its directives. In particular, they seem to be most concerned with food laws (eating only kosher food), in addition to having more than a little interest in such matters as Sabbath practice.

The foundation for their beliefs and practices, as has been mentioned, was the Torah, especially texts like Leviticus and Deuteronomy. But in addition, the Pharisees distinguished themselves from the Sadducees because they believed in the authority of the entire Tanakh (The Torah, the Neviim, and the Ketuvim), the Law, the Prophets, and the Writings).

The Pharisees advocated an austere and sober lifestyle, strict obedience to the law, careful study of holy scripture and an intelligent, thoughtful, 'rationalist' approach to the world. Though they believed that God controlled the course of events, they also held that men could choose between good and evil, and, since the soul was immortal, the choices they made would determine their eternal fate. These were popular ideas - in contrast to the empty formalism of the Sadducees - and many local village priests were Pharisees. It is for this reason that Jesus was preoccupied with the opposition of 'Scribes and Pharisees' as a popular preacher, it was the Pharisees he encountered as competitors.

THE SADDUCEES

The Sadducees were the landed aristocrats of the Land of Israel; they were the priests and ran the Temple. They were the aristocrats in 'power' at the time the Temple was destroyed by Titus of Rome (c 70 AD) and because those who gained 'power' after that time were wary of connection with the Sadducees, the latter virtually disappeared from history after the Temple's destruction. They were less liberal than the typical Pharisee, which is to say they were politically and religiously conservative.

Josephus, a Jewish historian of the first century, claims that the Sadducees were boorish and believed only in the first five books of Moses, (Genesis, Exodus, Leviticus, Numbers, and Deuteronomy) and that they did not believe in the resurrection of the dead. When he attempts to provide an analogy of what Sadducees think to his largely Roman audience, Josephus says the Sadducees 'do away with Fate altogether, and remove God beyond… the very sight of evil… they maintain that man has the free choice of good or evil'.

The influence of the Sadducees was enormous, but limited largely to what took place in Jerusalem during the High Holidays. We do not know what percentage of Jews attended the major feasts. A good guess is that each family attended one of these festivals per year. The holidays were family events, replete with food (even some red meat) and fun and fellowship (like contemporary Jewish and Christian and

Muslim religious holidays), and we can surmise that many Jews attended, perhaps even into the hundreds of thousands. Most of the time the calendar, the events and the liturgical matters were established and administered by the Sadducees. Disputes between groups, even between leaders, stirred up the crowds at times.

Behind the Sadducees were the Romans, and the Sadducees found themselves as leaders of Jerusalem and of a nation in need of careful co-operation with Rome. During the lifetime of Jesus, the Roman Emperors were Augustus (Octavian) and Tiberius; the Roman-appointed leaders included Herod the Great (d. 4 BC) and Herod Antipas, as well as the procurator Pontius Pilate (26-36 AD).

In AD 66 the nationalist revolt which had been threatening for decades in Palestine broke out. The rebels eventually took control in Jerusalem and massacred the Sadducee élite, whom they regarded as collaborators with the Romans. The Jewish Christian Church, interestingly, fled from the city; it was sufficiently distant from the world of Jewish nationalism to wish to keep out of this struggle. The result of the revolt was in the long term probably inevitable: the Romans could not afford to lose their grip on this corner of the Mediterranean, and they put a huge effort into crushing the rebels. Jerusalem lay in ruins and no substantial Christian community was to return to it until the fourth century.

The catastrophe of Jerusalem's destruction had an important effect: it left the Jewish intelligentsia determined to make their peace with the Roman authorities, to preserve their religion and to give it a more coherent identity. Like the Jewish Christians, mainstream Judaism had to regroup. It established an assembly of religious leaders which was very influential in giving Judaism a unity of religious belief which it had not previously possessed. The

Sadducee leadership had been destroyed and so it was the Pharisee group which stamped its identity on surviving Judaism.

It is interesting to see this development reflected in the Gospels. Although it had been the Sadducees who had been responsible for the train of events leading to the death of Jesus, it is the Pharisees who come in for most of the abuse recorded by the Gospel writers. When the Gospels were compiled, the Pharisees were the leaders of Judaism, a living force to which Christian communities were strongly opposed. The growing coherence in Judaism and the narrowing in the variety of Jewish belief, meant that by the end of the first century AD a clear break had become inevitable between Christianity and Judaism.

THE ZEALOTS

If the Sadducees cooperated with Rome, another party found Rome insufferable. The Zealots, known more for their attitude toward Rome and their violence than anything else, were a party some think existed even at the time of Jesus, though many today conclude that this party had its specific origins in events and persons more toward the middle of the first century. At any rate, we know about them mostly through Josephus, and he chooses to make them the 'scapegoat' for the war with Rome that brought Jerusalem to its knees. What we do know about the Zealots is that they were a militaristically-inclined sect of Judaism. Whether the party existed or not at the time of Jesus is of less concern than that the 'spirit' of zealotry - violence is compatible with the work of God and can be used to establish the will of God - was part and parcel of first-century Judaism. That one of Jesus' own followers was called a Zealot probably means just that, although he may well have abandoned such a modus operandi to follow Jesus.

The Zealots were the military arm of early Jewish patriotism. For them the only solution to the humiliation of Roman rule over the Jewish homeland was to take up the old traditions of violence, and it was they who gave the impetus to the disastrous revolts which finally shattered Jewish life in Palestine by the second century AD.

THE ESSENES

The Essenes were a sect of Judaism that broke with the ruling establishment in Jerusalem, moved themselves out of the holy city and established their headquarters along the Dead Sea near Khirbet Qumran. They show all the characteristics of religious sectarian radical groups. They were rigid in hierarchical authority, and showed too much vindictiveness towards others with similar, but not identical, beliefs and practices. What stands out today is their distinctive way of reading the Torah, which always spoke about them and the times in which thy were living. Their conviction was that God was on their side and the 'holy war' that was imminent would vindicate them and their assortment of liturgical and communal practices.

The discovery of the Dead Sea Scrolls in 1947 gave the world access to writings of the Essenes themselves for the first time, after almost two thousand years. The resemblance of the Qumran's creed and conduct to the description of the Essenes written by ancient historians such as Josephus and Pliny the Elder would seem to justify a definitive identification.

Coin finds indicate that an isolated community (now generally accepted to be Essenes) lived at Kirbet Qumran from early in the second century BC until it was destroyed by Roman legions under Vespasian in AD 68. Archaeological work has shown that the main building there had two floors and included a strong stone tower. They also maintained on the site a water storage facility, a mill, a forge, and a writing area, and there was a cemetery with about twelve hundred graves.

The scrolls were written on papyrus, parchment, leather and copper. Carbon dating dates the scroll wrappings to between the first half of the second century BC and the first half of the third century AD. Most documents found proved to be part of their library, hidden during the Roman destruction between AD 67 and 73. The majority are supposed to have been written during the first century BC and first century AD, but some damaged documents were hidden in one cave by Samaritans massacred by soldiers of Alexander the Great way back in 331 BC. Others were hidden by fleeing fugitives of the defeated army of Bar Kokhba in their last suicide revolt against Rome in AD 132-135.

The main sources for knowledge of the Qumran community itself are the Manual of Discipline and the Damascus Document. Damascus was the name the sect gave to its place of exile, almost certainly a symbolic name and not identical with the Damascus we know today. A copy of this document had already been discovered in the famous Cairo genizah in the late nineteenth century, but only when the Qumran Scrolls were found, among which were fragments of a copy of the same document, was it clear that it dated from the Qumran period. Its similarity to the Manual leads us to the belief that they come from the same source.

The members of the order call themselves the Covenant, the Congregation, or the Party Council. The main idea of those in this community was to share everything, not only material things but spiritual things. Every member had to hand over all his belongings to the common fund, from which individuals would receive everything necessary for life. Members worked, prayed, and ate together, though there existed a kind of hierarchy in the order, and they were seated in their assemblies, called the Many, according to their rank. In any group of ten there had to be one priest. Voting and speaking were permitted to any member, regardless of his rank. Sessions of the community were held under strict rules that governed such matters as to who was to sit first and who was to speak to the Many. A young man could not marry before he was twenty, which was the age he was expected to have fully matured to take responsibility.

A special council of twelve men and three priests formed the executive board and there were overseers to supervise work, keep the accounts, and examine applications for membership. The judges consisted of four priests and six members who were knowledgeable in the law and judgements were made following a penal code. Even minor offences such as interrupting somebody's speech or sleeping during a session were fined with temporary excommunication from full membership, similar to a probation. Any novice had to pass three stages of initiation, a very similar parallel to Freemasonry.

It was the strong belief of the Essene community that they were the chosen ones who had entered a new Covenant with God because the Jews had become corrupt and unobservant of the law and had therefore broken the old covenant. They also believed that

God would soon send the Anointed One (the Christos, in Greek) or the Messiah (the Meshiach, in Hebrew). In contrast to other Jewish expectations of the Messiah, the Manual of the Essenes announces the appearance of two such men: a priest from the House of Aaron and a king from the House of David.

Many scholars have made suggestions for identity of the anointed one and the Messiah, but as always no firm proof can be established.

Hebrew University in Jerusalem then undertook the continuous publication of the manuscripts. In 1997, Geza Vermes' *The Complete Dead Sea Scrolls in English* appeared in London. Work on translating the scrolls is now virtually complete, and it can be stated with little doubt that much of what Jesus taught took form from that desert community.

The Jewish roots of Christianity no longer constitute such a problem for Catholic theologians as they did, say, a century ago. In 1986, in a speech on the historic occasion of his visit to the Great Synagogue in Rome, Pope John Paul II referred to the Jews as 'our elder brothers'. Yet the Church was reluctant to concede the presence of Christian concepts and language in Jewish writings officially dated to more than a century before Jesus, maybe because of the revelatory nature of Jesus' teaching - the fact that it came directly from his Father in Heaven - might compromise the Church. It wouldn't do, after all, to have Christian revelation actually born in the minds of the Jews 100 years before Jesus.

So how do we now look at the Essenes? They were both the heirs of an ancient spiritual tradition and the initiators of a new desert lifestyle, so closely entwined with early Christianity that we today know it as monasticism. To the people of that time the desert was both a place of temptation and devils and the only place where direct communication with God could be reached. Jesus claimed that the Kingdom of his Father was both in every man's heart and all around us. In this, as in many other cases, only the monastic choice of removal from the distractions of the material world enables understanding of what Jesus meant.

In fact, there are many similarities between Essene tradition and the life and teachings of Jesus.

THE DESPOSYNI

The 'Messianic' heirs or heirs of Jesus 'family' were called Desposyni, which is ancient Greek for 'heirs' or 'belonging to the Master'. This was a hallowed style reserved exclusively for those in the same family descent as Jesus. The word is not to be found used in any other context.

During the reign of the emperor Domitian 81-96AD the execution of all Desposyni was ordered by Imperial decree.

In 318 AD a Desposyni delegation journeyed to Rome and received an audience with Bishop Silvester. They claimed that the Bishop of Jerusalem should be a Desposyni, a hereditary member of Jesus' family. Their claims were dismissed; the Bishop was not going to cross swords with the Emperor Constantine. They were advised that the teachings of Jesus had been superseded by a doctrine more amenable to imperial requirement.

THE DESPOSYNI AND ISLAM

Islam is much closer to James' ideology than to Judaism or Christianity. It could be that James' ideology of faith and goodness ('believe and perform good actions') spread south to the Arabs and survived centuries later in Mohammed's Quran. The Romans, after all, persecuted the (real) Christians, the 'desposyni/desposini', and forced them to disband and flee. They could have moved south to escape. Muslims believe in the prophets and in Jesus, but claim that the 'books' were changed by evil people. Isn't this what a desposyni/desposini would claim today? Those books were indeed changed, forcing the whole Christian world to believe that Christianity started in Rome and that Paul's doctrine was the doctrine of Jesus. The original books were banned. Christians who knew about those books were forced in exile. What Muslims basically tell us is exactly what a surviving Jamesian Christian would tell us.

CHAPTER 10

The effects of the crucifixion

The crucifixion raised two problems for the future of the Jesus movement. First, his disciples and friends had to ask themselves whether their understanding of his life, the charismatic cures and the message of Jesus was correct. They obviously concluded that it was, as proved by their subsequent conduct. The success of their resumed charismatic activity of healing and exorcism, described in the Acts of the Apostles, which they continued in the name of Jesus, persuaded them that their crucified Master was still alive and active through them, powerful and ready to return soon. For them, he rose from the dead.

The second problem concerns after-death motivation. Could the feeling of urgency which haunted Jesus still affect his followers after the crucifixion? I believe it did. Jesus' conviction that his mission and the arrival of the Kingdom of God formed a single and continuous act was replaced in the minds of his disciples by a drama in two acts. The life of Jesus in the recent past (Act 1) was to be followed by the inauguration of the kingdom after his glorious second coming (Act 2). And by the time the feverish expectation of Christ's return began to cool down, spiritual encouragement and security were supplied by the early Church.

The early Christian Church, in the footsteps of St Paul, its founder, succeeded in removing the major obstacles impeding the spreading of Jesus' message. Jesus considered his mission to be restricted to Jews and explicitly ordered his envoys not to preach the gospel to Gentiles. The apostles, who were delivering a freshly-tailored message to Jews about the Messiahship of Jesus, opened the Church to all the nations on witnessing the progressive fiasco of the evangelisation at home, giving in to Paul's insistent pressure. The Pagans entered in droves, first diluting and soon entirely transforming the Jewish heritage of Jesus. They justified the change by the belief, arising from the late Gospel of John, that the Holy Spirit was sent by Jesus to hand out new revelation and dispense afresh 'all the truth' (John 14:16-17; 16:13).

But what of the Jews? Jesus was one of them, the chosen race, a member of their movement and a citizen of Judaea. There was hatred enough to go around in those days between the family of Herod and his supporters and the people of Judaea, the Jews. It flowed in equal measure from both sides, one to the other. But the Jews, most certainly, would not have hated Jesus, simply because he was one of them, the people who were God's chosen. He was a Jew.

They certainly did not crucify Him, either, because that was simply beyond their power. Crucifixion was a Roman punishment. Nor did the Jews as a mob ever scream for Jesus' blood and call down God's wrath upon themselves and their children for his death. That is the worst kind of madness to claim, and to believe.

Think about it calmly for a moment. Can you imagine any crowd of people, or even any mob, calling down the wrath of God upon their own heads and their children's heads, and doing it not only voluntarily but in unison, unrehearsed? It defies belief, yet people believed it and still do.

The Church tells you that. The priests tell you that. A monk will tell you that if you stop one on the road and ask him. And there is nothing, anywhere, to suggest otherwise, or to teach you otherwise, or to explain anything in alternative terms. Nothing. So what else can you do but believe what you are told?

Crucifixion was a commonplace event. It was the most common form of execution for criminals in Roman times, whether they were thieves, miscreants, murderers, rebels, political dissidents or deserters from the Roman armies. If you were wealthy or well connected, you might die quickly, beheaded or garrotted, but if your death was required by the state, as a public spectacle, a lesson and a deterrent to others, you were crucified and died slowly, in great pain. Jesus was condemned as a political criminal - a rebel. And that was how he died. And apart from the people who knew him and were close to him, no one really cared.

Jesus knew he was not the Messiah, the kind of saviour expected by the Jews, and he foresaw that his death would be a sign to the Jews of what would happen to them if they did not repent. But Judas was portrayed as the betrayer of Jesus, and also being a Jew he was castigated along with all the Jews for his death. The sacking of Jerusalem in AD 70 by the Romans all but killed Jesus' form of Judaism.

Fifteen of the 27 New Testament books were written by Paul and Luke, we are told. In them Jews are vilified for the rejection of Jesus. They have since been reviled by the Christian Church and grossly ridiculed.

Understandably, Christianity considers itself the transmitter to posterity of the legacy of Jesus, albeit one that has been converted by the Church into a Gospel for the whole human race. Yet on reading the original message, thinking and honest members of the various Christian faiths should perhaps feel the need for a thorough re-examination of the fundamentals of their belief, ethics and piety; a reconsideration which may demand a complete doctrinal restructuring, a new 'reformation'.

As for open-minded and unprejudiced Jews, the Jesus emerging from his authentic sayings must appear to them as familiar, friendly and attractive, a profoundly impressive figure who has something significant and unifying to offer, which Jews can share with mankind at large.

In 1965 the Roman Catholic Church acknowledged at long last that the Jews were not responsible for the death of Jesus.

How can we improve our understanding of Jesus? The following advice touches the heart of the matter: look for what Jesus himself taught instead of being satisfied with what has been taught about him.

My quest now is beginning to take shape. The importance seems to lie in not what or who he was, but what he said and did.

CHAPTER 11

The emergent early Church

It would be grossly inaccurate to speak of the 'early Church' in a manner that implies any degree of cohesion, organisation or shared beliefs until many decades after the fall of Jerusalem. The leaders of the original Christian community, or church, in Jerusalem, Peter and James, were both dead and Paul had simply vanished without trace. Their joint legacy was a collection of disparate small congregations dotted through the Middle East, founded by a wide variety of evangelists, each of whom had preached his own highly individual version of the 'Good News'. The leadership vacuum left by the destruction of the 'Christian' community in Jerusalem was not filled for some time.

The structure of the early Christian Church, when it did begin to take shape, displayed a high degree of earlier Essene teaching, tradition and practice. The emergent Church used a handbook known as the Didache, or 'the teaching of the Lord', as its model and passages from it were frequently quoted in letters to newer Christian communities. The Didache and the Community Rule of the Essenes, found among the Dead Sea Scrolls, are startlingly similar. The first 'Christian Church' in Jerusalem, for example, was led by a triumvirate of elders, based on the Essene model. The three leaders were referred to as 'the Pillars', and are listed as James the brother of Jesus, the 'first Bishop of Jerusalem', Simon-Peter and John. Thus the well-respected use of 'pillar' symbolism had evolved further from its Egyptian use as a sign of divinely inspired wisdom or Gnosis, through its signification of the divine presence during the Exodus, to symbolise a pillar as a 'righteous' individual who has attained enlightenment.

However, there is little sign of enlightenment to be found in the bitter disputes and quarrels between the leaders and theologians drawn from the many and varied strands of 'Christian' belief. It took over two centuries for order to begin to emerge from the chaos of those early years. These continual and venomous controversies simply reflected the complete instability of belief in the early centuries of the Church. Even with the later establishment of an accepted canon of New Testament writings, the controversies did not cease, but this did prove to be a turning point in Church history that favoured those who were trying to establish an institutional church.

By the end of the first century Pauline Christianity had lost sight of the real Jewish Jesus and of the original meaning of his message. Paul, John and their churches replaced him by the other-worldly Christ of faith. Within decades of his death, the message of the real Judaic Jesus was transferred from its Semitic (Aramaic/Hebrew) linguistic context and its Jewish religious framework to alien surroundings, in other words, the transference of the Jesus movement from its Jewish home territory to the primarily Greek-speaking pagan Mediterranean world. As a result the new Church, by then mostly Gentile, soon lost its awareness of being Jewish; indeed, it became progressively anti-Jewish.

CHAPTER ELEVEN

Another fundamental twist exerted an adverse effect on the
appeal of the Christian message to Palestinian and dispersed Jews.
Jesus, the religious man with the irresistible charismatic charm,
metamorphosed into Jesus the Christ, the object of the Christian
religion. The prophet from Nazareth proclaiming the nearness of
the Kingdom of God did not mean much to the average new recruit
from Alexandria, Antioch, Ephesus, Corinth or Rome. Their gaze
was directed towards a universal saviour.

And so from the second century the growing Christian Church,
instructed by eminent minds trained in Greek philosophy such as
Iranaeus of Lyons, Clement, Origen and Arthanasius of Alexandria,
substituted the religious manifesto of the real Jesus for an incarnate
Christ and his revelation as the eternal only Son of God, and the
mutual tie between the divine persons of the Holy Trinity. The
Scriptures, including the Old Testament, were searched for
apparently suitable quotations and interpreted allegorically to
prove the conclusions reached by philosophical reasoning. This
procedure was made all the easier for these great Hellenistic
thinkers, since their Bible of both Testaments was in the Greek
language, with which they were familiar and which they could
easily manipulate. They could do so freely, since by that time there
was no longer any Jewish voice in Christendom to sound the alarm.

If Christianity had not taken root in the provinces of the
Roman Empire, it would have remained a tiny Jewish sect. It can
also be argued that even if the historical Jesus had no intention of
approaching the Gentiles, his essential message contained an
explicit universalistic element. So, once the primitive Church
decided that non-Jews could be admitted into the fold without first
compelling them fully to embrace the Jewish way of life, it was

logical to attempt a 'translation' in the broadest sense of the Christian message for the benefit of the Gentile world.

Christianity laboured under a serious handicap in understanding and commenting on the Old Testament. The Greek-speaking Eastern half of the Church was at one remove from the text read by Jesus, but the western Church, where the Greek text had to be translated into Latin, was already at two removes both from the Gospel and the Hebrew Scriptures. When its greatest luminary, St Augustine (354-430), who knew neither Greek nor Hebrew, let alone Aramaic, needed information about the Hebrew original of some unclear passage in the Old Testament, he had to contact St Jerome, the only Christian Hebraist of the age, who at that time lived in Bethlehem at the other end of the Mediterranean world.

To this linguistic and cultural separation of Christianity from the world of Jesus must be added another dark factor, the growing anti-Judaism of the Church. The same Jerome, the Hebrew expert of Christendom, describes the sound made by Jewish worshippers in the synagogue as the grunting of a pig and the braying of donkeys. In a similar vein, St John Christendom, Augustine's other contemporary, compared the synagogue of the Christ-killing Jews to a brothel, a wild beasts' den, the devil's citadel, a precipice and abyss of perdition, fit for people who 'live only for their belly and behave no better than pigs and goats'.

This passage expresses in a nutshell the idea that would develop into what we call Pauline Christianity. It was blasphemy to the Jews: the eternal and only God fathers a son with a mortal woman, and this son, who is also God, enters this world with the purpose of becoming a human sacrifice in order to save humankind from damnation. No wonder James the Righteous and his Jerusalem

Church were horrified. Paul then declared that Christianity was for everybody, not just for Jews, and that did it - the line of separation was drawn. His ideas were in effect much more attractive to Pagans than to Jews, because mythical Greek and Roman Gods had many sons with mortal women.

The fundamental split between 'Pauline' and Jerusalem Christianity is well known today, but about 200 years ago, the accepted idea was that there had only ever been one form of Christianity, taught by Jesus and continued by his Apostles, and also by Paul.

With amazing gall, Paul even calls the preachers of 'the other Jesus' 'false brothers' - quite astonishing given their closeness to Jesus. He specifically avoided evangelising in places where other Apostles had already established their missions.

From what little we know of the Jerusalem group (almost entirely from the unreliable Acts with a few scraps from Paul's Epistles) its members lived communally, pooling property and money. They saw themselves as a sect within Judaism, not a breakaway movement, observing the Jewish law and worshipping at the Jerusalem temple. Even so, the Jewish authorities looked upon these dissidents with suspicion, at times taking draconian action and even executing the group's leaders - which was where Paul came in. Exactly why they disliked the Jewish Jerusalem Christians is unclear.

As the early records are so heavily Pauline in attitude, there is no way we can be absolutely sure exactly how the Jewish believers viewed Jesus, but evidently they saw Him as the Messiah prophesied in the Jewish scriptures, the divine king who would deliver his people from oppression. But Paul preached a radically different idea, in which Jesus' death became the whole point; he acknowledged that he fulfilled the criteria laid down by the great Jewish prophets by which the Messiah would be recognised, but argued that God had changed his mind about the nature of the role. He was no longer sent to physically deliver the Jewish people but to usher in the Day of Judgement - the end of the world. It was Paul who created the concept of Jesus as redeemer.

Another vital difference was that Paul believed that the 'good news' and the possibility of salvation offered by Jesus' sacrifice was not preserved exclusively for Jews, but available to any man or woman who accepts its truth. This fundamental difference between Paul's vision of the religion and that of the Jerusalem community accounts for the discussion in the Letters of issues such as the relevance of the Laws of Moses and whether, for example, male Christians should be circumcised. For Paul, faith in Jesus Christ had replaced acceptance of the Law as the 'qualification' to become one of God's chosen.

But Paul changed everything from what it was then to what it is today, from Jewish to Gentile. It was all Paul's doing. He stripped what was there in Jerusalem - the movement that Jesus and his followers called the Way - of all its Jewishness, and thereby of all its true meaning, and turned it into something inoffensive to the Jews, an idea bland enough to be accepted by the Romans. He stripped away all the rigid, unyielding, and unpopular Jewish morality and rewrapped the story in the style of his ancient Greek ancestors, with their love of fantastic, dramatic, fictitious, and completely implausible tales. And in so doing, he changed Jesus from a simple Jewish man of high ideals and stern patriotism into the only Son of God, born of a virgin, thus following the widely used stories of history from Isis, and Osiris, Dionysus, Buddha to Mithras and others.

The newly approved Gospels were accorded the respect of a new 'Divine Law' which demanded universal acceptance and respect. The concept of law implied authority, but whose authority? The Church's! Who wielded that authority? The men who led the Church, of course. The 'Pillars' of the first Christian community in Jerusalem had a degree of authority and charisma deriving directly from their association with Jesus. That was now invested in the bishops and deacons of the new Gentile Church.

Heresy remained an ever-present problem. It was largely solved by St Augustine of Hippo when he defined it as the distortion of a revealed truth by a believer or an unbeliever. The pivotal term, a revealed truth, was itself defined by the Church hierarchy as what the Church itself had declared to be revealed truth. This useful, if somewhat circular and self-serving definition, was then used by Church leaders to establish a total monopoly on all access to the sacred. The Church's very need to survive caused it to refute anything it viewed as heretical with increasing venom, and also led to the rise of dogmatic statements of belief which papered over areas of dispute with dictatorial rigidity. The growing and ever more powerful Roman Church could afford no rivals, either within Christianity or in the pagan world, and campaigned vigorously and effectively for the closure of temples and centres of worship of rival faiths, hijacking these well-established sacred sites for its own use. Thus the great Greek mystery temples of classical antiquity were abolished and their oracles silenced for all time.

With the decline of the Roman Empire, the Church became the principal lawmaker for the newly converted peoples of Europe, and their customary laws were given written form by the clergy, who were the scribes, codifiers and final arbiters. Thus, being the self-appointed guardians of history, the priests wrote down the oral legends and myths of the various tribes, omitting all that was offensive to their Christian teaching, retaining this, adding that, subtly changing people's ancient histories and creating the mould for a new, essentially Christian, culture.

In this pervasive way the Church was not only to distort the histories of entire peoples, but also devalue any pagan rivals in the religious field. This all-embracing process was strengthened by the incorporation of pagan festivals into the emerging Christian calendar: Easter took over from the festival of Astarte, the Phoenician goddess of love and fertility, the feast of St John the Baptist replaced the much older pagan celebrations of the summer equinox and the celebration of the winter equinox was amalgamated with the birthday of Mithras on 25th December, to become the feast of Christmas.

Much of Mithras' own mythology was incorporated into the Christian story, for legend recalls that at his birth shepherds adored Him, and that after performing a variety of good deeds for his followers, he too celebrated a last supper with them before ascending to heaven. Mithras, in the form of Sol Invictus - the god worshipped by Constantine the Great - was supposed to return to Earth at the end of time and judge the human race; a chain of events that seems a trifle bizarre for anyone who believes that Christianity is either unique or very different from its predecessors.

During the latter half of the second century and continuing into the third, relations were strained between Jewish and Gentile Christian communities. The early Church had produced the canon of the New Testament, whereas the Jewish Christian community remained faithful to its own Hebrew gospel. Although little is known about the development of Jewish Christianity from the middle of the second century AD until the rise of Islam in the sixth century, the church father Epiphanius (c 315-403) records that communities existed as far away as Mesopotamia. He writes further that these Jewish Christians had synagogues and elders like the Jews, and engaged in similar religious practices.

After Constantine the Great became Emperor of Rome and made Christianity an approved religion, things began to move very much faster. The Council of Nicaea in 325 AD was convened by Constantine to end all controversy over the nature of Jesus, strengthen the power of the clergy and condemn heresy in all its forms. In reality it gave the Church a power base that it has continued to use, enlarge and exploit ever since.

The time span between the crucifixion of Jesus and the final selection of the canonical text was 364 years. To put this into a latter-day perspective, from the present date this number of years would take us back to the 1640s, when the Stuart King Charles 1 was on the throne of Britain. 1642 was the year of Galileo's death in Italy, and the year when Georgeana (now York, Maine) became the first incorporated city in America, 133 years before the War of Independence. If Jesus had been crucified in 1642, it would be like having the New Testament confirmed in 2006.

During the early centuries of Christianity countless literary works were produced to promote and uphold the Faith, but in the final event only 27 documents were approved by the Catholic bishops, and even they were subject to editing and amendment before being considered wholly suitable. These now familiar works served to project a divine and elusive image of Jesus as required by the new Church of Rome, but in contriving this, the bishops managed to subvert and override many of the beliefs of the original Jewish Christians. In this newly-structured version of the Faith, the humanity of Jesus and the female element of his mission were subsumed by an ecclesiastical department of the imperial régime.

Fortunately, the texts of numerous Christian documents produced between the time of Jesus and the days of Constantine are still accessible. This makes it possible to determine what Christianity once was, as against what it became. The official ecclesiastical view is that a majority of these documents cannot be considered authentic because they were not approved by the Council in AD 397. The fact that the early Christians considered their documents appropriate to their belief was discounted on the basis that the original religion of Jesus was not itself authentic, since Jesus was a Nazarene Jew and did not follow the rule of Rome!

What we have here is a situation whereby the revised 4th century style of Christianity was not established because of Jesus, but almost in spite of Him. In practical terms, the very purpose of Christianity as a diversely-scattered fellowship was nullified by the new régime. The emperors had long been revered as deities on Earth, and in this respect the figure of Jesus posed a challenge for Constantine in Rome. He explained to Christians that he was the one who had secured their freedom in the Roman Empire, and therefore it should be him and not Jesus who ought to be regarded as the saviour of the faith. Christians of all schools now had a choice of being free or persecuted. As a result their long-standing customs and ideals were lost, devoured by Jesus' Roman enemies. Christianity ceased being a way of life based on the teachings of

Jesus and became an institutionalised religion governed by the doctrines of the Church of Rome.

THE COUNCILS

Initially there was strong disagreement among Christians about what Christianity was all about. The Christian dogma was formalised by a series of councils, whose conclusions were largely arbitrary. The council of Nicaea (325) mandated that only four gospels were true; the others were heretic. The council of Ephesus (431) sanctioned that the divine nature of Jesus was superior to his human nature. The council of Calcedonia (451) accepted Pope Leone I's theory that Jesus was both human and divine (and this was based on Greek philosophy, not on historical evidence or on the gospels' testimony).

THE HISTORIANS

Other than the gospels, we know of early Christianity mainly through the Jewish historian Josephus (37-96 AD), but he himself became a Roman citizen and even an advisor to two emperors. Two centuries later, Eusebius and Irenaeus wrote about the origins of the Christian religion. Both of them basically codified Christianity as we know it. Irenaeus makes the oldest known claim that there are only four official gospels and the others are work of the devil. Eusebius (who was working for Constantine and even wrote his biography) compiled a history of the Roman Church from Peter on (Eusebius wrote that the Emperor was the vehicle of God on earth).

THE EARLY CHRISTIANS

Rome was obviously not the place where Christianity had been born, nor the cultural centre of the world. Christianity first spread in Palestine and Syria, then east to Armenia (the first country to convert) and to Greece, the cultural centre of the Empire. When the apostles dispersed Peter went to Rome, but others went elsewhere. Notably, Thaddeus went to Armenia.

Later, Paul went to Greece. The first community to call themselves Christians was in Syria. The man whom most (including Paul) considered the head of Christianity was James the Just, who remained in Palestine. These were all equal centres of Christianity. It was only after the Roman conversion that the Roman branch of Christianity became the official one, and the lineage back to Peter (the Popes) was recognised as the only lineage worth knowing. It was then that only four gospels (probably written in Greece between 66 AD and the end of the second century) were accepted as true, even if for centuries many others had circulated. After that the competing branches of Christianity were persecuted and annihilated.

CHAPTER 12

❦

The formation of the early Christian Church and the writing of the Gospels

The early Christian movement needed to have some kind of theological structure if it was going to survive and grow. The proliferation of conflicting Gospels risked leading it to a potentially fatal fragmentation. It needed a leadership that would be impossible to achieve if each community had its own beliefs and its own Gospel.

By the end of the second century, a power structure started to take shape. A three-rank hierarchy of bishops, priests, and deacons emerged in various communities, claiming to speak for the majority and believing themselves to be the guardians of the only true faith. They were actually very brave in what they were trying to do, and they were probably genuinely scared that without a set of widely-accepted and rigid rules and rituals, the whole movement would wither away and die.

When being a Christian meant risking persecution and even death, the very survival of the Church became contingent on the establishment of some kind of order. This grew until, around the year 180 and under the leadership of Irenaeus, the Bishop of Lyon, a single, unified view was finally imposed. There could be only one Church with one set of beliefs and rituals. All other viewpoints were rejected as heresy. Their doctrine was straightforward: there could be no salvation outside their true Church; its members should be orthodox, which meant straight thinking; and the Church should be Catholic, which meant 'universal'.

This meant that the cottage industry of Gospels had to be stopped. Irenaeus decided that there should be four true Gospels, using the curious argument that, as there were four corners to the Universe and four principal winds, so there should be four Gospels. He wrote five volumes entitled the *Destruction and Overthrow of Falsely So-called Knowledge,* in which he denounced most of the existing works as blasphemous, settling on the four Gospels we know today.

Apart from the Gospel of Peter, none of the Gnostic Gospels had a Passion narrative, but the four Gospels Irenaeus chose did. They spoke about Jesus' death on the Cross and about his Resurrection; they linked the story being promoted to the fundamental ritual of the Eucharist, the last supper. But they didn't start off that way. In its earliest version, the first of them to be included, the Gospel of Mark, doesn't talk about a virgin birth at all, nor does it have the Resurrection in it. It just ends with Jesus' empty tomb, where a mysterious young man, a transcendental being of some kind, like an angel, tells a group of women who come to the tomb that Jesus is waiting for them in Galilee. This terrifies these women. They run off and don't tell anyone about it - which makes you wonder how Mark or whoever wrote that Gospel would have ever heard about it in the first place. But that's how Mark originally ended his Gospel. It's only in Matthew, fifty years later, and then in Luke, ten years after that, that elaborate post-resurrection appearances were added to Mark's original ending, which is then itself rewritten.

It took another two hundred years - to the year 367, in fact - for the list of twenty-seven texts that comprise what we know as the New Testament to be finally agreed upon. By the end of that century, Christianity had become the officially approved religion and possession of any of the texts considered heretical was held to be a criminal offence. All known copies of the alternative Gospels were burned and destroyed.

All, that is, except for the ones spirited away to the caves of Nag Hammadi, which do not show Jesus to be supernatural in any way. They were banned because the Jesus of these texts was just a roving wise man who preached a life of wholehearted acceptance of fellow human beings. He is not here to save us from sin and from eternal damnation. He is here to guide us to some kind of spiritual understanding. And once a disciple reaches enlightenment, and this notion must have given Irenaeus and his cronies a few sleepless nights, the master is no longer needed. The student and the teacher become equals.

The four canon Gospels, the ones in the New Testament, see Jesus as our Saviour, the Messiah, the Son of God. Orthodox Christians, and Orthodox Jews, for that matter, insist that an unbridgeable chasm separates man from his Creator. The Gospels that were found in Nag Hammadi contradicted this: for them, self-knowledge was the knowledge of God; the self and the divine are one and the same. Even worse, by describing Jesus as a teacher, an enlightened sage, they considered Him a man, someone we all could emulate, and that wouldn't do for Irenaeus and his lot. He couldn't just be a man; He had to be much more than that. He had to be the Son of God. He had to be unique, because by his being unique the Church became unique, the only path to salvation. By painting Him in that light, the early Church could claim that if you weren't with them, following their rules, living the way they wanted you to, you were doomed to damnation.

So what can we extract from the Gospels that is original material, given that they have been altered, amended and extended by the Church over many years?

To understand how we get from Jesus to the Gospels, we must understand that Galilean Judaism was predominantly an oral culture and not a written one like ours. In oral cultures, events are watched and speeches and sayings are heard. The ordinary person begins to make sense of it by reciting it or by repeating it, and when he or she gets together with others, they work on a given rendering of that event or speech or story. It needs to be observed. Oral cultures see, hear and remember, and what they focus on are the 'big facts', the 'major sayings' and the 'big picture'. But they come to reciting whatever they choose to recite, and their given performance will 'colour the situation' or 'set the context' and these colourings and shadings will either be typical or specific, though no one would worry about whether or not the contextual shadings are precisely what was done on that specific occasion.

According to the most current research, early pre-Christianity reflected tremendous diversity. While we may think of modern Christianity as divided into many branches of Protestant, Roman Catholic, and Eastern Orthodox varieties, there were many more groups in the early Jesus movement within the first two hundred years after Jesus' life. Many people held very diverse ideas about what Jesus said and did. We could call these people Jewish Christians or Christian Jews. Neither term identifies a single orthodox group or family of groups in the first or second centuries.

According to one source, there were hundreds of different versions of Jesus' words, hundreds of 'Gospels', in the first three centuries after his death.

As the remembered words and acts of Jesus were gradually put into writing, diversity began to diminish. The process by which an oral transmission turns into a written one always involves selection, and the selection each group of followers makes determines its stand on important issues. In addition, those who could not read were largely left out of the decision-making process.

With many written Gospels in existence, the diversity within early pre-Christianity continued for three hundred years, until Constantine realized that a stable empire could not be built upon hundreds of conflicting interpretations of who Jesus was. In 325 AD he ordered a council of bishops and theologians to gather at Nicaea (in what is now Turkey) to settle once and for all who Jesus had been and what he had said and done. The theological portion of the debate centred on whether Jesus was human, divine, or some combination of both. There was reportedly a certain pressure on all who attended; if Constantine did not get the agreement of opinion he wanted, he might withdraw his support from Christianity altogether.

Given this pressure, various compromises were made. For instance, since the sun god was very popular in Roman culture, the council declared the Roman 'sun' day to be the Christian Sabbath. This day of the week had no particular significance for Jesus or his early followers. Likewise, the council adopted the traditional celebration of the birth of the sun, around the time of the winter solstice, for the celebration of Jesus' birthday.

The canonical Gospels display the workings of four different minds, from four different backgrounds, choosing to emphasise independent points for their own particular purpose. Clearly they were written to be circulated within certain communities, only later reaching a much wider audience. Naturally there are common motivations - the desire to spread the 'good news' and present Jesus in as positive a light as possible. But there are others, and one with far-reaching consequences was the writers' desire to portray the new religion in as Roman-friendly a light as possible. This led them to put a certain spin on the story, and in particular to misrepresent the events surrounding Jesus' crucifixion.

All four Gospels place the blame for Jesus' arrest, condemnation and execution squarely on the Jewish leaders in Jerusalem, disregarding the Roman authorities, in the person of Pilate. However, as modern historians are very well informed about the laws and customs in Roman-occupied Palestine, it is now obvious that the New Testament version is by no means the whole truth. Crucifixion was a Roman penalty specifically reserved for rebels against Rome's authority, and it punished political, not religious, transgressions.

Trying to establish their religion in the Roman Empire - and especially against the backdrop of Nero's first persecution and the Jewish Revolt - the Gospel writers had to allay any official suspicions, but they could not admit that the religion's founder had been sentenced to death by those same Roman authorities as this was hardly calculated to win them over. So the burden of blame was shifted to the Jewish leaders (who were not exactly popular with Rome) and thus all Jews - a charge that is particularly strong in the Gospel of John.

These subtexts become increasingly important when we turn

our attention to the question of who wrote the canonical gospels, and when - and their comparative reliability. Having studied the origins of the Gospels for over two centuries, historians and other experts have been unable to agree on when they were written and even by whom. There is nowhere near enough information.

Nowadays only fundamentalists indulge in the luxury of believing that the Gospels were fixed from the beginning and never changed. The texts have manifestly been amended many, many times by a host of hands, bent on tweaking the message and recreating Jesus in their own image. The classic example is the story of the adulterous woman ('Let anyone of you who is without sin be the first to throw a stone'), which many regard as Jesus' finest hour. In modern Bibles this episode is found in John, in chapter 7-8, and is often quoted as an example of Christ's wisdom and compassion. However, the incident was conspicuous by its absence in bibles before the twelfth century. It was first added to Luke, only later being transferred to John. Many argue that it was a genuine story about Jesus that had been passed down the generations, and therefore deserves a place in the Gospels. Perhaps so, but there is no proof, and the fact remains that some eight hundred years after the earliest known copies of the New Testament the text was still being changed.

It was not until the Council of Trent in 1545 that the Roman Catholic Church decreed that no more alterations or additions should be made to the Bible. Even so, the editing process continues. For example, because the passage known as the 'longer text of the Eucharist' in Luke (22:19-20) is now believed not to have been part of the original text, it is left out of some modern translations, among them the New English Bible. And if the four Gospels have changed since the earliest surviving copies, there is every likelihood they also changed even more before these copies were made.

The word 'Gospel' means good news. There are four Gospel accounts in the New Testament:

MATTHEW, MARK, LUKE AND JOHN

The first three Gospels are sometimes called the 'synoptic' (same view) Gospels. This is because they each cover teaching and miracles by Jesus that are also covered in another account. John, writing later, recounts Jesus' other words and miracles that have a particular spiritual meaning.

The similarities and difference between the three Synoptic Gospels has given rise to many debates and theories. The classic solution is the 'two source theory', which maintains that Mark is an independent composition and that Matthew and Luke relied on Mark and inserted or combined with it material from another unknown or hypothetical source or compilation consisting mainly of sayings. For identification purposes this unknown source has been designated as Q, representing Quelle, the German word for source.

All four gospels present Jesus as both the Son of God and the son of man. Between them they record his baptism, the feeding of the 5000 from five loaves and two fishes, Mary's anointing of the Lord Jesus, his prayer in the garden of Gethsemane, his betrayal, trial, crucifixion, death, burial and resurrection. However, each writer does so in a slightly different way, recording additional details or emphasising one aspect more than the others.

Both the Jewish Christians and the Gentile Christians in the generation after Paul collected their treasured recollections of Jesus into Gospels, the Jewish Christians into their Sayings Gospel Q, and the Gentile Christians into their Narrative Gospel Mark. One main reason that the Sayings Gospel Q did not become a book within the New Testament is that the New Testament is the book of the Gentile Christian Church, not the book of the Jewish Christian Church. We know about the Sayings Gospel Q only because, as a last expression of moving towards unity, both confessions decided to merge it and the Narrative Gospel Mark into a single Gospel, each from their own perspective, of course. Matthew is from the perspective of the Jewish Christian Church, Luke from that of the Gentile Christian Church. So it has been possible to reconstruct the Sayings Gospel Q rather accurately, as a team of scholars have done, though no manuscripts have survived because it soon ceased to be copied by the Gentile Christian Church.

It is perhaps a reflection of today's emphasis on a Jesus of faith that most modern Christians, practising and non-practising, are quire unaware of the sort of conflicts that have divided the world of Gospel studies during the last century or so. Few realise, for instance, that despite the fact that the Canonical Gospels bear the names Matthew, Mark, Luke and John, these names are mere attributions and not necessarily those of their real authors. The earliest writers who referred to the Gospels significantly failed to mention names of authors, it being apparent that each Gospel, both those surviving and those that have failed to survive, was originally designed as The Gospel for a particular community. A canon of the four recognised Gospels only gradually came into general usage, at the same time acquiring associations with specific names from Christianity's earliest years. It should also be born in mind that none of the earliest texts had any of the easy identification features they bear now. Everything was written in capital letters. There were no headings, chapter divisions or verse divisions; these were refinements which were not to appear until the Middle Ages. To make matters more difficult for the modern scholar, there was practically no punctuation or space between words.

THE GOSPEL ACCORDING TO MARK

Mark's is considered to be the first of the written Gospels. It is really the one that establishes the life of Jesus as a story form. It develops a narrative from his early career, through the main points of his life, and culminates in his death. And, as such, it sets the pattern for all the later Gospel traditions. We know that both Matthew and Luke used Mark as a source in their composition and it is also probable that even John knew something of Mark in tradition. So Mark is really the one that sets the stage for all the later Christian Gospel writings.

It is also fairly well accepted that Mark's Gospel was a product of the Christian community in Rome (which is probably how the connection with Peter crept in).

Historians have shown that Mark has been constructed from many individual stories and recollections, assembled into a single narrative with short connecting passages. In other words, Mark had basically written the Gospel's 'plot' by connecting up individual stories about Jesus. However, Mark is not without a plan, organising his narrative thematically. For example, an episode in which Jesus addresses the spiritual blindness of those around Him is followed by his curing a blind man.

Startlingly, in Mark there are no post-resurrection appearances; the last passages tell of Mary Magdalene and two other women finding Jesus' tomb open, his body gone and a man dressed in white who informs them he has risen from the dead. The story ends with the women running off. Beyond the mysterious man's word, there is no attempt to convince the reader that Jesus really had risen (although clearly Mark himself believed in the Resurrection).

Turn to the last verses of Mark today and you will indeed find stories of the risen Christ's appearances, but sadly they were added much later, simply because their absence was so glaring - not to mention embarrassing. (Whoever took it upon himself to add them based his version on Luke's Gospel.) Neither of the two earliest complete versions of the New Testament, the Codex Sinaiticus and Codex Vaticanus, included any post-Resurrection episodes. But was Mark truly unaware of these momentous happenings, or was what he wrote about Jesus after the resurrection deemed unacceptable later, and hastily removed? Or was his original ending somehow lost?

Without knowing the exact circumstances in which Mark's Gospel was composed and handed down, nobody can answer these questions conclusively. But it is very odd that what is for Christians the single most important event in Jesus' life is missing.

THE GOSPEL ACCORDING TO MATTHEW

In the Church's formative years - the second and third centuries - Matthew was by far the favourite Gospel, and the most often quoted, which is probably why it comes first in the New Testament.

The evidence suggest that Matthew was written after the Jewish Revolt, its basic theme being that the failure of the Jews to recognise the true nature of Jesus was the cause of their downfall, which indicates that it was written after the downfall in 70 AD, although the Gospel never explicitly mentions it.

Early Christian writers all ascribed the Gospel to Jesus' disciple Matthew, the tax collector who joined him in the early days. But since it was recognised that Matthew draws upon Mark's Gospel (among other sources), this has been impossible to sustain. (And as this Matthew appears in the Gospel, why doesn't the writer use the first person?)

Matthew's Gospel is the most Jewish-oriented of the four, as it assumes more familiarity with Jewish customs and appeals far more to the scriptures. It is also more specific than any of the other Gospels about Jesus' alleged fulfilment of Old Testament messianic prophecies. Although on a few occasions Mark points out that an event in Jesus' life had been prophesied, Matthew does so much more often and more emphatically. Clearly his intention was to persuade Jews, or affirm this belief of a Jewish-Christian community, that Jesus was their Messiah according to the criteria laid down in their own scriptures.

THE GOSPEL AND ACTS ACCORDING TO LUKE

Both Luke's Gospel and his Acts of the Apostles were written to and for one Theophilius, presumably a high-ranking Roman official, as he is addressed as *kristos*, meaning roughly 'Your Excellency'), apparently in response to his request for a briefing on the emergent religion. But the writer's underlying agenda was 'to claim for the Church its rightful place in the Roman world, demonstrate that it was no threat to the Roman order, and make a case for its positive contributions to society'. Luke was influenced, among other considerations, by the desirability of showing that Christianity was politically innocent.

To suit his aim of persuading Theophilius that Christians were beyond suspicion, Luke plays down the ambiguous passages that might clash with the Roman way - sometimes so transparently as to verge on the comic. For example, both Mark and Matthew describe a scene where Herod Antipas, the Roman-appointed ruler of Galilee, hears rumours that Jesus is John the Baptist risen again, and is afraid. In Luke this becomes 'and was anxious to see Him'.

Although Luke's Gospel follows almost exactly the same storyline as Mark and Matthew, it relates certain events and sayings of Jesus that appear in neither. Indeed, academic detective work has established that Luke incorporated material from some earlier sources not available to either of them.

THE GOSPEL ACCORDING TO JOHN

Despite all the reservations, understanding the origins, orientation and purpose of the three synoptic Gospels is relatively easy, but in John nothing is quite as it seems.

John, by contrast with Matthew and Luke, is a complex piece of writing, weaving together many themes and layers of symbolism, besides drawing on several literary gestures, not just Jewish traditions. With the synoptics, basically what you see is what you get, but with John's Gospel, everything is shrouded in layers of paradox and mystery. In the writer of John we have an author who is seeking to tell a well-rounded, multi-layered story without any loose ends.

This is the only one of the New Testament Gospels that explicitly claims to be derived from the eyewitness account of one of Jesus' followers, the mysterious 'beloved disciple'. It ends with the bold statement, after Jesus has said farewell, 'This is the disciple who testifies to these things and who wrote them down. We know that his testimony is true'. However, the use of the third person makes it clear it was not actually set down by the disciple but based on his written memoirs, although the Gospel writer was clearly not above exploiting him to add authority to his own theological perspective. In the end, it is just another of the Fourth Gospel's many mysteries.

In fact John's Gospel possesses so many mysteries, paradoxes and puzzles that we might be forgiven for thinking that the author deliberately set out to confuse us. For example, in the synoptics most of Jesus' activity tales place in Galilee and other places outside Judaea and it is only at the end that he makes his fateful journey to Jerusalem, where he causes a major upset in the Temple by attacking the traders. But in John's Gospel he makes several visits to Jerusalem, initially right at the beginning of his ministry - and it is then that he causes mayhem in the Temple. Which are we to believe? It is not just a question of John's Gospel being out-voted by the other three, since Matthew and Luke are based on Mark so if he got something wrong they would too.

As we have seen, there is evidence, from both early traditions and modern academic analysis, that Mark created his storyline when putting together isolated stories about Jesus, so his plot is not to be taken too literally. But does that mean we should totally accept John's Gospel? Unfortunately, no. Seemingly the author of John tweaked his chronology to fit the cycle of Jewish festivals. So sometimes John's Gospel is more credible than Mark's, sometimes vice versa.

Much more importantly, the Fourth Gospel presents Jesus in a fundamentally different way. Although to Mark, Matthew and Luke he is the Son of God, he is also essentially mortal man in the mould of the prophets, becoming something more transcendental only when he resurrects. But right from the beginning John unequivocally has Jesus as the 'word made flesh' and 'the Logos… pre-existent and one with God'. This is similar to the way Paul talks about Jesus.

His character is different too. In Mark, Matthew and Luke, Jesus talks directly about himself (using 'I') just nine, seventeen and ten times respectively - but in John he does so 118 times. In the Fourth Gospel Jesus speaks much more about his own importance and uniqueness: clearly the writer saw Him not merely as God's messenger but actually as the message.

THE OTHER GOSPELS

In recent years, a new wave of 'Historical Jesus' research has emerged in the wake of the discovery in 1945 in Egypt of the ancient manuscripts that are known today as the 'Nag Hammadi library' and as 'Gnostic Gospels' and then of the Dead Sea Scrolls in 1947.

We've listened to the winners, and their story doesn't make sense. So let's listen to the losers and see if their story makes any more sense.

Many Gospels were written, including and besides the four official ones. The four official Gospels were written in Greece in

Greek, the earliest (Mark's) dating from the year 70 and the last one (John's) dating from the second century after Christ. (The oldest manuscript of the Gospels that we found dates from the fourth century, but we have fragments that have been dated from the mid second century and we can deduct the date of composition from references in the texts.) There is general agreement that three of the official ones (the 'synoptic' Gospels) derive from a common source, whereas John's is inherently different. One hypothesis is that John's and this common source derive, in turn, from a pre-existing text, called 'Q', that has never been found. One of the banned Gospels, the Gospel of Thomas, has been considered a potential candidate for 'Q' or for something closer to 'Q' than anything else we have found.

John's Gospel is markedly different from the other three Gospels: it names many people who are anonymous in the other three Gospels and it includes two episodes (the wedding at Cana and the raising of Lazarus) that the other Gospels seem curiously unaware of. It sounds a very contentious issue.

Texts outlawed by Rome paint a very different picture of Jesus' teaching, especially the ones written by the Gnostic Christians. Sometimes Jesus appears as a sort of revolutionary, sometimes as a sort of Buddhist-type thinker. In the most ancient texts he rarely appears as the Jesus who makes miracles and ascended to heaven. Sometimes he barely appears at all, while others (James, Paul) are the predominant characters. Peter, the most famous of Jesus' followers, is actually a very minor figure in early Christian documents.

Today it is difficult to understand why some Gospels were banned. Several of the banned Gospels are apparently consistent with the dogma: why ban them? In 325 Christianity had become the religion of the Roman empire and it was not nice to emphasise that it was the Romans who had killed Jesus; in 325 Christianity had taken the beliefs that would become the Catholic dogma, and it was not nice to emphasise that Jesus had a brother (although even the official Gospels say so) or that Mary Magdalene was always with Him (although even the official Gospels say so) and it was nice to undermine Jesus' miracles. Most of the other Gospels may have been considered redundant (they didn't add anything meaningful to the story) and dangerous (they could stress aspects of Jesus' story that the Church would rather downplay).

The Gnostic Christians were persecuted after Rome converted to Christianity, and most of their texts were burned. The Church also outlawed all other histories of Jesus but the four official ones.

It is also likely that the Gospels as we know them have been heavily rewritten after they were originally written. Papias of Hierapolis in 110 talks of the Gospel of St Matthew as a collection of oracles - not of miracles. All four official Gospels were written after Paul wrote his letters. Paul's letters are the oldest Christian documents. But Paul admits he never met Jesus. Irenaeus (at the end of the second century) is the first Christian writer who mentions the dogma of the four.

In the second century, Clement of Alexandria admits that two versions of Mark's Gospel existed but one was being suppressed, because it contained two passages that should not be viewed by average Christians. Thus the texts were being chosen, edited and purged for the first two centuries of the Christian era. That process had been continued and by the time Irenaeus wrote that there were only four Gospels. Irenaeus' choice was formalised in 325 at the council of Nicaea, where these four Gospels became the official dogma of the Roman Church and all other histories of Jesus were banned.

Irenaeus picked only a fraction of the available literature on Jesus. He excluded some of the most popular texts, such as the Gospel of Thomas and the Gospel of the Hebrews (by far the two most popular texts among early Christians). Either the memory was lost of what was old and what was new, (Irenaeus claims that Mark and Luke were eyewitnesses, which of course they were not) or the Church was already at work completely reinventing the story of Jesus to suit whatever ideology.

Important as the four Gospels of Matthew, Mark, Luke and John are, we have the wrong impression of what the early Church and early Christianity were about unless we bear in mind that they were so obviously altered over 300 years until they became canon. At the same time we ought to remember the living diversity of traditions and writings which preceded the formation of the canon, and which until comparatively recent times had been deliberately removed from circulation, with all possible traces removed. They are as much a part of the early history of Jesus and the Church as the accepted New Testament canon, which was not agreed on until nearly 350 years after Jesus died.

It is now patently obvious that the earliest form of Christianity was not one unified belief and that the earliest Christian Church contained an entire spectrum of attitudes and of understanding of Jesus, living together in a state of peaceful existence. The imposition of a standard orthodox belief came later, with the concentration of authority in the hands of the Roman Church. We now know that the Roman Church introduced its own literature opposing the diversity of traditions. The effect of this was to strengthen the collective belief within the organised Church and drove those that held the old 'apostolic' beliefs out from the Church, ultimately branding them as heretics.

This transformation progressed to the point where by the fourth century AD Augustine declared that he would not have accepted the truth of Christ and the Gospels at all if the Catholic Church had not informed him of the true belief.

CHAPTER 13

❧

The religion of Jesus

Jesus tried to convey to his audience, and especially to the inner circle of his followers, how to draw near to God. The basic vision of Jesus was centred on the divine Kingdom of God. His vocation was to persuade his Jewish contemporaries to strive wholeheartedly to find and achieve this Kingdom. Jesus was really interested in the action to be followed in the perfect observance of the Torah to reach the Kingdom, which is depicted by Jesus as the ultimate spiritual value. He was concerned in his teachings with the ways and means which would secure admittance into the Kingdom.

JESUS THE SON OF MAN

The early evangelists or Christian writers set out to interpret Jesus' sayings against a background of many variations, for instance Jewish, Essene, Hellenistic and Oriental, and to show his utterances as a part of his mission. None of them makes an attempt to make an example of his teaching as such. On the other hand there are many passages in the Gospels which repeat traditions of the words of Jesus. We now know that collections of 'sayings of the Lord' constituted the earliest prototypes of Gospel writing and form. If we accept that the sayings are the earliest recollections at our disposal (and surely this is corroborated by their extended form in the Gospels), then we can to some extent see how the utterer of these sayings, Jesus, saw himself, rather than how the evangelists later saw Him.

We can now take this a stage further and make a link to some of the lost texts referred to previously, the mystical sequence of seeking - finding - wondering - reigning - resting.

Seeking and finding - John the Baptist baptised Jesus, the culmination of his seeking, finding his destiny, his kingdom.

Wondering - Jesus tells his disciples 'My kingdom is not of this world'.

Reigning - He reigns as two in one, the Priestly Messiah and the Kingly Messiah, thus uniting both strands of thought.

Resting - His teaching of the attainment of the Kingdom of God is the central theme of Jesus' teaching, the self-fulfilment, the inner self, the I, all of which when attained will bring the spiritual rest.

The ministry of Jesus we know of is concerned entirely with teaching how to seek and find the Kingdom of God that is present in the world all the time. It is within each and every one of us, and it is there to be found - once we have stopped wondering what it is we can discover and do to throw off all the earthly baggage we have accumulated since birth and return to the innocent state in which we were born. Then, and only then, will we be reborn and reign in the knowledge and love of God which will enable us to rest in peace.

What is important at this stage is to affirm Jesus' claim of the innocence of the newborn child and his insistence that we must try to regain that innocence to find our true selves within us. For instance the Celtic church believed that we were all born free of sin, but in 597 AD, when Augustine came to England by order of the Pope, the Synod of Whitby accepted the Roman Catholic version that we are all born with sin and Jesus came into the world to save us from our sins.

The mystery Gospels of both Thomas and Phillip in a way confirm the character of early Christian mystery. A transformation of conscience is suggested, which can in turn transform man's vision on earth and reveal the Kingdom. There is a tendency in both Gospels to revert to Gnostic beliefs deriving from the older mystery rites, but in the hands of Jesus they have acquired new meaning of man's maturing individuality to quote from the Gospel of Thomas logo 67. He who knows the all but fails to know himself lacks everything. In logo 77 Jesus said 'I am the light that is over them all - I am the all. The all has come forth from me and the all has attained unto me. Cleave the wood I am there, raise up the stone and you will find me there. The all is the light of the world is here in everything we touch and do. The divine, the Kingdom is here among us all the time'.

CHAPTER 14

❧

Aramaic gospels

After the death of Jesus, his church, or followers to be more precise, were led by James his brother. But these followers of Jesus were Judaeo Christians who were soon castigated as heretics by the non-Jewish majority of the Church for not believing in the divinity of Jesus.

The Gospels then, which purport to tell the story of Jesus, have to be analysed to grasp the significance of the events and teaching contained in them. We should therefore start ideally with the language used by Jesus in the teaching. He spoke Aramaic, a Semitic tongue used by most of his compatriots which is closely related to Hebrew, the language of the Jewish Bible (the Old Testament). But the four Gospels, Matthew, Mark, Luke and John, have survived only in Greek.

Scholars maintain that they were composed in Greek and are not translations from a semitic original. The closest we can get to Aramaic is a quote in the second century attributed to Bishop Papias by the church Historian Eusebios in the fourth century AD that the evangelical Matthew was 'acquainted' with a collection of Aramaic sayings of Jesus. This of course could be the lost 'Q' or even the Gospel of Thomas.

During the first centuries of Christianity the vast majority of the church were Greek speaking non Jews inhabitants of the Roman empire. They needed to have the teachings of Jesus in Greek. As a result the Aramaic originals of the sayings of Jesus have been allowed to fade from memory or have even been deliberately ignored.

THE FIFTH GOSPEL (THE GOSPEL OF THOMAS)

If there is one candidate for the title of 'The Gospel', since unquestionably it is at least the equal in age and authenticity of the canonical books, then it is the Gospel of Thomas, attributed to the disciple of that name. A collection of Jesus' sayings, this book has been known in full only for sixty years. The first hints of its existence came from a number of papyrus fragments found between 1897 and 1903 in the major early Christian centre of Oxyrhynchus (modern El Bahnasa) in Egypt. What startled scholars was that not only did it contain several sayings attributed to Jesus not found in the Gospels, but the fragments could be dated to between 150 and 200AD, making them the oldest writings about him known at that time. However, it was another fifty years before a full copy of this lost work was found among the collection of documents discovered at Nag Hammadi in Egypt in 1945.

The Gospel of Thomas is something of a thorn in the flesh for those who believe the current New Testament is nothing less than God's own word. An analysis of its language reveals that it was composed well before 100 AD, at about the same time as the canonical Gospels were taking shape. But there are clues that point to it *predating* them.

The book is a collection of 114 sayings described, in the opening lines, as 'the hidden words that the living Jesus spoke', written down by 'Didymus Judas Thomas'. Thomas is Aramaic for 'twin' and Didymus also means 'twin' in Greek, so it is really just a translation of his name, or rather nickname. Some of the sayings are presented as statements by Jesus, while others are in the form of a question-and-answer session with the disciples, like other Gnostic books. About a third echo or parallel sayings in the New Testament, but many are completely new.

Some of the sayings are simpler forms of parables that occur in the synoptic Gospels, suggesting that the writers of Mark, Matthew and Luke elaborated - and, even more significantly, in some cases misunderstood - the original lesson. For example, in the 'consider the lilies' passage, Luke and Matthew have 'They do not labour or spin', but in Thomas it is 'They do not card or spin', carding being the preparation of wool for spinning. Therefore Thomas seems to have a more accurate version of the original saying, which became slightly muddled by the time it reached Luke and Matthew - and, like all common sayings material in those Gospels, got here via Q. In other words, Thomas gives a purer and therefore earlier version, showing that it must have predated even Q. The fact that the Gospel of Thomas appeals to the authority of two apostles, James the Just and Thomas himself, whose roles were soon eclipsed by those associated with Rome, Peter and Paul, also points to an early date.

The implications of this are truly far-reaching. At the very least the Gospel of Thomas should be taken as seriously as the canonical Gospels are now taken by New Testament scholars and non-Catholic theologians. The Catholic Church, however, has condemned it as heretical. To them, had God meant Christians to read it, it would have been in the New Testament. This is a very trite answer implying that God censures and writes every written word the Church says he does.

One of this Gospel's most interesting features is how it portrays Jesus' disciples. First, and more strikingly, they included women, two in particular, Mary (almost certainly the Magdalene, although not explicitly stated) and Salome, among his questioners. Secondly, while Thomas, Mary and Salome ask intelligent, searching questions that show they understand Jesus' teaching, those posed by Peter and Matthew (besides various unnamed disciples) reveal that they have little idea of his mindset, giving Jesus the chance to correct them. There is a distinct impression that a few favoured disciples constituted an inner circle - and while this includes the only two named women, it emphatically does not include Peter. This is strikingly different from the way the disciples are portrayed in the New Testament.

Further, the Gospel of Thomas illustrates concerns which are usually judged to belong to the first century, disagreements about apostleship, uncertainty about the role of James the Righteous, interest in sayings of Jesus and sayings collections, and so forth. Sayings in the Gospel of Thomas also seem to be transmitted in a form earlier than the form we have in the canonical Gospels. Such may be noted, for instance, in parables: Thomas preserves parables of Jesus simply as stories, but the New Testament Gospels append allegorical interpretations to the parables in an effort to explain them and apply them to new situations. If the composition of the Gospel of Thomas may be given a date in the first century, then Thomas may take us back to a place that much closer to the historical Jews and the Gospel of Thomas. Together with the sayings, Gospel Q may provide strong evidence for Jesus as a great teacher of wisdom.

The Jesus of Thomas is also somewhat different from the Jesus of the New Testament Gospels, and it would appear that the Gospel of Thomas is not fundamentally dependent upon the New Testament Gospels but is an independent and primary source for the Jesus tradition. Jesus in the Gospel of Thomas performs no physical miracles, reveals no fulfilment of prophecy and announces no apocalyptic kingdom.

In the Gospel of Thomas and the Thomas tradition, it is what Jesus says and not how He dies that is important, and the words and wisdoms of the living Jesus bring insight, light, and life. The Gospel of Thomas proclaims a gospel of wisdom by inviting readers to encounter Jesus and his sayings and find an interpretation of the sayings that will enlighten their lives. Then they 'will not taste death.' Jesus in the Gospel of Thomas is not unlike the Buddha in Theravada Buddhism. Jesus and the Buddha point the way, but it is up to those who follow to labour at the task of understanding and living.

The Gospel of Thomas also sheds light on aspects of the life and work of the historical Jesus. Before Church dogma, before the formulations of Christology, before the honorific titles bestowed upon Jesus, there was Jesus the Jewish man of wisdom walking the roads of Galilee with his friends, speaking in parables, stories and other utterances about God's presence and God's reign, and showing God's presence and power through acts of faith healing and exorcism.

Along with many 21st century scholars, I believe that many of those who wish, for historical reasons, to minimize the significance of the Gospel of Thomas and marginalize it in the discussion of who Jesus was and how the early Church developed, assign it a later date of composition for that reason. Conversely, many of those - and I am one of them - who wish to employ the Gospel of Thomas in the study of Jesus and Christian origins support their use of the text by arguing for an earlier date of composition.

We have already seen that many of the logos in the gospel of Thomas are used and expanded in the canonical Gospels. Thus the eye of reason would date Thomas before the canonical Gospels and not after them. If for example Thomas' sayings were derived from the canonical Gospels there would not be so much of their stories missing. If Thomas is an earlier composition it logically follows that we already know that the stories of Thomas were enriched and extended and in addition probably up to 75% of the canonical texts are later additions.

In Thomas' version of the Parable of the Wicked Tenants (see extract below), the owner of a vineyard sends a servant to collect fruit from his tenants, but they just assault the servant. The same happens with a second servant, so the owner sends his son, but the tenants kill him. The parable concludes at this point with the characteristic words 'He who has ears, let him hear.' But the Synoptic version of the parable (Mark 12.1-11 and parallels in Matthew and Luke) has a whole succession of servants (representing the prophets of Israel), all of whom are beaten or killed before the owner sends his son, who also dies (Mark 12.5-8).

In addition, the parable adds that the tenants will be replaced, and there is a quotation from the Hebrew Bible (Mark 12.10-11). It has been suggested that the simpler form in the Gospel of Thomas represents Jesus' original teaching, in which the vineyard stands for the ancestral land of Israel in Jesus' own time. The two servants symbolise its population, who are opposed by foreign occupation, and the son is Jesus, Israel's Messiah. The Synoptic version, it is claimed, has expanded this into a picture of the disobedience of Israel down the ages, with the succession of killed or beaten servants representing the biblical prophets and the expulsion of the tenants symbolising God's rejection of Israel in favour of the gentiles. The son is Jesus as a universal saviour, rather than a national one. Similarly, the Parable of the Net in Matthew 13 is an allegory of the Last Judgement, but this theme does not occur in the Gospel of Thomas, where the emphasis is on the fisherman as the model of the man who acts according to wisdom (see extract below).

However, caution is necessary before such examples in Thomas are accepted as the 'authentic' teaching of Jesus. Much in the Gospel of Thomas represents the common currency of Gnostic thought and the work should probably be considered - certainly in its extant Coptic form - as a broadly Gnostic composition. Thus the theme of the Kingdom of Heaven is as prominent in Thomas as it is in the canonical Gospels, but in Thomas it is a wholly present and spiritual reality, rather than the New Testament's kingdom of the future. In Thomas, entering the kingdom is the equivalent of the disciple's discovery of his or her own divine nature. Thomas's version of the Parable of the Net emphasises one large fish which is preserved, and similarly its account of the Parable of the Lost Sheep describes the straying animal as the biggest of the flock. The fish and the sheep both probably refer to the true Gnostic, who alone is the recipient of salvation. In Thomas, the words 'He who has ears to hear, let him hear', which also occur in the canonical gospels, are certainly a call to human beings to recognise both the truth about Jesus and their true nature as belonging to the divine world in unity with the supreme father.

SAYINGS FROM THE COPTIC GOSPEL OF THOMAS

These are the secret words which the living Jesus spoke, and which Didymus Judas Thomas wrote down.

1. And he said: He who shall find the interpretation of these words. shall not taste death

2. Jesus said: He who seeks, let him not cease seeking until he finds; and when he finds he will be troubled, and when he is troubled he will be amazed, and he will reign over the All.

10. Jesus said: I have cast a fire upon the world, and see, I watch over it until it is ablaze.

31. Jesus said: No prophet is accepted in his own village, no physician heals those who know him.

47. Jesus said: It is not possible for a man to ride two horses or stretch two bows; and it is not possible for a servant to serve two masters,   unless he honours the one and insults the other.

8. Man is like a wise fisherman who casts his net into the sea; he drew it up from the sea full of small fish: among them he found a large food fish, the wise fisherman; he threw all the small fish into the sea, he chose the large fish without difficulty, He who has ears to hear, let him hear!

65. A good man had a vineyard; he leased it to tenants, that they might work in it and he receive the fruits from them. He sent his servant, that the tenants might give him the fruits of the vineyard. They seized his servant, beat him and all but killed him. The servant went away and told his master. His master said, 'Perhaps they did not know him.' He sent another servant; the tenants beat the other also. Then the master sent

his son. He said, 'Perhaps they will have respect for my son.' Those tenants, since they knew that he was the heir of the vineyard, they seized him and killed him. He who has ears let him hear.

107. The kingdom is like a shepherd who had hundred sheep; one of them, the biggest, went astray; he left the ninety-nine and sought after the one until he found it. After he had laboured, he said to the sheep, 'I love you more than the ninety-nine.'

As a final thought, consider the following Gospel of Thomas, logo 34: 'Jesus said: If a blind man guides the being of a blind man both of them fall to the bottom of the pit'.

Here Jesus refers to spiritual blindness. The being of a person is something very deep within him and a special quality is needed to guide it. False guidance at that level would result in a calamity (i.e. the fall to the bottom of the pit). It is a dig at the religious leaders of the day who have no clue about what he is teaching and his meaning.

Now if you think long and hard upon what Jesus meant, you might realize it means that you can talk to God in your own mind, and in your own prayers. Think about that for a moment, and about what it means to organised institutional Churches. If a man can talk to God in his own mind and pray in the security of his own bosom, what need has he of priests, or of a church - any church? Especially one with a strict code or creed about what you must believe. No wonder the Gospel of Thomas was considered heretical and was repressed.

CHAPTER 15

❦

The Council of Nicaea 325 AD and the Creeds

THE COUNCIL

Constantine the Great was Roman Emperor from 306-337 AD. In 323, after the Battle of Chalcedon, he became the sole head of the Roman world.

Tradition tells us that he was converted to Christianity suddenly and by a miracle. One evening, before the battle of Milvian Bridge, he saw a radiant cross appearing in the heavens, with the inscription, 'By this thou shalt conquer.' The tradition is first mentioned by Eusebius in his *De Vita Constantini* , written after the emperor's death. This miracle has been defended by the Roman Catholic Church, but cannot stand the test of critical examination. Constantine may have seen some phenomenon in the skies; he was no doubt convinced of the superior claims of Christianity as the rising religion; but his conversion was a change of policy, rather than of moral character.

Long after that event he killed his son, his second wife, several other relatives and some of his intimate friends, in passionate resentment of some fancied infringement of his rights. In his relation to Christianity he was cool, calculating, always bent upon the practically useful, always regarding the practically possible. He retained the office and title of *Pontifex Maximus* to the last, and did not receive Christian Baptism until he felt death close upon him. He kept pagans in the highest positions in his immediate surroundings, and forbade everything which might look like an encroachment of Christianity upon paganism. Such a faith in such a character is not the result of a sudden conversion by a miracle: if it were, the effect would be more miraculous than the cause. Judging from the character both of his father and his mother, it is probable that he grew up in quiet but steady contact with Christianity. Christianity had, indeed, become something in the air which no one occupying a prominent position in the Roman world could remain entirely foreign to. But the singular mixture of political carefulness and personal indifference with which he treated it presupposes a relationship of observation rather than impression. Constantine knew Christianity well, but only as a power in the Roman Empire, and he protected it as a wise and far-seeing statesman. As a power not of this world, he hardly, if ever came to understand it.

His first edict concerning the Christians (Rome 312) is lost. By the second (Milan, 313) he granted them not only free religious worship and the recognition of the state but reparation of previously incurred losses. Banished men who worked on the galleys or in the mines were recalled, confiscated estates were restored, etc. A series of edicts, 315, 316, 319, 321 and 323, completed the revolution. Christians were admitted to the offices of the State, both military and civil; the Christian clergy was exempted from all municipal burdens, as were pagan priests; the emancipation of Christian slaves was facilitated; Jews were forbidden to keep Christian slaves, etc. An edict of 321 ordered Sunday to be celebrated by cessation of all work in public. When Constantine became master of the whole empire all these edicts were extended to the whole realm, and the Roman world more and more assumed the aspect of a Christian state.

One thing, however, puzzled and annoyed the Emperor very much - the dissentions of the Christians, their perpetual squabbles about doctrines and the fanatical hatred that this engendered. In the Roman Empire the most different religions lived peacefully beside each other, and here was a religion which could not live in peace with itself. For political reasons, however, unity and harmony were necessary; religious stability is an aid to social and public stability. In 325 the Emperor convened the fist great ecumenical council at Nicaea to settle the Arian controversy. It was the first time the Christian Church and the Roman State had met face to face, and the impression was very deep on both sides.

The Emperor stood there in all his glory among the three hundred and eighteen Bishops, only one sixth of all the Bishops of the so called Christian religion. He learned something from those people. He saw that with Christianity was born a new sentiment in the human heart hitherto unknown to mankind, and that on this sentiment the throne could be rested more safely, than on the success of a court-intrigue, or the victory of a hired army.

After the Council of Nicaea, he conversed more and more frequently and intimately with the Bishops. His interest in Christianity grew with the years, but, as was to have been foreseen, he was sure to be led astray. He was more and more drawn over to the side of the Arians, and it was an Arian bishop who baptized him, reputedly on his deathbed.

So what actually occurred at the Council of Nicaea? Constantine called for a council meeting to be held in Nicaea with the Bishops of the Christian Church to resolve escalating quarrels and controversy mounting to a bitter degree of disunity among the church leadership concerning theological issues. The falling Roman Empire, now under Constantine's rule, could not withstand the division caused by years of hard-fought 'out of hand' arguing over doctrinal differences. Constantine saw it not only as a threat to Christianity but as a threat to society as well. Therefore, at the Council of Nicaea, Constantine demanded that the Christians settle their internal disagreements and become Christ-like agents who could bring new life into a troubled, beaten-down empire. He and the bishops had reason to worry about the future survival of Christianity within the Roman world empire, let alone the survival of his world empire. The Council of Nicaea was the meeting to settle differences, to become like-minded.

At the council there were not only Christian leaders from Alexandria, Antioch, Athens, Jerusalem and Rome but the leaders of the many other cults, sects and religions, including those of Apollo, Demeter/Ceres, Dionysus/Bacchus/Iosos, Janus, Jupiter/Zeus, Oannes/Fagon, Osiris and Isis and 'Sol Invictus', the Invincible Sun, the object of Constantine's devotion. The purpose of this council was to unify the various competing cults under one universal or 'catholic' church, which, of course, would be controlled by Constantine and Rome. As noted, Rome claimed the ultimate authority because it purported to be founded upon the 'rock of Peter.' Thus, the statue of Jupiter in Rome was converted into 'St Peter,' whose so-called bones were subsequently installed in the Vatican. In a typical religion-making move, the gods of these other cults were subjugated under the new God and changed into 'apostles' and 'saints.'

The main theological issue and focus had always been about Christ. Since the end of the Apostolic Age and the beginning of the Church Age, saints began questioning, debating, fighting and separating over the question, who is the Christ? Is He more divine than human or more human than divine? Was Jesus created/made or begotten? Being the Son of God, is He co-equal and co-eternal with father God, or less and lower in status than the Father? Is the Father the One and only True God, or are the Father, the Son, and the Holy Spirit the One true God? 'True God of True God,' 'One Being, Three Persons', a tri-unity called 'Trinity'? Jesus said, 'Who do you say that I am?' (Matthew 16:15).

The two main protagonists in the argument were Arius and Athanasius. Arius argued that the very fact that Jesus had called God his 'Father' implied a distinction between them, since paternity involves prior existence; he also quoted Gospel passages that stressed the humanity and vulnerability of Christ. Athanasius took the opposite view: Jesus was divine in the same way as God the Father, an equally controversial idea at the time, which Athanasius backed up with his own proof texts.

At the beginning of the controversy, there was no orthodox teaching on the nature of Christ and nobody knew whether Athanasius or Arius was right. Discussion had raged for over two hundred years. It was impossible to prove anything from scripture, since texts could be found to support either side. But the Greek fathers of the Church did not allow scripture to dominate their theology. In the Creed he formulated after the Council of Nicaea, Athanasius used an entirely unscriptural term to describe Jesus' relationship with God: he was *homoousion*, 'of one substance' with the Father. Other fathers based their theology on religious experience rather than a detailed reading of the Bible, which could not tell us everything about a God who transcended all human words and concepts.

Once the Nicaea Council meeting was under way Constantine demanded that the 300 bishops make a decision by majority vote defining who Jesus Christ was. Constantine commanded them to create a 'Creed' doctrine that all of Christianity would follow and obey a doctrine that would be called the 'Nicene Creed', upheld by the Church and enforced by the Emperor. The Bishops voted to make the full deity of Christ the accepted position of the Church. The Council of Nicaea voted to make the Trinity the official doctrine of the Church.

The die had been cast. In the future it would become the norm for matters of individual Christian belief to be decided by a council of bishops.

The Council of Nicaea did not invent the doctrine of the deity of Christ. Rather, the Council of Nicaea affirmed the Apostles' teaching of who Christ is - the One true God in Deity and Trinity with the Father and the Holy Spirit.

In the final event, the notion of the Trinity of God was upheld by a majority vote, following which Arius and his supporters were banished. Some delegates, including Bishop Eusebius, had striven to the last for a form of compromise, but they were compelled to relent fully in favour of the ruling. And so it was that with God designated as both the Father and the Son, Jesus the man was conveniently bypassed as a figure of any practical significance. The Emperor was now regarded as the messianic godhead - not only from that moment, but as of right through an inheritance deemed reserved for him 'since the beginning of the world'!

The findings of the council marked the turning point from which Christianity became the world religion we know now. Constantine was clearly grateful for his victory and made it part of his policy to set Christianity on course. Altogether more obscure, however, is the relationship between his brand of Christianity and the intentions of Jesus. Certainly Constantine does not appear to have been recognizably Christian before his victory. Only six years before the Milvian Bridge battle he had had hundreds of Frankish rebel prisoners torn to pieces in an arena. He had stood by without apparent qualms while Galerius, following up Diocletian's anti-Christian policy, had supervised the burning of Christian sacred texts and the mutilation of those who refused sacrifice to the pagan gods. Even after his victory the triumphal arch erected in his honour, which stands to this day alongside the Colosseum, was adorned with traditional Pagan symbols. A commemorative medallion struck by Constantine in 313 AD portrays him as Invictus Constantinus alongside the image of Sol Invictus, the God of a Pagan cult imported from Syria a few decades earlier by the Emperor Aurelian. Even eleven years after winning the battle at the Milvian Bridge Constantine had already vanquished his rival Licinius, former Emperor in the East. He then killed his wife (by having her boiled alive in her bath) and his own son - hardly the action of a true follower of Jesus. It was only when he was approaching death that he asked for, or was accepted for, Christian Baptism. As was still the custom, he received this naked, thereafter renouncing the purple of his Imperial rank.

It is maintained that during the Nicene Council the names Jesus and Christ were put together for the first time in the phrase 'Jesus Christ' or 'Christ Jesus,' uniting two of the major factions, with Jesus representing the Hesus of the Druids, Joshua/Jesus of the Israelites, Horus/Iusa of the Egyptians and IES/Iesios of the Dionysians/Samothracians, and Christ representing the Krishna/Christos of India, the Anointed of the Jews and KRST of Egypt, among others. It is thus alleged that the phrase 'Jesus Christ,' which had never been a name, does not appear in Greek or Latin authors prior to the first Council of Nicaea. In the centuries after the purported advent of the Christian saviour, at least 21 councils were convened to establish Church policy and doctrine, many of which were, as noted, bloody melees. It was a long, slow process that eventually unified the numerous warring factions to a large extent.

Today what many scholars and followers of Jesus consider to be the sheer futility of the Nicene Council, and all others that set out to provide a formula for Christianity, has been beautifully expressed by Birmingham University lecturer Frances Young:

'There are as many different responses to Jesus Christ as there are different fingerprints... To reduce any living faith to a set of definitions and propositions is bound to distort it. Attempts to produce Creeds are inevitably divisive or compromising. Eusebius of Caesarea signed the Creed of Nicaea for the sake of Church unity, but he was clearly embarrassed about it. What we need is not new Creeds, but a new openness which will allow manifold ways of responding and elucidating that response.'

'A new openness' and a casting aside of barriers. A self-abnegation. Is not this what Jesus and his kingdom of God were all about? Perhaps as today's Christians we should recognise that the real Jesus was more fully human than many care to contemplate.

Equally, today's Jews may need to adjust to the view that God *did* speak through Jesus of Nazareth two thousand years ago, and that while he nay not have seemed to be the Messiah their forebears were wanting or expecting, he was, and remains to this day, what God intended.

The destruction of the library and all its works at Alexandria by Bishop Theophilus on the instructions of Emperor Theodosius in 391 AD was the death knell of opposition to the church policy. Alexandria was the most important cultured centre of the ancient world, but the archives were an anathema to the newly-devised Church teaching. In all over half a million irreplaceable documents representing the minds and thoughts of the ancient world were destroyed. In one fell swoop the vast wisdom of the ages was lost for all time. The result of course was that the Roman Catholic Church was now free to make up its own history to interpret its own science and to establish its own philosophy.

In 390 AD the Apostles Creed was produced in the vain hope of uniting the different factions of the Church, mainly between East, West, Constantinople and Rome. The debate and disagreement rambled on for centuries. The final split between East and West occurred in 867 AD when the Eastern Church announced it had maintained the true Apostolic succession and the Patriarch of Constantinople excommunicated the Bishop of Rome. The Catholic Church decreed that the Holy Spirit proceeded from the Father and the Son, but the Eastern Church maintained that the Holy Spirit proceeded from the Father through the Son. The split was now complete.

In 451 AD at the Council of Chalcedon it was agreed by both Eastern and Western bishops that Jesus had been fully human and fully divine. In Rome it gradually became established that one man, the Bishop of Rome, had the right to make decisions for all Christendom. Those in the East objected to the idea of Roman supremacy and went their own ways, but in the East Christian doctrinal practice remained intact until the 16th century, when the great Martin Luther issued his challenge by nailing up his 95 Theses on the door of the Schlosskirche at Wittenberg.

In the years to come the taking of bread and wine in the Western Church became taking the physical body and blood of Christ known as transubstantiation.

THE NICENE CREED

Every week, in Christian churches throughout the world, countless Protestant, Roman Catholic and Eastern Orthodox believers, in surprising unity, repeat this formula, the so-called Nicene Creed. It represents part of their common profession of faith. Although few reflect on it this way, it also represents the point of division between Christianity and every other form if belief. Jews and Moslems would have little difficulty in accepting the initial words:

> *We believe in one God,*
> *The Father, the Almighty,*
> *Maker of heaven and earth…*

Although Moslems would tend to balk at the concept of God as 'Father', those relating to Jesus are of a different order. They demand the belief that a man who to all appearances was merely an obscure Jewish teacher of two thousand years ago, has in fact been co-creator and co-ruler of our multi-million-galaxy universe throughout its entire existence. Such a concept has not only been dismissed as hopelessly irrational by atheists and agnostics, it has also quite understandably been rejected by Jews and Moslems as incompatible with their fundamental belief in the singularity of God.

The Church of England's book of Common Worship records The Nicene Creed as follows:

We believe in one God,
The Father, the Almighty,
Maker of heaven and earth,
Of all that is
seen and unseen.

We believe in one Lord, Jesus Christ,
The only Son of God,
Eternally begotten of the Father,
God from God, Light from Light,
True God from true God,
Begotten, not made,
Of one being with the Father;
Through Him all things were made.
For us and for our salvation He came down from heaven,
Was incarnate from the Holy Spirit and the Virgin Mary
and was made man.
For our sake He was crucified under Pontius Pilate;
He suffered death and was buried.
On the third day He rose again
In accordance with Scriptures;

He ascended into Heaven
And is seated at the right hand of the Father.
He will come again in glory to judge the living and the dead,
And his kingdom will have no end.

We believe in the Holy Spirit,
The Lord, the giver of life,
Who proceeds from the Father and the Son,
Who with the Father and the Son is worshipped and glorified,
Who has spoken through the prophets.
We believe in one holy catholic and apostolic church.
We acknowledge one baptism for the forgiveness of sins.
We look for the resurrection of the dead,
And the life of the world to come.
Amen.

THE APOSTLE'S CREED

The Apostle's Creed is the creed most widely used in Christian worship in the Western world. Throughout the Middle Ages it was generally believed that this Creed had been composed by the Apostles on the day of Pentecost and that each of them contributed one of the twelve sections. This appears to be a legend dating back to somewhere between the 4th and 6th centuries. However it still has good reason to be called the Apostle's Creed, because its content is in agreement with apostolic teaching.

The earliest evidence for its present form is St Pirminius in the early 8th century, although it appears to be related to a shorter Roman creed which had itself derived from other earlier and simpler texts such as the 'rule of the faith' or the 'tradition', which were based on the Lord's baptismal command in Matthew 28:19. The Creed was widely used by Charlemagne (the first Holy Roman Emperor) and was eventually accepted at Rome where the old Roman Creed or similar forms had survived for centuries.

The Creed seems to have had three uses, first as a confession of faith for those about to be Baptised, secondly as a catechism (an instruction for new Christians in the essentials of the faith), and thirdly as a 'rule of faith' to give continuity to orthodox Christian doctrine. In the West by the early Middle Ages it was widely employed at baptism. The Anglican Book of Common Prayer uses it at Baptism and daily Morning Prayer and Evensong except on the 13 days of the year when the Athanasian Creed is to be used instead.

The Creed is Trinitarian in form but the heart of the Creed is its confession concerning Jesus Christ and the events to do with his conception, birth, suffering, death, resurrection, ascension and coming judgement.

BOOK OF COMMON PRAYER

I believe in one God the Father Almighty,
Maker of heaven and earth,
And of all things visible and invisible:

And in one Lord Jesus Christ, the only begotten Son of God,
Begotten of the Father before all worlds,
God of God, Light of Light, Very God of Very God,
Begotten not made,
Being of one substance with the Father,

By whom all things were made:
Who for us men, and for our salvation came down from heaven,
And was incarnate by the Holy Ghost of the Virgin Mary,

And was made man.
And was crucified also for us under Pontius Pilate.
He suffered and was buried.
And the third day he rose again according to the Scriptures,
And ascended into heaven.

And sitteth on the right hand of the Father.
And he shall come again with glory to judge both the quick and the dead:
Whose kingdom shall have no end.

And I believe in the Holy Ghost,
The Lord and giver of life,
Who proceedeth from the Father and the Son,
Who with then Father and the Son together is worshipped and glorified,
Who spake by the Prophets,
And I believe one Catholic and Apostolic Church.
I acknowledge one Baptism for the remission of sins.
And I look for the resurrection of the dead,
And the life of the world to come.
Amen.

The Apostle's Creed has often been at the centre of doctrinal controversies. There are literally hundreds of expositions of its content. Its beauty lies in its simplicity.

In the Western Churches the Apostle's Creed is probably the

most popular of all ancient creeds. In eastern Orthodoxy, however, it is regarded as a 'Western' Creed and plays no major role.

THE ATHANASIAN CREED

This creed is of uncertain origin. It was supposedly prepared in the time of Athanasius, the great theologian of the fourth century, but many scholars have theorized that it seems more likely that it dates from the fifth or sixth centuries because of its Western character.

The first evidence of the creed appears to be a sermon of St Caeserius of Aries and it is similar to a relatively recently discovered manuscript of St Vincent of Lerins, prompting the theory that it was composed in southern Gaul. There is also evidence that its primary liturgical use was as a hymn.

The Creed contains a clear and detailed statement of the Trinity (eg the Father is God, the Son of God, and the Holy Spirit is God; and yet there are not three Gods but one God. It also upholds the full deity and humanity of Christ, his death for sins, resurrection, ascension, second coming and final judgement.

The Book of Common Prayer requires that it be read on thirteen designated occasions during the year. In many Anglican congregations it is read aloud in corporate worship on Trinity Sunday.

ATHANASIAN CREED

Whoever wants to be saved should above all cling to the Catholic faith.

Whoever does not guard it whole and inviolable will doubtless perish eternally.

Now this is the catholic faith: We worship one God in Trinity and the Trinity in unity, neither confusing the persons not dividing the divine being.

For the Father is one person, the Son is another, and the Spirit is still another.

But the deity of the Father, Son, and Holy Spirit is one, equal in glory, coeternal in majesty.

What the Father is, the Son is, and so is the Holy Spirit.

Uncreated is the Father; uncreated is the Son; uncreated is the Spirit.

The Father is infinite; the Son is infinite; the Holy Spirit is infinite.

Eternal is the Father; eternal is the Son; eternal is the Spirit: And yet there are not three eternal beings, but one who is eternal; as there are not three uncreated and unlimited beings, but one who is uncreated and unlimited.

Almighty is the Father; almighty is the Son; almighty is the Spirit; And yet there are not three almighty beings, but one who is almighty.

Thus the Father is God; the Son is God; the Holy Spirit is God: And yet there are not three gods, but one God.

Thus the Father is Lord; the Son is Lord; the Holy Spirit is Lord: And yet there are not three lords, but one lord.

As Christian truth compels us to acknowledge each distinct person as God and Lord, so Catholic religion forbids us to say that there are three Gods or lords.

The Father was neither made nor created nor begotten; the Son was neither made nor created not begotten; but was alone begotten of the Father; the Spirit was neither made nor created, but is proceeding from the Father and the Son.

Thus there is one Father, not three fathers; one Son, not three sons, one Holy Spirit, not three spirits.

And in this Trinity no one is before or after, greater or less than the other, but all three persons are in themselves, coeternal and coequal; and so we must worship the Trinity in unity and the one God in three persons.

Whoever wants to be saved should think thus about the Trinity.

It is necessary for eternal salvation that one also faithfully believe that our Lord Jesus Christ became flesh.

For this is the true faith that we believe and confess: That our Lord Jesus Christ, God's Son, is both God and man.

He is God, begotten before all worlds from the being of the Father, and he is man, born in the world from the being of his mother - existing fully as God, and fully as man with a rational soul and a human body; equal to the Father in divinity, subordinate to the Father in humanity.

Although he is God and man, he is not divided, but is one Christ.

He is united because God has taken humanly into himself, he does not transform deity into humanity.

He is completely one in the unity of his person, without confusing his natures.

For as the rational soul and body are one person, so the one Christ is God and man.

He suffered death for our salvation. He descended into Hell and rose again from the dead.

He ascended into Heaven and is seated at the right hand of the Father.

He will come again to judge the living and the dead.

At his coming all people shall rise bodily to give an account of their own deeds.

Those who have done good will enter eternal life, those who have done evil will enter eternal fire.

This is the catholic faith.

One cannot be saved without believing this firmly and faithfully.

Having read the Athanasian Creed it is not difficult to understand the confusion in simple uneducated minds caused by the Trinity and why it is such a difficult subject for any minister to explain to their congregation.

THE HOLY SPIRIT AND THE TRINITY - A PERSONAL VIEW

So where have my studies brought me, and how can I satisfy myself on the meaning of the Trinity as set out by the Church?

The hardest things for most Christian religious teachers to explain to their congregations are the Holy Spirit and the Trinity.

In 'Christianity, the Complete Guide' edited by John Bowden, under the heading of the Holy Spirit, is an explanation of the term five pages long. For me the first few words are the key to an understanding within my own belief.

I quote: 'Throughout the History of the Christian Church the Holy Spirit (once referred to by the more archaic term Holy Ghost) has been an experience rather than a topic of thought, discussion or speculation'.

I have always had problems with a strict belief in the Church's explanation of the Trinity, the three in one, the Father and the Son and the Holy Spirit all being one and the same. But now I see things in a different light stemming from my understanding of creation.

God created the earth and he put life on earth. He created us in his own likeness but he did not give us the capacity to use all of our brains - in fact we use less than 10% of the brain's capacity.

I believe that this was the message that Jesus tried to get across to his disciples and ultimately to us all. He said, 'I will teach you how to find God, through your true self which is within you'. That which is implanted in every one of us is for me the Holy Spirit. The purpose in life is to find that spirit within us so that we each can find our true self and communicate and unite with God, our Creator.

It is Jesus and his original teachings, not those invented years after his death, that will guide me on the way. He is the supreme example. Through the Holy Spirit within him he found God and could communicate with God.

Let me put it this way. On one level there is God my Creator and on another lower level there is me. My aim is to be able personally to communicate with God. I believe that the only way I can achieve this is through the teachings of Jesus, who himself was able to communicate with God. His teaching will show the way. That communication for me is the Holy Spirit, the realisation of the true self within me.

I believe it was that message that his Disciples failed fully to understand and that frankly most of us still fail to understand, and get to grips with.

JESUS OF HISTORY - CHRIST OF FAITH

The Jesus of History is an individual, a man who lived out his life in a certain specific geographical location. The Christ of faith is beyond the reach of historians, since there is no way of dealing with the transcendental, what people claim to know and think in their mind. This can never be weighed or assessed.

Christianity, more than any other religion, demands the belief that certain events really did happen at specific times in real locations. In most other religions it is the revelation and not the circumstances surrounding it which is important.

To put this into context, what to us is more important at a church service? Is it where it is held and when, who is there, what time of day, what people did before the service, yesterday, today or even what they are going to do tomorrow? On the other hand is it the sermon, the lesson the preacher is trying to get his congregation to understand?

Put back in the context of the time of Jesus, surely the most important thing is not where he came from, where he went, what happened in between, who was there, but what he *said*.

Jesus apparently wrote nothing himself, or if he did we are not privy to it. None of the early writers make reference to him setting out his thoughts in writing. He is only ever described as giving his teaching orally. No words were written, or if they were they have never been preserved by any writing of his contemporaries. What we have is a collection of writings described as the New Testament, finally agreed as canon in the latter half of the 4th century AD.

The first known of these writings are by someone who knows nothing about Jesus and had no wish to know. He of course was Paul, the persecutor turned zealot who created a new and potent religion in the name of a man he never knew. He did this by interpreting the life of Jesus and his mission in his own vivid and mystical way. What is really strange about Paul's letters is that they make no attempt to describe Jesus or the background of his life. This new spiritual teaching (it was not a religion) called itself 'The Way', a common description for religions in the first century AD. The term 'Christian' had yet to be coined. According to the Acts of the Apostles, the term Christian was first used to describe believers in Antioch in Syria, probably in a mocking, insulting way.

At this stage of developments we reach the crossroads: the Jesus of History or the Christ of Faith? Paul believed that those who had known and followed Jesus, even members of Jesus' family, and most significantly Peter, had got it all wrong. Only he knew the truth! It is hardly surprising that this lofty and elitist attitude was to cause major ructions among the followers of Jesus.

Christianity as we now know it is unquestionably based on Paul's interpretation of Jesus' mission, and from the beginning this requires faith in Paul's mystical experiences. Even today Christianity considers that this faith is paramount as a requirement to be a Christian.

The historical Jesus as recognised by his family and followers was essentially Jewish. They saw him as a Messiah prophesied in Jewish scripture, the divine King who would deliver his people from oppression. Paul however argued that God had changed his mind about the role of Jesus; he was no longer sent to deliver the Jewish people but to usher in the Day of Judgement, the end of the world. It was Paul who created the concept of Jesus as the Redeemer who was sent to redeem us from our sins!

Today's scholars' prevailing view is that the movement founded by Jesus was entirely Jewish and that Paul customised it, creating a Religion totally different from what Jesus intended. So effective was Paul's creation that all four Gospel writers put the blame for the arrest of Jesus, his condemnation and execution squarely on the shoulders of the Jewish leaders in Jerusalem, with the Roman authorities acting at worst out of expediency. However modern historians are well acquainted with the laws and customs in Roman occupied Palestine at the time. It is now obvious that the New Testament version contained in the Gospels does not represent the whole truth. Crucifixion was a Roman penalty specifically reserved for rebels against Rome's authority and it punished political, not religious transgressions.

Trying therefore to establish this religion in the Roman Empire especially against the backdrop of persecutions and Jewish revolt, the gospel writers had to allay any official suspicions. They could not admit that the Religious Founder had been sentenced to death by the same authorities who they were trying to win over. So the burden of blame was shifted on to the Jewish leaders (who at the time were hardly popular in Rome) and therefore all Jews. This is particularly evident in the Gospel of John.

The formative period of Christianity has been understood more by scholars since the discoveries of the 'lost material' in the middle of the 20th century. This formative period was characterised by a great conflict between two opposing approaches, 'pistis' (faith) and 'gnosis' (knowing).

Pistis was Paul's approach and the belief that mere humans find it impossible to comprehend God's will, but that salvation can be found by trusting in Jesus. In the faith system an organised church is needed, sanctioned by God, with a distinct hierarchy to guide the believer and help with any crisis of faith.

Gnosis however depends on a personal understanding and experience of and with Jesus. It does not require any organisation (ie church) as salvation is in one's own hands. God is within each and every one of us.

It is perhaps hardly any wonder that Gnosis lost the battle. Faith's victory means that history has been biased and written in its favour, the Church thus portrayed its approach to Christianity as the authentic version taught by Jesus himself, while Gnosticism condemned as a contamination of the religion that bore little or no relation to its true meaning.

CHAPTER 16

∾

St Paul - hero or villain?

Saul of Tarsus, better known as St Paul in his Epistles, claims that he was a Roman citizen and a Pharisee who spent some considerable time vigorously persecuting the followers of Jesus in the years immediately after the crucifixion. Yet after his miraculous conversion on the road to Damascus, this zealous opponent of Jesus' followers did a complete religious turnaround and changed his religion and his name. Following an unexplained period of three years in Arabia he then joined James the Just and his followers in Jerusalem, apparently learning the 'true way' as taught by Jesus. He travelled widely as an evangelist, yet despite his undoubted evangelical zeal, he became the subject of scathing criticism by James' and Jesus' disciples in Jerusalem.

Christianity as it is today is really what Paul wanted it to be, but Paul was not one of the twelve and candidly admitted that he never met Jesus in person. Paul, a Roman citizen and proud of it, favoured equal treatments for Jews and non-Jews, but there is no evidence that this was also the view of the other Christians.

Surprisingly Paul only wrote two facts about Jesus' life: that he was crucified and that he had several brothers, including one named James, whom he also refers to, implicitly, as the leader of the Christians. Either he didn't know much about Jesus, or whatever he knew was expunged from the New Testament as embarrassing to the Roman dogma. It is interesting that the Roman dogma (Christianity as we know it today) is based on Paul's understanding of Jesus' message, even if Paul was the least acquainted with Jesus of all the early leaders. But he was the only one who was a Roman citizen, and who preached Christianity for all, not just for the Jews.

The New Testament includes Paul's letters as an appendix, but they may be the reason the New Testament is the way it is: first Paul coded Christian religion as a Greek and Roman-friendly dogma, then some Gospels (written in Greece in Greek) were chosen as the official ones because they reflected that dogma. Paul's letters date from about the year 50, while the earliest gospel is from 60-70. Paul's letters came first and it sounds as if the Gospels were chosen and edited to justify what Paul wrote (as if to say 'you see? That's precisely what Jesus had said').

Paul's letters may be the real foundations of modern Christianity, whereas original Christianity perished in the Roman persecutions of the desposyni/desposini (Jesus' heirs and blood relatives in Palestine) following Constantine's conversion.

Paul represented a different kind of Christianity from the one preached in Palestine. He was very young when he was admitted in the Agora of Athens. He must have had good credentials, otherwise educated people would not even have listened to him. Paul was a Roman citizen, and younger than the Apostles (he was not one of the twelve). There are speculations that he may have been a member of the Herodian family. He represented the view that Christianity was not only for Jews but for everybody.

James the Just was the leader of the early Christians in

Palestine. His importance was recognised by early Christians and by Paul himself, who treated him like a leader and seemed more interested in James' leadership than in Jesus' teachings.

New Testament accounts and other sources make it abundantly clear that there was a fundamental difference between 'the Way', as interpreted by James and the original disciples, and the new version taught by Paul. The conflict is mentioned in the account of the Council of Jerusalem in the Acts of the Apostles. James the Just and the disciples had an absolute dedication to the Torah, a strict prohibition against mixing with the gentiles and rigid adherence to the dietary laws of Judaism.

Paul preached that everybody could be a member of the sect. James probably preached that only Jews could be members. Paul was in favour of opening Jerusalem to Roman citizens. James was against foreigners. James was the product of a resistance that had lasted centuries, first fighting against the Greeks and then the Romans.

Paul was probably not a traitor but a pragmatic; he wanted to win and realised that compromise was essential. James was an idealist who wanted to the right, no matter what. Martyrdom is not inherent in Paul's preaching, it is in James' ideology.

James is but one of many blood relatives of Jesus who left their mark on early Christians in the Middle East. When Rome converted, they were virtually wiped out. Some were killed, some were forced to disband and they disappeared from Christian genealogy.

James' life ended in the years immediately preceding the Jewish rebellion of 66-70 and his stoning may have been related to the upheaval that cause that war, which in turn may have been related to his fundamentalist ideology, which in turn may have been a source of conflict with Paul.

Documents of that era spend more time talking of Jesus than of anyone else. In the New Testament he is hardly mentioned, as if someone carefully removed any reference to the man who was the most influential Christian of the era.

An inscription in stone, found in 2002 near Jerusalem and written in Aramaic, with the words, 'James, son of Joseph, brother of Jesus', is the oldest known reference to Jesus; it is dated 63 AD.

Paul mixed almost exclusively with gentiles and, in his view, the Covenant and its laws no longer applied. Circumcision was no longer necessary for converts and he taught that faith, and faith alone, was all that was required. The word 'treachery' occurs in the texts of the Dead Sea scrolls, referring to the factional strife within the community. The dispute obviously hinged on Paul's preaching to the gentiles and his repeated denial of the validity of the Torah. This led to a dramatic confrontation between a man called 'the Liar', namely Paul, and 'the Teacher of Righteousness', who at that time may have been James the Just. Paul was accused of not walking in the way of perfection as commanded by God and of transgressing the word of the Torah, and as a result, Barnabas, who had been his constant companion up to this time, deserted him. Paul himself tells us this in his Epistle to the Galatians which also lists his total repudiation of the Law, his teaching that salvation is by faith alone and his denial of the Torah, which he claimed was worthless.

Any analysis of the differences that separated the teachings of Paul and those of James and the other disciples in Jerusalem clearly demonstrates that Paul had not only committed blasphemy in respect of his controversial views on the Torah but that it was he who was responsible for the 'deification' of Jesus. The original disciples of Jesus, members of his family and Jews in general would have been outraged at the mere idea that Jesus was divine. To orthodox Jews this idea was the ultimate sacrilege.

The Gospels do not record any claim by Jesus to divine status. He never even claims the title of 'Son of God', indeed 'Son of Man' is the only title he uses himself.

It was Paul who taught the notion that contradicted all of Jewish tradition from the time of Abraham onwards, that at Golgotha Jesus had become the 'sacrificial lamb' and had 'died for us'. This idea was not merely repulsive in Jewish eyes, it was in complete contradiction to the experience of the patriarch Abraham. Since the time of Abraham, no Jew could perform a human sacrifice or become one, and those that transgressed this teaching were castigated for it. The sacrifice of an innocent man for the guilt of others also went against the basic religious principle that the innocent should not suffer for the guilty, enunciated centuries earlier by the prophet Ezekiel. Thus Paul repudiated the Law, condemned circumcision and circumcisers - ie all Jews - brought back the pagan concept of human sacrifice, and then deified Jesus. Few, if any, Jewish disciples had anything more to do with him and Paul wrote that his colleagues and companions after his expulsion were Judaeo-Greeks such as Timothy, whose mother was a 'believing Jewess' and who was also a Roman citizen.

Paul's letters express considerable resentment and bitterness about his treatment and display his pain and anger at the charge that he was a liar and not a true apostle. 'Am I not free? Am I not an apostle? Have I not seen Jesus our Lord?... Even though I may not be an apostle to others, surely I am to you! In a later letter he writes: '... and for this purpose I was appointed a herald and an apostle - I am telling the truth I am not lying.'

His visions have been described as dreams. The name Christ did not exist until Paul first used it, years after Jesus was dead, speaking of him as Jesus, the Christ. 'Christos' was an obscure Greek word, meaning a redeemer of things, before Paul personalized it to Jesus to indicate the supposed divinity. So the argument condemning the Jews as the slayers of Christ is a total fabrication. It is a lie, created for political purposes.

So let us begin with the absolute truth - the Jews did not crucify the Christ. Let us go even further than that: the Jews did not *hate* the Christ, because the Jews had never *heard* of the Christ.

The various Pauline epistles contained in the New Testament form an important part of Christianity, yet these 'earliest' of Christian texts never discuss a historical background of Jesus, even though Paul purportedly lived during and after Jesus' advent and surely would have known about his master's miraculous life. Instead, these letters deal with a spiritual construct found in various religions, sects, cults and mystery schools for hundreds to thousands of years prior to the Christian era. The Pauline literature does not refer to Pilate or the Romans, or Caiaphas, or the Sanhedrin, or Herod or Judas, or the holy women, or any person in the Gospel account of the Passion, and what is more it never makes any allusion to them; lastly, it mentions absolutely none of the events of the Passion, either directly or by way of allusion.

Is it conceivable that a preacher of Jesus could go throughout the world to convert people to the teachings of Jesus, as Paul did, without ever quoting a single one of his sayings? Had Paul known that Jesus had preached a sermon, or formulated a prayer, or said many inspired things about the here and the hereafter, he could not have helped quoting, now and then, from the words of his master. If Christianity could have been established without a knowledge of the teachings of Jesus, why then did Jesus come to teach, and why were his teachings preserved by divine inspiration? If Paul knew of a miracle-working Jesus, one who could feed the multitude with a few loaves and fishes, who could command the grave to open, who could cast out devils and cleanse the land of the foulest disease of leprosy, who could, and did, perform many other wonderful works to convince the unbelieving generation of his divinity - is it conceivable that either intentionally or inadvertently he would have never once referred to them in all his preaching? The position, then, that there is not a single saying of Jesus in the Gospels which is quoted by Paul in his many epistles is unassailable, and certainly fatal to the historicity of the Gospel Jesus.

The Pauline epistles were regarded by James as blasphemous and insulting, as they denigrate circumcision, circumcisers and the Law. It is not surprising, therefore, that this quarrel did not end with Paul's expulsion from the first Christian community in Jerusalem. Indeed it soon turned from bitter, verbal argument to an act of murderous violence.

Today's prevailing view among researchers is that the movement founded by Jesus was entirely Jewish, and that Paul created a religion that was totally different from what his Saviour intended. According to this view, through an accident of history the Jerusalem version was wiped out by the Romans at the end of the Jewish Revolt in 70 CE, when the population was either slaughtered or carried off into slavery. However, the story is much more complicated than that.

For a start, the Jewish Christians appear to have survived the fall of Jerusalem. In the second century the Church Fathers condemned as heretical a Christian sect known as the Ebionites (from the Aramaic *ebionim*, 'the poor',) who interpreted Jesus' life and mission purely in terms of his being the Jewish Messiah. The Ebionites - who were still being condemned two centuries after that - were possibly remnants of the Jerusalem Church (Paul once describes the group led by Jesus the Just as 'the poor').

Christianity was entirely Jewish until Paul came along and generated an entirely new religion out of what had been just another Jewish sect.

THE PAULINE MYTHOLOGY

The main culprit, and the one whose writings might be blamed for the corruption of Jesus' legacy in the Mediterranean regions, appears to have been St Paul. But having said that, it may be that he can be excused in many respects. Some of the writings attributed to Paul are spurious fabrications. Apart from that, the peculiar nature of his original undertaking outside his homeland involved him in a competitive world of religious extremes that would have been entirely unfamiliar to him.

Paul makes his first New Testament appearance as one Saul of Tarsus in The Acts of the Apostles during the years following the crucifixion of Jesus. He is first encountered in Jerusalem consenting to the stoning of a disciple called Stephen, who had prophesied that Jesus would destroy the Temple. Thereafter, Saul approached the High Priest and received a commission to pursue and arrest the disciples of Jesus in Damascus and bring them bound to Jerusalem. The biblical story of Paul (Saul) begins therefore with him being an enemy of Jesus' apostles and an emissary of the Temple elders.

His Hebrew name was Saul, whilst his given Roman equivalent was Paul. The details that he was originally from Tarsus, and trained as a Pharisee are given in Acts 22:3 and 26:5.

The year AD 37 had been one of administrative change throughout the Roman Empire, and especially in the Holy Land. Emperor Tiberius had died and the new Emperor, Gaius Caligula, dismissed Pontius Pilate and installed Antonius Felix as Governor of Judaea in his stead. In Jerusalem, Joseph Caiaphas had been replaced as the High Priest by Theophilus and a whole new administration was in place - more answerable to Rome than ever before.

As Jesus had long maintained, the Jews could never overthrow Roman occupation while divided from the gentiles. Paul, on the other hand, was equally sure that association with gentiles represented a weakness that left the Jews vulnerable and exposed. The account in the Acts suggests that, in AD40 (seven years after the crucifixion of Jesus), Paul went to confront the Nazarenes at a conference in Damascus, Syria, with a mandate from the High Priest in Jerusalem. This cannot have been the case: the Jewish Sanhedrin Council of elders had no jurisdiction whatever in Syria. It is likely that Paul, a supporter of the House of Herod, was operating for the King's administration in an attempt to suppress the Nazarenes. However, before he had a chance to make his presence felt, he was apparently confronted by the voice of Jesus asking, 'Saul, Saul, why persecutest thou me?' (Acts 9:4-5).

Jesus subsequently instructed the disciple Ananias to enlighten Paul in the Nazarene philosophy, but Ananias hesitated, knowing that Saul was an enemy agent: 'Lord, I have heard by many of this man, how much evil he hath done to thy saints at Jerusalem'. Nonetheless, the disciple obeyed.

From this experience, Paul forsook his Hebrew sympathies and emerged as a fully-fledged Hellenist. At once he began preaching in Damascus - but there was a problem, for the people could not believe that the man who had come hotfoot to challenge the Messiah was now promoting him instead. The Nazarenes were confused, distrustful and angry to the extent that Paul's life was threatened and the disciples had to spirit him out of the city. By AD 43 Paul was a fervent evangelist, but his conversion had been so traumatic and his change of heart so far-reaching that he regarded Jesus not just as an earthly Messiah with an inspiring social message but as the manifest son of God, a heavenly power-lord.

Paul's missionary journeys took him to Anatoia (Asia Minor) and the Greek-speaking areas of the eastern Mediterranean. But his dramatically revised version of the gospel was that an awesome Saviour would soon establish a worldwide regime of perfect righteousness.

Through Paul's imaginative teaching, a whole new concept of Jesus arose. No longer was he simply the long-awaited Messiah who would reinstate the Davidic line and free the Jews from Roman oppression. He was now the heavenly saviour of the whole world.

While James and the apostles were preaching their less fanciful messages, Paul had strayed into a realm of pure fantasy. In his unbridled enthusiasm, he rekindled an ancient myth and uttered a string of self-styled prophecies that were never fulfilled. Yet for all that, it is Paul who dominates the bulk of the New Testament beyond the Gospels. Such was the power of Paul's teaching that Jesus, the Christ, was transformed into an aspect of Almighty God, while Jesus of the House of Judah was lost to religious history altogether.

Paul's allotted task was to further Hellenic-Jewish instruction among the gentiles of the Mediterranean coastal lands, and to take Jesus' message to those Jews who lived outside their homeland in the Diaspora. Instead he ignored the root objective and (as was perhaps inevitable) contrived his own cult following. For Paul, the veneration and outright worship of Jesus was sufficient to ensure redemption and entry into the Kingdom of Heaven. All the social values professed and urged by Jesus were cast aside in Paul's attempt to compete with a variety of pagan beliefs.

Throughout the ancient Mediterranean world, there were many religions whose Gods and prophets were supposedly born of virgins and defied death in one way or another. They were all of supernatural origin and had astounding powers over ordinary mortals. To be fair to Paul, he certainly encountered problems Jesus had never faced in his native environment. Paul's route to success against such odds was to present Jesus in a way that would transcend these paranormal idols. In the event he created an image of Jesus so far removed from reality that Jewish society regarded him as a fraud. Notwithstanding this, it was the transcendent Jesus, the Christ, of Paul's invention who later was to become the Christ of Orthodox Christianity.

CHAPTER 17

❦

The assault on James, and Paul's arrest

From a lost work comes the accusation that Paul assaulted James the brother of Jesus and tried to kill him, apparently throwing him headlong down the steps of the Temple and breaking his legs. The Acts of the Apostles claims that this was because he had inflamed the Jewish mob at the Temple by preaching the Gospel. The truth however would appear to be that this was a protective arrest to save the Roman citizen Paul from a mob that wished to kill him for his attempt on the life of James the Just, who was supremely popular with the people.

When warned of another plot to kill him, the Roman arresting officer took Paul to Caesarea under an escort of 200 soldiers, 70 cavalrymen and 200 spearmen. This was a suspiciously large escort for a Jewish blasphemer whom the Romans would normally have left to the court of the Sanhedrin and the inevitable sentence of death by stoning.

No Christian scholars have ever questioned why such an expenditure of scarce military resources should be employed to protect Paul at a time of potential rebellion. Yet, the most probable answer can be found within the New Testament: Paul is not only a Roman citizen but a member of the Herodian ruling family and a long-term friend of Rome. These uncomfortable facts can be found in one of Paul's own letters, where he wrote: 'greet those who belong to the household of Aristobulus. Greet Herodian my relative.'

Aristobulus was the son of Agrippa II's brother, Herod of Chalcis, whose son was known as 'Herodian' or the 'Littlest Herod'. These politically-charged family links explain how Paul became a member of the temple guard authorised by the high priest to persecute the followers of Jesus. Paul, or Saulus, as the Romans and Herodians knew him, had friends and relatives in very high places.

The community at Antioch was mainly drawn from members of the Herodian family. These Herodian and pro-Roman links go some way to explain why Paul neutered Jesus' message so thoroughly. He stripped it of all Jewish and nationalistic intent and then diluted it further with a series of instructions to obey all lawful authorities. Paul, like Herod the Great, wore his Judaism very lightly. If that were not so, it is difficult to conceive how any Jew of a studious and devout Pharasaic background could preach the anti-Semitic and anti-Torah message he repeatedly stressed in his Epistles.

He took the story of the virgin birth, for one thing, from several sources. Mithras, the Roman soldiers' god, for example, was born in a stable, delivered of a virgin. And Horus, the god-son of Isis and Osiris, was born of a virgin too, and destined to die to expiate the sins of mankind. Paul named Jesus the Son of God in that tradition and cited his resurrection as the sign of his divinity. Paul made Jesus the Christ an immortal.

Thus Paul's message of subservience to 'lawful' Roman authority and his preaching of a New Covenant that denied the Torah was the complete negation of the teaching of Jesus and his brother and successor James. James' almost strong Jewish stance had distinct political dimensions. His pro-Torah, nationalistic, anti-Herodian and anti-Roman policy inevitably resulted in a head-on collision with the authorities in Jerusalem - the Sadducee high priests- and their principal ally, Paul's influential relative King Agrippa II.

The inevitable collision occurred after King Agrippa appointed a new Sadducee high priest, Ananus, who convened a meeting of the Sanhedrin to try James for blasphemy. *The Mishna Sanhedrin* listed procedures for the execution of men deemed popular with the people and recommended that the priests gather around the condemned man to jostle him and cause him to fall from the temple wall. Then the victim was to be stoned and have his brains beaten out with clubs. This is precisely what happened to James. The brother of Jesus was cast down from the temple wall and stoned and then given the *coup-de-grace* with a fuller's club.

It was after this traumatic murder that the Ebionites and the other members of the ma'madot, led by James' 'cousin' Simeon, left Jerusalem and crossed the Jordan into Pella. These descendants of the family of Jesus, known as the *Desposyni*, retained the hereditary leadership of the Ebionites for the next 150 years. In Jerusalem and Judea, opinion among the Jews was sharply divided. The Zealots actively fomented rebellion against Rome, the Sadducees, 'Hellenisers' and Herodians tried every means within their power to oppose any rising, while others simply wanted to live and worship in peace. However the murder of James proved to be the catalyst; with his death, the die was now cast and preparations for war soon came into the open.

Despite the fact that the church has always insisted that Paul was martyred in Rome, being beheaded in or about the year 66 AD and citing 'oral tradition' as their source, one famous contemporary historian tells a very different story about Saul, the kinsman of

Agrippa. Josephus writes that when the Jewish Zealot forces occupied Jerusalem in 66AD 'The men of power [the Sadducees], perceiving that the sedition was too hard for them to subdue… endeavoured to save themselves, and sent ambassadors, some to Florus (the Roman Procuror)… and others to Agrippa, among whom the most eminent was Saul, and Antipas, and Costovarus, who were of the king's kindred.'

The messengers to Florus and Agrippa were to request prompt military action by the Romans to subdue the rebellion before it got out of hand, a motivation completely in accord with Paul's oft-expressed philosophy of 'obey lawful authorities'. When this attempt failed, the insurrection became unstoppable and when, in the early months of the insurrection, the Jews repeatedly defeated the Romans, Saul is mentioned by Josephus again, this time as a member of a deputation sent to the Emperor Nero at Corinth, then called Achia: 'Cestius sent Saul and his friends, at their own desire, to Achia, to Nero, to inform him of the great distress they were in.'

After this meeting Nero appointed Vespasian as commander of the legions in Palestine. After four years of prolonged and bitter fighting, Jerusalem was besieged, and it fell to the Romans amid unprecedented scenes of carnage. The city's surviving inhabitants were put to the sword, crucified or sold into slavery. The Holy City itself and the Temple were razed to the ground. At a stroke the Jewish people were deprived of the central shrine of their religion, the home of the Lord God of Israel, and the spiritual heart of their culture and traditions was destroyed.

Everything had now irrevocably changed for the Jews, for the true followers of Jesus and for the entire world. Paul's followers now had the field to themselves. All who could testify to the true teachings of Jesus were either dead, on the run from the Romans, or scattered and in hiding.

CHAPTER 18

❧

The lost testaments, hidden gospels and scrolls and ancient texts

THE LOST TESTAMENTS

Insofar as St Paul exaggerated the image of Jesus for the benefit of his Pagan audience, there is no doubt that the later church fathers manipulated Paul's writings to suit their personal endeavours, just as St Clement brazenly corrupted the gospel of Mark. Even during his own lifetime, Paul had occasion to warn people about fictitious letters purporting to be from him, and it was not uncommon for epistles to be fabricated for propagandist purposes.

Paul's letters to Timothy, Titus and Philemon have been the subject of particular linguistic scrutiny, and it is doubtful that they represent authentic missives from his own hand. These individually-addressed correspondences (known as the Pastoral Letters) are very different in language, style and vocabulary from the sermon-like epistles addressed to community congregations such as the Corinthians, Galatians and Thessalonians. There are numerous elements of these personally-addressed letters which relate to doctrinal writings of the 2nd century that would have been unknown to Paul, and many scholars now believe they were written some considerable time after Paul's death.

Paul emerges from all this as both the culprit and the victim. The founding doctrines of the Church of Rome were based on the opinions of the pre-Roman Church Fathers. Their primary works of inspiration are said to have been the epistles of St Paul and, in many respects, Church dogma rests entirely on these Pauline teachings. They constitute some 30 per cent of the New Testament, yet not one fragment of any such letter exists in Paul's own hand. Similarly, there are no original 1st century documents for any of the works selected by Athanasius and the 4th century bishops for New Testament inclusion - yet the world's libraries and museums are bursting with tens of thousands of documents from much older times. Of the original 27 New Testament scriptural texts not one is known to have survived, although numerous other gospels and tractates which the Church does not acknowledge have been unearthed in the past century or so, including dozens of Dead Sea Scrolls texts.

It seems inconceivable that no discovery has yet been made of manuscripts that would transform the New Testament into an historically-documented reality. If the church fathers of the 2nd and 3rd centuries had such documents in their possession, then one might justifiably wonder what happened to them. Were such important documents - on which a major world religion was founded - truly lost by the very men who established that religion? One possibility is that perhaps such items do exist, but that they might have been purposely destroyed for the very same reason.

In the past hundred years, scholars have searched for a 'hidden Gospel'. By examining various textual strands in the books of Matthew, Mark and Luke they have identified hypothetical sources which the writers of these books used. The most well known, Q, consists essentially of the duplicate portions of Matthew and Luke which do not also appear in Mark. The hypothesis runs as follows: most scholars now consider Mark to be the earliest written Gospel of which we have a copy. If the authors of Matthew and Luke were not aware of each other's work, then the portions of these two books that do not use Mark as a source and that overlap must have used another source: Q.

Like the Gospel of Thomas, Q is proposed to be a collection of sayings, aphorisms, and parables, with very few actual events recorded in it. Many scholars now consider these early textual strands to be the products of the various evolving Jesus movement communities.

But there is yet another story of a 'hidden Gospel', one rarely told. At the time of the council of Nicaea, the eastern areas of what are now Turkey, Syria and Iraq were controlled by the Persian Empire. In this region, a group of early Christians had established themselves securely by the time of the destruction of Jerusalem by the Romans in 70 AD. The early Jewish Christians in Persian lands were largely of Semitic extraction and all were Aramaic-speaking. Since the Persians were enemies of the Romans, and since the Romans persecuted the Christians, the Persians decided to let these Christians practise their religion in peace. These early Christians built schools, libraries, and places of worship in the Persian Empire, with Persian support.

For the first four centuries of the Christian era, Aramaic-speaking Christians in these lands had copies of early scriptures which they could study and contemplate in their homes openly and without fear of reprisal. In the earliest days these included the Gospel of Thomas, which may have been compiled in what is now

Syria, and which reflects a view of Jesus as a wisdom figure and a teacher rather than as a saviour.

The version of the scriptures these Jewish Christians used originated around Edessa in what is now eastern Turkey and came to be known as the Peshitta –meaning simple, straight, and true. The Peshitta included the basic Gospels-Matthew, Mark, Luke, and John- but in a form of Aramaic close to the dialect that Jesus himself would have used.

Since they spoke and worshipped in the same language that Yeshua spoke, these Aramaic Christians felt (and their descendants still feel) that the Peshitta is a version of the original Aramaic words of Jesus, and that they stayed very close in spirit to his original message. While some Aramaic-speaking Jewish Christian groups went along with the council of Nicaea, most soon broke contact with the rest of both Roman and Eastern Orthodox Christianity over the increasingly complex Creeds and the forceful attempts to impose a single theology on all Christians. Little was heard from or reported about them in Europe for the next fifteen hundred years, while Christianity in the West underwent its own political and theological evolution.

As modern Assyrian Christian writer Abraham Rihbany commented:

The Syrian Christians of Semitic stock have had very little to do with the development of the 'Creeds of Christendom'. Theological organizations has been as foreign to the minds of the Eastern Christians as political organization. They have always been worshippers rather than theologians, believers rather than systematic thinkers......The Christian Church had its simple forgoing with a group of Jewish followers of Jesus Christ in Palestine....

The Creed of the theologians consists of many articles'; The Creed of Christ only two: 'love the Lord thy God with all thy heart, and thy neighbour as thyself.'

Another Aramaic Christian scholar, George Lamsa, pointed out the irony that most Christians in Europe were not allowed or able to read the scriptures until well after the advent of the printing press in the Middle Ages; until that time only priests were allowed to see the scriptures. Even the possession of a translation of the Gospels in a vernacular language like English was a crime punishable by death. On the other hand, a thousand years earlier, Aramaic-speaking Christians had copies of the Gospels in Aramaic in their homes and for their open use.

THE DEAD SEA SCROLLS

The Dead Sea Scrolls were discovered in 1947 in the Judean desert at Khirbet Qumran, by a shepherd boy from a Bedouin tribe. In all, following proper archaeological excavation, it is estimated that at one time there were in excess of sixty jars containing scrolls secreted in the caves the boy discovered.

The Dead Sea Scrolls, or Qumran manuscripts, turned out to be a library or collected sacred literature of a settlement of Jewish Essenes dating from the 1st and 2nd centuries BC. Some were familiar books of the Old Testament, but others were esoteric writings of the Essene elders. Precious little was known about the Essenes before the discovery of the scrolls. The only references came from historians like Josephus - Pliny the elder and Philo Judaeus. These authors had made it known that there was a sceptical esoteric movement within Judaism in the last centuries

BC and in early Christian times; so little was known that modern day scholars only mentioned them in passing until 1947 when the discovery was made.

As soon as details of the contents of the scrolls became known it was obvious that the Essenes had studied the Old Testament and interpreted it in a mystical sense. They designed their beliefs on the understanding of the OT from the other major religious parties in Judaism, namely the Sadducees (the aristocratic priestly party) and the Pharisees (the representatives of Rabbinic Judaism). The Essenes considered that there was a hidden esoteric meaning in the older writings which could only be understood by one who had been illuminated (initiated into the belief). Illumination or initiation consisted of a period of lengthy period of spiritual probation, followed by rites of baptism and instruction in secret knowledge (gnosis). The baptism was total submission in water, representing a dying and then rebirth to a higher life.

The Essene God was the God of knowledge. It was he who awoke the feelings in the breast of the initiate. Initiates were permitted then to partake of a meal of bread and wine. Thus there flourished in the heartland of Judea a gnosis with its own initiation ceremony, a sacramental meal and an esoteric understanding of the Jewish scriptures. Here was proof that Palestine at the time of Jesus and immediately before was home to a gnostic belief.

Research is still going on to piece together fragments of the scrolls, and because of this it is not feasible to list all the texts known to have been found. A substantial number of them are commentaries on various books of the Old Testament as well as other Judaic works known as apocrypha. Some however are worthy of comment.

THE COPPER SCROLL

This lists 64 sites where treasures of gold, silver and precious religious vessels are hidden. Many of the sites are in Jerusalem and others in the surrounding countryside. So far these depositories have not been found.

THE COMMUNITY RULE

This follows the rituals and regulations governing life in the desert community. It includes a hierarchy of authority for the community and instructions for the master of the community and various officers subordinate to him.

THE WAR SCROLL

This is a very specific manual of strategy and tactics in war. It was intended for use against attackers principally the Romans.

THE TEMPLE SCROLL

This deals with the Temple at Jerusalem with the design furnishings, fixtures and fittings of the Temple. It also outlines details of rituals performed in the Temple. It is a kind of alternative Torah.

Because of these discoveries archaeologists, historians are able to provide a much better idea of the people and of what life was like for the Jews at the time of Jesus.

THE NAG HAMMADI TEXTS

Since the discovery of the Nag Hammadi library the world of the historical Jesus and the early religions in existence at the time of Jesus have begun to look very different.

The Nag Hammadi library was first discovered in December

1945 by an old Arab peasant in Upper Egypt. He had gone out with his brothers to dig for *sabakh*, a soft soil they used to fertilize their crops. Their digging unearthed an earthenware jar almost a metre high. They smashed the jar and found inside thirteen papyrus books bound in leather. In all 52 texts were subsequently found, including a collection of early Christian Gospels, some previously unknown or unheard of.

They included:

- The Gospel of Philip
- The Gospel of Thomas
- The Gospel of Truth
- The Gospel to the Egyptians
- The secret book of John
- The secret book of James
- The Apocalypse of Paul
- The letter of Peter to Philip
- The Apocalypse of Peter.

In all the texts have been split into 5 groups by historians:
1. The Thomas group of texts
2. The Sethian school of thought
3. The Valentenian school of thought
4. The Hermetic Heritage
5. Gnostic texts that are difficult to classify.

Why then were the texts buried and why have they remained almost totally unknown for nearly 2000 years? These texts and others besides which circulated at the beginning of the Christian era were denounced as heresy by Orthodox Christians in the middle of the second century AD. Bishop Irenaeus, who supervised the church at Lyon in c. 180 AD, wrote five volumes entitled 'The destruction and overthrow of falsely so-called knowledge'. To him they were a 'blasphemy against Christ'.

It is now believed that the texts were hidden by Pachomonian monks who occupied a monastery close by.

The Nag Hammadi library seems to have been concealed according to archaeologists in the latter part of the 4th century AD, but why?

A momentous event happened in the year 367 AD which may suggest why they were concealed. In that year the Archbishop of Alexandria, Athanasius (soon to become the champion of Orthodox Christianity), wrote a letter to be read in the Churches of Egypt. In it he listed the 27 books of the New Testament to be treated as canon. He also condemned the heretics and their despicable writings. Apocryphal texts, he maintained in his letter, are 'a fabrication of the heretics to deceive the guileless'.

All known copies of the alternative gospels were burned and destroyed. All, that is, except for the ones spirited away to the caves of Nag Hammadi, which do not show Jesus to be supernatural in any way.

They were banned because the Jesus of these texts was totally different. He is not here to save us from sin and from eternal damnation; He is here to guide us to some kind of spiritual understanding. And once a disciple reaches enlightenment - and this notion must have given Irenaeus a few sleepless nights - the master is no longer needed. The student and the teacher become equals; the four canon gospels, the ones in the New Testament -

they see Jesus as our Saviour, the Messiah, the Son of God. Orthodox Christians - and orthodox Jews, for that matter - insist that an unbridgeable chasm separates man from his Creator. The Gospels that were found in Nag Hammadi contradicted this: for them, self-knowledge is the knowledge of God; the self and the divine are one and the same. Even worse, by describing Jesus as a teacher, an enlightened sage - they consider Him a *man*, someone anyone can emulate, and that wouldn't do for the Church. He couldn't just be a man. He had to be *unique*, because by His being unique, the Church becomes unique, the only path to salvation. By painting Him in that light, the early church could claim that if you weren't with them, following their rules, living the way they wanted you to, you were doomed to damnation.

On reflection this must surely be a classic case of the pot calling the kettle black. With what we know now about the composition of the Canonic Gospels and how much they have been amended and added to over the years, who can we believe. The problem is of course that history records the acts of the winners and the Orthodox Church was winning.

Consider as an example Luke 2 verses 29-32, which is also recorded in the Nunc Dimitus as follows:

Lord now lettest thou thy servant depart in peace
According to thy word
For mine eyes have seen they salvation
Which thou hast prepareth before the face of all thy people.
To be a light to lighten the gentiles
And to be the Glory of thy people Israel.

How can this have been original material when Jesus' teachings were meant only for the ears of the Jews? It was Paul who solicited the gentiles!

But of all the Church's many cover-ups one stands head and shoulders above them all. Since the very beginning of their religion, orthodox Christians through the Church have been trying to suppress the facts about the extent of the influence that John the Baptist had over Jesus. The reason for this age-old conspiracy is obvious - but nonetheless shocking: the claims about Jesus on which first their faith, and later their power structure, was built would fall apart if they admitted the truth. These facts were true.

Their first act of censorship was adding a qualification to Jesus' statement. Matthew 11:11 says 'Truly I say to you that among those born of women there has never arisen one greater than John the Baptist'. The added rider was 'yet whoever is least in the kingdom of heaven is greater than he'. As can be seen, this was added because Jesus' own words undermined the very image of Him that Christians were trying to promote. Their claims that Jesus was the One would simply have been invalidated.

We had always assumed that the all-important phrase was added very early. However, the discovery of the 'Hebrew Matthew' shows that it originally had no such disclaimer. The Pseudo-Clementine literature also reveals that the unedited words of Jesus were still being used against Christians by the devotees of John the Baptist at least until the middle of the second century. The first Christians' fear was in fact justified - the John sect was using Jesus' own words to prove its case. Censorship must have been more systematic, involving the alteration of more manuscripts.

Thus the Nag Hammadi library has thrown a totally new light on the activities and teachings around the time of Jesus.

Scholars have produced many theories about the events of the first century AD. It remains true that the best-attested Gospel with the most authentic and original provenance is probably the gospel of Thomas, but this early record of the sayings of Jesus was dismissed by the Church because it dared to suggest that the spirit of Jesus was everywhere, and not a prerogative of the ecclesiastical establishment: 'Split a piece of wood, and I am there. Lift up a stone, and you will find me'.

Even more of a thorn in the side of the Church is item 12 in the Thomas Gospel: The disciples said to Jesus, 'We know that you will depart from us. Who will be our leader?' In responding to this, Jesus did not mention St Peter as the Bishops would have preferred. If he had, it is a fair guess that the Gospel of Thomas would be embraced within the body of approved Christian literature. In fact, Jesus did not name any of his apostles; he had no vision whatever of an apostolic succession. Instead, he proclaimed that the leadership of his mission should rest firmly with his own brother, and he answered 'No matter, where you are, you are to go to James the Just'.

ANCIENT TEXTS

Notwithstanding all tradition and scholarly opinion concerning the authorship dates of the canonical gospels, the fact is that not one single original manuscript is available for analysis. The earliest complete canonical texts date from the 4th century. They are considered to be copies from older originals, but this cannot be proved except by way of circumstantial evidence.

The relevance of this is that various other gospels and Christian texts do exist from earlier times in the 2nd and 3rd centuries. Although these documents are older than the oldest extant canonical texts, they too are stated historically to be copies from much earlier originals. In the light of this, it is difficult to comprehend how the Church can persist in maintaining that its own selected and approved texts are more authentic than the rest when there is no confirmation of this. Perhaps the Gospels of Matthew, Mark, Luke and John are indeed older than the non-canonical Gospels of Peter, Thomas, Philip and others- but they might not be. The most important fact to note is that all these individual texts were in Christian usage before the New Testament was compiled and, historically, they are equally valid as evidence of Christian beliefs and practice in the days prior to Roman intervention.

The very oldest biblical compilation held in the Vatican Library dates from no earlier than the 4th century and is known as the Vatican Codex (the *Codex Vaticanus*). These manuscripts, written in Greek, are bound in a series of 759 papyrus folios with two or three columns to a page. Additionally there are 30 dubious folios from a later date which were added in the 16th century to replace some that were missing from the original collection. There have long been disputes as to the origin of the Vatican Codex, but the most common opinion is that it was produced in Egypt.

Many of the sayings of Jesus - as reported in the Gospels of Matthew, Mark and Luke - are repeated word for word, even to the detail of their parenthesised elements. Moreover, a good many of these entries also appear in the non-canonical Gospel of Thomas, which actually adds to them giving a total of 114 sayings purportedly spoken by Jesus.

The Gospel of Thomas was a vital handbook for the early

Christians, although it was not selected by the Bishops for the New Testament. There were a number of reasons for its exclusion, not the least of which was that it dealt specifically with the teachings of Jesus, and made no mention of his birth, death and resurrection which became so crucial to the Roman portrayal of the Faith in later times. It also contradicted the new Catholic teaching that Jesus was only acceptable by way of adherence to the Church.

Additionally, the Gospel of Thomas contained an item concerning Mary Magdalene in which Peter complained about her presence in the apostolic fraternity of males. In response, Jesus confided that she would become an equally living spirit in their company. But there was no room for anything concerning female equality in the newly-devised, male-dominated Church of Rome. As a consequence of this - along with the 4th century notion that access to Jesus was a strict prerogative of the Bishops - the Gospel of Thomas was deemed inappropriate for the canon.

It has been argued recently that Thomas does not have the same provenance of antiquity as the canonical Gospels, but this is simply not so. Extant Greek manuscript sections of Thomas date from around AD 200, well over a century earlier than any canonical manuscript. In addition, the Gospel of Thomas is known to have existed in Syriac or Aramaic writing in the second half of the 1st century. It stems from precisely the same era attributed to the gospel of Mark, and might indeed have been one of that Gospel's original sources. A comparison of the sayings in Thomas with their parallels in Matthew, Mark and Luke has led linguistic scholars to deduce that the Thomas verses have a more primitive construction. Also that this Gospel more closely resembles the ultimate key source for the synoptic Gospels - an earlier Gospel now known as 'Q' (relating to the Teutonic word *quelle*, meaning 'source').

There is absolutely nothing in the Gospel of Thomas or Q to indicate the notion that Jesus died for people's sins and rose again, but the early Christians who used these books clearly believed in a different concept of his perpetual existence. In fact, so too did the Romans, and it is documented from imperial times that the emperors took the most extreme measures to persecute and exterminate those messianic dynasts whom they called the Heir of the Lord.

To gain an insight into the extreme change of attitude to Christianity taken by Constantine and his officials, it helps to understand how Christians and their 'deadly superstition' were perceived by the Romans in earlier times.

The Senate and its ambassadors were able to claim religious supremacy over the Christians following Rome's military conquest and destruction of Jerusalem by the legions of General Titus in AD 70. Just two years after the mass slaughter of Christians by Nero, a Jewish revolt had erupted against the Roman overlords of Judea in AD 66. As far as the Romans were concerned, Christianity was born out of liberal Judaism, and was perceived as a Jewish cult which shared the same god. This god was traditionally reckoned to be the all-powerful protector of the Israelite nation and yet, to the Romans, their Roman gods were clearly more powerful because, following the crushing of the four-year revolt, the Judaeo-Christian God was seen to have been defeated.

Joseph ben Mattathias, a Pharisee scholar, was one of the leading figures of the Judaean rising. Better known these days by his Romanised name, Flavius Josephus, he was the appointed military commander of Galilee. In the years subsequent to the revolt he wrote The Wars of the Jews (AD 92). By comparing his work with *The Annals of Imperial Rome*, the parallel histories of the Jews and Romans give us first-hand perspectives from the two opposing cultures.

By the time of the Bar Kochba revolt in 132 AD, significant divisions had appeared in the Christian movement. Although a suppressed underground society in Rome, they maintained the tradition of appointing bishops to lead them and, from AD 136, Hyginus was their bishop in Rome. Hyginus was at odds with some of the bishops in other lands, the main dispute between the various factions concerning the matter of Jesus' personal divinity. There were two predominant groupings at the debate: the followers of Hyginus, who had spread into parts of Gaul (later France), Spain and North Africa, while the alternative Nazarene sect was scattered through Asia and the Middle East, and also, to a lesser extent, in Britain and Gaul. In essence, the Hyginus Christians followed teachings that were said to have emanated from St Paul, whereas the Nazarenes preferred the more direct teachings of Jesus and his brother James, who had been the first Nazarene bishop in Jerusalem.

During the period of Christian history, a number of powerful figures emerged in the ranks outside Rome, not the least of whom was Iranaeus, the Bishop of Lyon in Gaul. In about AD 177, he challenged the Nazarene concept that Jesus was a man and not of divine origin, as the Hyginus teaching implied. He also condemned the Nazarenes for preaching the gospel of Matthew, which he considered to be Jewish rather than Christian. In endeavouring to enforce his opinion, Iranaeus went so far as to pronounce in his treatise *Adversus Haeresus* (Against Heresies) that Jesus was himself a heretic, who had been practising the wrong religion! Jesus, he claimed, was personally mistaken in his beliefs.

Additionally, he wrote of the Nazarenes, whom he classified as ebionites:

'They, like Jesus as well as the Essenes and Zadokites of two centuries before, expound upon the prophetic books of the Old Testament. They reject the Pauline epistles, and they reject the apostle Paul, calling him an apostate of the law.'

The Nazarenes recognised the absurdity that Jesus' teachings should take second place to those of Paul. In retaliation, they denounced Paul as having been a 'renegade and a false apostle', claiming that his idolatrous writings should be rejected altogether. Thus, even 222 years before the New Testament was completed, the original Christians were themselves divided in opinion as to which scriptural texts they preferred.

Since they spoke and worshipped in the same language Yeshua spoke, these Aramaic Christians felt (and their descendants still feel) that the Peshitta is a version of the original Aramaic words of Jesus, and that they stayed very close in spirit to his original message. While some Aramaic-speaking Jewish Christian groups went along with the council of Nicaea, most soon broke contact with the rest of both Roman and Eastern Orthodox Christianity over the increasingly complex creeds and the forceful attempts to impose a single theology on all Christians. Little was heard from or reported about them in Europe for the next fifteen hundred years, while Christianity in the West underwent its own political and theological evolution.

As modern Assyrian Christian writer Abraham Rihbany commented:

'The Syrian Christians of Semitic stock have had very little to do with the development of the 'Creeds of Christendom.'

Theological organizations has been as foreign to the minds of the Eastern Christians as political organization. They have always been worshippers rather than theologians, believers rather than systematic thinkers. The Christian Church had its simple forgoing with a group of Jewish followers of Jesus Christ in Palestine... The Creed of the theologians consists of many articles, The Creed of Christ only two: 'love the Lord thy God with all thy heart, and thy neighbour as thyself.'

The Jesus tradition is Jewish. It must now be self-evident that there is a vast gulf between the Jesus of history and the Jesus of faith. The strict custodians of Christian theology insist that the two are identical, but any historian who looks honestly at the data can easily discover that they are not. We have already seen how the Vatican, for example, has long been forced to maintain its position through suppression and manipulated expression. But this hard-line position is becoming harder and harder to maintain - the strain is showing, cracks are beginning to appear. It would seem inevitable that at some stage the pressure will become too much, that the entire construction will collapse under the weight of its erroneous assumptions, blatant untruths and deliberate misreadings. This of course must not be allowed to happen. Too many people have a 'blind' faith that is still guided by a Church seeking to sustain itself. Gradually the truth must be realised to allow the story to be retold to make it compatible with the other mainstream religions. After all - we all believe in one God!

There is a need among people today for some sense of purpose and direction or way to give more meaning to life. As we enter the third millennium AD with its greater knowledge and understanding of all things, people, and particularly young people, are not prepared to accept blind faith in anything, let alone Christianity, with its many weaknesses and flaws. They are more aware now than ever before that Christianity is a far-from-accurate transcription of what happened nearly 2000 years ago.

For two millennia, Christians have expected Christ's second coming to be a physical return to our planet and that he will wander among us once again and put everything right, restore peace and fulfil the ancient dream and purpose of a Messiah. But perhaps the second coming can be interpreted in a different way; perhaps it means the Spirit of Jesus will be able to enter every human mind, enabling a new form of life and living to come into being.

If we want to consider this further, we ought to have a greater knowledge of the events of the beginning.

Archaeological discoveries including the Dead Sea Scrolls at Qumran and the Gnostic Gospels at Nag Hammadi have brought some of the events of the beginning of Christianity and the people involved closer to us.

CHAPTER 19

❦

Druids and Christians

Although a form of early Christianity entered Britain in the middle 1st century, it is evident that this did not constitute a wide-scale conversion to a new faith. Despite the fact that Linus and his sister Gladys were embraced by the Christian fraternity in Rome, there is no record to suggest that Cymbeline, Arviragus or Boudicca became Christians. Their way of life was built on Druidic principles and the Britons maintained their old beliefs for another few centuries while Christianity evolved alongside. According to the Roman biographer Suetonius (AD c 100), Emperor Claudius had not used the term Christian in his AD 43 edict against the Britons; he cited only Druidism and the Jews of Christus. The term Christian appears to have been first used a year later at Antioch in Syria.

The style of Christianity that came into Britain with Joseph of Arimathea, and into Gaul with Philip and Mary Magdalene, was a Nazarene concept that seems to have been, in some ways, compatible with the Druid culture.

As Nazarene Christianity gained a foothold alongside Druidism in the West, the emergent culture gave rise in the 6th century to an amalgam that became known to later historians as the Celtic Church. By that time, the Church of Rome was firmly established and the bishops looked for the slightest excuse to denounce the

Druid priests and Celtic monks, finding the mark of sin even in their hairstyles. They wore long hair flowing from the backs of their heads, with the fronts of their heads shaved across from the temples. The alternative Roman tonsure, as introduced by Pope Gregory 1 and brought to England by St Augustine in 597, was a circlet of short hair around an otherwise clean-shaven head, supposedly representative of a holy crown. According to Rome, the Celtic hairstyle was a heretical symbol.

HOSTILITY OR HARMONY

An essential difference between Druidism and Christianity was that the druidic order was not a religion. Rather more akin to the Essene community, the Druids maintained their own government, courts of law, educational colleges and surgeons. The members of the order were its statesmen, legislators, priest, physicians, lawyers, teachers and poets. Diogenes Laertius, a 3rd century chronicler of philosophies, wrote that the three main Druidic tenets were 'to worship the gods, to do no evil, and to practice manly virtue'.

In the Gallic and Celtic realms, where it is known that Christianity flourished from 1st century times, the main factor which allowed this to happen so naturally appears to have been the jointly-held Pythagorean beliefs of the Druids and the Nazarenes. Both expressed belief equally in an afterlife and in a heavenly Otherworld. Immortality of the soul (rather than of the body) was around as a concept long before Jesus' time.

Native Britons were then confronted by two threats: their kingdoms had been usurped by Germanic invaders, and now their ancient Celtic religion was being subsumed. As the land filled from its eastern shore with Angles and Saxons, the Britons were forced westwards across the island to the far reaches of Wales and Cornwall and northwards into the regions of Cumbria, Northumbria and Strathclyde.

Some time after Augustine's arrangement with King Aethelbert, a tablet was placed above the vestry fireplace at the London church of St Peter's in Cornhill explaining:

'In the year of our Lord 179, Lucius, the first Christian king of this island now called Briton, founded the first church in London, well known as the church of St Peter in Cornhill; and founded there the archiepiscopal seat, and made it the metropolitan church and the primary church of his kingdom. So it remained for the space of four hundred years until the coming of St Augustine... Then, indeed, the seat and pallium of the archbishopric was translated from the said church of St Peter in Cornhill to Dorobernia, which is now called Canterbury.'

The greatest of all travesties is that as Roman Christianity overran Celtic Christianity, the literature of the latter was systematically destroyed. Not a scrap survives of any Gaelic writing by St Columba. During medieval times, many ancient Celtic manuscripts from before 600, including the works of Columba, were rewritten in Latin and presented as original documents. *The Cathach* of St Columba, who died in 597, provides a good example of this subterfuge. The 58-folio work, held by the Royal Irish Academy from shortly after its discovery in 1813, is reckoned to be the oldest Irish illuminated manuscript in existence. It is said to have been a copy made by Columba himself from manuscripts given to him by St Finian prior to 561. Palaeographic evidence proves, however, that the document was written long after Columba's death.

CHAPTER 20

❧

Pagans and Celtic Christianity

By the 6th century, Christianity of the Roman style had made little impact in Britain, and throughout the 500s the Celtic Church prevailed. In 574, Britain's most kingly installation by way of a Celtic Christian rite was performed when St Columba of Iona anointed King Aedan mac Gabran of Dalriada. It was not until 597 that St Augustine arrived from Rome, and not until 664 that the Catholic bishops enforced some of their doctrines at the Synod of Whitby. The Vatican maintains that King Oswiu of Northumbria conceded at this Synod to the papal authority of St Peter in order to gain admission to the Kingdom of Heaven. But when the presumed papal supremacy was tested on the stalwarts of the British Church, they asserted that they recognised no such authority. They reiterated the words of Dianothus, Abbot of Bangor. At a conference with St Augustine in 607, Dianothus had stated that he and his colleagues were prepared to acknowledge the Church of God, 'but as for other obedience, we know of none that he whom you term the Pope, or Bishop of Bishops, can demand'.

The introduction of Roman Christianity into Britain was largely facilitated by the Saxon King Aethelbert of Kent. Aethelbert's wife swayed her husband to the Roman faith. When St Augustine arrived in 597, Aethelbert gave him a palace in

Canterbury as a centre for the new Church in Angle-land, and, moreover it is mostly in Latin - a language that was unknown in Ireland during the saint's lifetime and which was never used by the Gaels. With its inclusion of Bible sections from the Latin *Vulgate*, the *Cathach* was either a pure fabrication or a substantial corruption of Columba's original work, since the text is wholly Romanised to comply with post-Augustanian teaching after the Synod of Whitby. Other such works followed, including the 7th century *Book of Durrow* and the 9th century *Book of Kells*. Historically they are all important, and they are individually wonderful in artistic terms, but they are all Roman Church fabrications, produced to subvert the Old Faith of Britain and Ireland.

It was not as if the Celtic churchmen were unaware of the impending threat posed by Pope Gregory and Augustine, but there was little they could do to prevent it because the Saxons had already driven them from the region where Augustine landed. Apologetic Church history records that his mission was designed to convert the Saxon invaders but, according to the 8th century priest Bede of Jarrow, Augustine's papal brief was to subjugate 'all the Bishops of Britain'. The intention is made transparent because the Saxons had no Bishops.

The story of loss and destruction is the same throughout Western Europe, and constitutes the reasons why the era became known as the Dark Ages; its history was literally plunged into darkness. Within the Britannic Church communities of those times there had been prominent adepts of old wisdom - abbots and culdees such as St Ninian, St David, St Patrick, St Columba and St Kentigern, all of whom were denounced by the Roman Church for their so-called wizardry and pagan beliefs. Even the later papal establishment regarded them as necromancers and sorcerers, but this is not the way things are currently portrayed. The teachings of these men were so firmly cemented in society that the Church was obliged in time to recognise them. A thousand years after their lifetime the Vatican officials decided to bring them into the Orthodox Saintly fold, so that the truth of their establishment would be lost forever.

In 590 Pope Gregory 1, a lawyer, was called Gregory the Great. He changed the course of Church history and promoted the newly-formed Catholicism of the west as distinct from the composite of Eastern and Western which prevailed before his time.

In 591 Pope Gregory maligned Mary Magdalene, giving rise to her non-biblical representation as a sinful harlot. He subsequently amended the original Catholic Mass, invented the concept of a horned devil, sacked all lay staff from the Lateran palace, redefined matters of ecclesiastical discipline and took overall control of the military. Then, in 597, he sent St Augustine to England with a brief to overawe and decimate the Celtic Church. From the time of Gregory 1, the Church and the Roman state became one again, as it had been in high imperial times, and a new form of empire began - an international realm of absolute spiritual dominion by the Popes.

The Vatican achieved destruction of the 'King Structure' in France and in 751 AD it enforced a new practice whereby kings and queens within the Catholic domain were henceforth crowned by, and made subordinate to, the Pope. The effects of this were felt not only in France but in England, which (subsequent to the arrangement between St Augustine and King Aethelbert) had also become a Catholic realm. In earlier times monarchs on both sides of the water had reigned by virtue of bloodline inheritance, but this desposynic tradition was curtailed when the rules of hereditary status were dogmatically changed by a strategy that has since become known as the greatest documentary fraud in sovereign history.

In order to tackle the problem of heritable interest, Pope Zachary came up with a plan to gain supremacy over all the kings and queens of Christendom. In the year 751, without revoking his source, he produced a previously unknown document that was purported to be more than 400 years old and carried the signature of Emperor Constantine. It proclaimed that the Pope was Christ's personally elected representative on earth, with a palace that ranked above all the palaces in the world. His divinely-granted dignity was stated to be above that of any earthly ruler and only he, the Pope, had the power and authority to 'create' kings and queens as his subordinate. The charter made it forcefully clear that the Pope held the office as Christ's chosen deputy, granting him the style *Vicarius Filii Dei* (Vicar of the Son of God).

The document became known as the Donation of Constantine, and its provisions were immediately enforced by the Vatican as being an edict from Jesus Christ himself. Consequently, the whole nature and structure of monarchy changed from being an office of community guardianship to one of absolute rule. Henceforth European monarchs were crowned by the Pope, becoming servants of the Church instead of being champions of the people.

Zachary's plan was to change all kingly tradition by granting territorial dominion to future kings who would operate under his supreme authority. The defunct Roman Empire was a relic of history, but Zachary had a new concept - a Holy Roman Empire controlled from the Vatican. His first initiative was to depose the long-standing royal house of France, the Merovingians of Gaul.

Papal troopers seized King Childeric 111 and, as a humiliation to signify the loss of his kingship, his hair was cut brutally short. He was then incarcerated in a monastery dungeon, where he died four years later.

There was no thought by anyone at the time that the Donation of Constantine might be a forgery. Even the anti-papists who sought to criticise its content did not question its authenticity. The best they could do was to maintain that Emperor Constantine had no right to have signed away the Western Empire in this fashion. But the fact was that, although the opening and closing sections of the *Donation were* cleverly constructed in the 4th-century style of Constantine's day, its more central themes, such as the descriptions of imperial and papal ceremony, were representative of a much later era. Its New Testament references relate to the Latin *Vulgate* Bible - an edition translated and compiled by St Jerome, who was not born until AD 340, some 26 years after Constantine supposedly signed and dated the document. Apart from this, the language of the Donation, with its numerous anachronisms of form and content, is that of the 8th century and bears no relation to the writing style of Constantine's day. It is as different as modern English is to that of William Shakespeare - with a similar span of time in between.

CHAPTER 21

❦

The Da Vinci Code

On a recent visit to Buckfastleigh and the Abbey, I spent some time in the shop casting my eyes over many of the publications sponsored particularly by the Roman Catholic Church. One pamphlet in particular aroused my curiosity; it was entitled 'Answering the Da Vinci Code'. As a matter of interest and insight into modern Church thinking, I list below some of the points made in the pamphlet:

An unholy mixture of fact and fiction
The plot follows the adventures of a Harvard Professor of 'Symbology' who follows a trail of clues and puzzles from a murder scene in the Paris Museum where Leonardo Da Vinci's *Mona Lisa* is kept, through to the discovery of the Holy Grail. Along the way the reader is drawn into a conspiracy-fuelled alternative understanding of religion, Jesus Christ, the Catholic Church and any number of other people and institutions once held sacred.

Why the controversy?
While the book is intended primarily as a work of fiction, the author claims that 'all descriptions of artwork, architecture, documents and secret rituals in this novel are accurate' (p16). Thus

Dan Brown claims to introduce the reader to real historical research and investigation which led to the following startling conclusions:

- Jesus is not God.
- Jesus was married to Mary Magdalene and had a child with her.
- Jesus intended Mary Magdalene and not Peter to lead the Church.
- Mary Magdalene represents the 'sacred feminine', a kind of pre-Christian goddess.
- The Roman Emperor Constantine decided the Canon of Scripture (the official list of books included in the Bible) and made Christ into a divinity.
- A secret society named the Priory of Sion is attempting to keep this truth alive and protect Jesus' descendants from ruthless *Opus Dei* killers.

Many of the ideas above find their origin in a heresy of the first centuries after Christ known as gnosticism. The Gnostics believed that salvation was achieved through secret knowledge (*gnosis* in Greek). Gnosticism denied that Christ was God.

What is the Canon of Scripture?

After the death of Jesus and the resurrection, early followers influenced by Paul began to write the books of the New Testament, and these were attributed for example to the Apostles. These books were kept and copied and read in the early Churches. In the second and third centuries, Gnostics and other heretics wrote their own versions of the Gospels and attempted to have them accepted as genuinely being written by the Apostles. In response to these false writings the Churches drew up a list of authentic books that had come from the Apostles, called the 'canon'. This exercise was done for the first time in the *Munatorian Canon* some 150 years before Constantine.

Was Jesus' Divinity a late invention?
While there were a number of heretics in the early Church who questioned Christ's divinity (and others his humanity) the truth that Jesus is God was always present in the earliest documents of the Church, in the Gospels and the letters of St Paul.

Was Jesus married with children?
In a world obsessed by sex, Jesus' celibacy for the Kingdom (Mt 19:12) raises many difficult questions; in the past few decades this has resulted in various attempts to assign Jesus a wife or lover. Mary Magdalene has been put forward by revisionist history and feminist myth as the most likely candidate. There is no evidence for a marriage and speculation about a relationship derives from the heretical Gnostic texts called the 'Gospel of Philip' and the 'Gospel of Mary', written to support the Gnostic sects. One text refers to Mary as Jesus' 'companion' which has been stretched to mean his sexual partner, and the other speaks of Jesus favouring Mary above the other disciple and kissing her on the mouth. Both these texts were written between one and three centuries after the four accepted Gospels and 'along with other Gnostic gospels like the Gospel of Thomas' are full of bizarre stories and beliefs that were never accepted by the early Church, hence they were never accepted into the canon of scripture.

How important is Mary Magdalene?
Mary Magdalene has always been honoured by the Church. Her

feast day (22nd July) has been kept since the earliest times and she has been given the title of 'Apostle to the Apostles' in recognition of the fact that it was she who brought the news of the resurrection to the other disciples.

In the Da Vinci Code however, *she* is the Holy Grail (the 'cup' that held the blood of Christ) for she gives birth to the bloodline of Christ. She represents the 'sacred feminine', a continuation of the Goddess worship dominant in pre-Christian Pagan religion; she is also the intended head of the Church, as it says in the code 'it was not Peter to whom Christ gave directions with what to establish the Christian Church. It was Mary Magdalene... Jesus was the original feminist'. (DVC p334) The Church depicted by Dan Brown is one that has always been anti-pleasure, anti-sex and anti-woman, and has done its utmost to suppress Goddess worship and oppress women in general from its very beginnings. Mary Magdalene is set up as a female antagonist to a male chauvinist caricature of the Church: unfortunately historical accuracy and genuine research fall by the wayside.

The Da Vinci Code: threat or opportunity?
Great reading or not, *The Da Vinci Code* makes some false, misleading and downright offensive claims about Christ, his Church and some perfectly legitimate associations like *Opus Dei*. Its ideas are neither new nor original, but for those lacking a solid knowledge of the history of the Church and the scriptures they can cause doubts and confusion. Jesus is belittled and his Church portrayed as corrupt and deceitful. *The Da Vinci Code* illustrates how important it is for believers to know their faith and its history, so that every conversation can become an opportunity to dismiss

the book's neo-gnosticism, which contains no hope, and give the real good news that Jesus Christ is the son of God who died and rose again for our salvation.

I have now read the book several times and most of the books written about it. I have also seen the film. As for the pamphlet, I am reminded of the words of that famous wartime song - 'Who do you think you are kidding Mr Hitler?'

This pamphlet was issued by an organisation which for nearly 1400 years proposed to its followers and the whole world that Mary Magdalene was a prostitute. As proclaimed in 591 AD by Pope Gregory II, it was only with the discovery of the hidden literature 50-60 years ago, and even then not until 1969, that the Vatican reversed its position on this. Pope John Paul II then acknowledged Mary Magdalene, bestowing on her the title of Apostle to the Apostles. What a total climbdown - leading us to reflect on how much more of the church's so called beliefs and teaching need revising.

Recently I was asked what my reaction was to *The Da Vinci Code* and my reply was - it is a brilliant novel.

Somewhere along the line the Church has I think lost the plot. They concentrate too much on trying to prove who Jesus was and what he did; Mary Magdalene became a prostitute to strengthen Jesus' position. To forgive her for the sins of her trade was a further embellishment of his status as a God. At the same time it demeans the feminine connection to a male-dominated institution.

As far as marriage is concerned we forget that Jesus was Jewish. We are saying no more than a 'Jewish man gets married and has a child.' How can any later theological position alter the overwhelming probability of that simple human action? An action, we should remember, in accordance with the teachings of the

Hebrew Scriptures - the Old Testament - as well as the social standards of the day. Blasphemy? I don't think so.

It is self-evident that the most severe reaction against exploring such ideas come from those with the most to lose - those whose religious beliefs depend more upon maintaining a difference between faiths rather than seeking harmony among them. We can, and should, continue to ask these critics 'Why do such ideas frighten you so much?'

For me it is not important. I care not if He was married or if He had five wives and fifteen children. What's important is what He said, what His message was: 'I can show you how to find the kingdom of God which is within you.'

Let us remember that the historical Jesus lived long before any theologians or institutions concocted theories about him.

CHAPTER 22

❦

Some other beliefs and religious societies

PAGANISM

Where the Vatican now stands there once stood a pagan temple. Here Pagan Priests observed sacred ceremonies which the early Christian Church found so disturbing that they tried to erase evidence of them ever having been practised. But what were those shocking pagan rites, gruesome sacrifices, or obscene orgies, as we have been led to believe? And why? The truth is far stranger than this fiction we have been fed.

Where the gathered faithful now revere Jesus, the ancients worshipped another god-man who like Jesus had been born miraculously on 25th December before three shepherds. In this ancient sanctuary congregations once glorified a pagan redeemer who, like Jesus, was said to have ascended into heaven and to have promised to come again at the end of time to judge the quick and the dead.

Where the Pope now celebrates Mass, pagan priests also celebrated a symbolic meal of bread and wine in memory of their Saviour, who just like Jesus had declared: 'He who will not eat of my body and drink of my blood so that he will be made one with me and I with him, the same shall not know salvation.'

For two thousand years the West has been dominated by the

idea that Christianity is sacred and unique, while paganism is primitive and the work of the devil. To even consider that they could be part of the same tradition has been unthinkable.

Pagan spirituality was actually the sophisticated product of a highly-developed culture. The real spirituality of the people expressed itself through the mystery religions which spread throughout the ancient Mediterranean, inspiring great minds who regarded them as the very source of civilisation.

Each mystery tradition had exotic outer mysteries consisting of myths and stories which were common knowledge and rituals which were open for anyone to participate in. There were also esoteric inner mysteries, a sacred secret known only to the initiated and which enabled them to bring about personal transformation and spiritual enlightenment.

At the heart of the mysteries were myths concerning a dying god-man who was known by many different names.

Egypt - Osiris
Greece - Dionysus
Asia Minor - Attis
Syria - Adonis
Italy - Bacchus
Persia - Mithras

In essence they were one and the same being telling the same story, albeit in different forms. As a modern comparison take Shakespeare's *Romeo and Juliet* and the musical *West Side Story*, the same theme but different words.

What do all the various versions of a dying god-man have in common?

1. He is God made flesh - the Saviour and Son of God.

2. His Father is God, his mother a mortal virgin.

3. He is born in a cave or a humble cowshed on 25 December (a pagan festival) in the presence of three shepherds.

4. He offers his followers a chance to be born again through the rites of baptism.

5. He turns water into wine at a marriage ceremony.

6. He rides triumphantly into town on a donkey while people wave palms to honour Him.

7. He dies at Eastertide (a pagan festival) as a sacrifice for the sins of the world.

8. After his death he rises on the third day and ascends to Heaven in glory.

9. His followers await his return as promised.

10. His death and resurrection are celebrated by a ritual meal of bread and wine which symbolise his body and blood.

The Chambers dictionary defines the word pagan as follows: 'A person following any (especially polytheistic) pre-Christian religion, a person who is not a Christian, Jew or Muslim, and is regarded as uncultured or unenlightened' (polytheistic means a plurality of gods).

Paganism is now practically a dead religion, or rather exterminated. It did not simply fade away into oblivion but was actively suppressed and annihilated. Its temples and shrines were desecrated and demolished, its great sacred books burned. No living lineage has been left to explain its ancient beliefs; all that can be done is to try to attempt some reconstruction from archaeological evidence and texts that have survived. Paganism was the spirituality which inspired the magnificence of the pyramids at Giza, the architecture of the Parthenon, the legendary sculptures of Phideas, the powerful plays of Euripides and Sophocles and the wonderful philosophy of Socrates and Plato.

Pagan civilisations built vast libraries. Its astronomers knew the earth was a sphere which, along with the planets, revolves round the sun. They had even estimated its circumference to within one degree of accuracy.

Most people associate paganism with witchcraft or myths of the Gods of Olympus. Pagan spirituality did embrace both; they practised their traditional worship to maintain the fertility of the land and that of the gods to maintain the power of the status quo.

There was however a third, more mystical, expression of the pagan spirit which inspired the great minds of the ancient world. They were initiates of various religions known as mysteries and they underwent a secret process of initiation which profoundly transformed their state of consciousness.

At the heart of pagan philosophy is an understanding that all things are one. The mysteries aimed at awakening within the initiate the sublime experience of this oneness. Every initiation was aimed at the unification with the world and with the deity.

THE SPIRITUALITY OF PAGANISM

The landscape of religious belief is constantly changing, and a kind of revolution is taking place. The Third World and parts of the Eastern world are developing a form of Christianity. But it is Christianity with a difference. They are using their own social background and their pagan roots and adapting the Christian message to suit their own particular background. This is creating new ideas, new spiritual experiences. In their countries people are changing the way they think about religion and religious practice. They are using their past to help them adapt to their belief in the future.

Humanity has many basic things in common. All humans experience the cycles of day and night, the changing of the seasons and universal laws like gravity, motion, the speed of light and thermodynamics. Humanity has also developed senses and the experience of a body with its birth, death and physical and emotional needs. We are connected as a race in sharing these realities, but we have not always during our development been able to recognise the truth.

Some people of deep spiritual faith have been able to recognise the truth. Paganism in its purest form relates the human conscience to its beginnings, even to the cosmos itself. It allows individuals to find their own path of belief, their own unique point of intersection with the Universe and all living things. It does not require this belief to be recorded, coded and repeated as a dogma (ie a creed). In paganism, responsibility for matters of belief rest solely with, and directly on, each individual. It cannot be avoided even by choosing not to act, for in so doing you have exercised a choice.

Paganism asserts that the individual has the right to examine any idea or belief; it can be tested, examined, looked at from any angle, taken up or discarded. You are not obligated, you have the freedom of choice, you have the right or power to decide, because you are responsible for the ultimate choice you make. This is the fundamental principle of paganism.

CHAPTER TWENTY TWO

HOW DID PAGANISM MERGE INTO CHRISTIANITY?

It was during the years of the Roman Empire that the word 'Christian' gradually came into use to describe those who followed Jesus of Nazareth. Ancient Rome tolerated monotheism and even in some forms accepted Yahweh, the God of Israel. However even Christians did not go to the temple, did not participate in Roman state religious observances and did not worship the accepted gods. So the Romans declared them godless and that they must therefore be atheists.

The early years of Christianity were marked by a great deal of variety of belief. Each so-called Christian group had its own idea on who Jesus was, what his ministry meant and how best to emulate him. Beliefs and practices differed greatly and not all early Christians accepted the resurrection of Jesus as a literal event. They organised themselves in different ways, and women had equal participation. Many did not have a concept of Jesus as 'the Christ'. And this is just in the West. China had an active early Christian population and had no concept of original sin, just like pagans and the Celtic church.

With the discovery of the Dead Sea Scrolls, thousands of new writings were discovered. It is now estimated that the document known as Q which is accepted as being quoted by Matthew and Luke may have consisted of 225 verses. The Gospel of Thomas also discovered was very provocative, also being a 'sayings' Gospel, and 35% of its sayings or logos are now suspected of featuring in Q as well. So it is now accepted among scholars that early Christian writings were in this form of genre.

It is interesting to note that the early 'Christian' writings, Q for

244

example, do not include the following:

- The baptism of Jesus
- An encounter between Jesus and the authorities
- A plot to kill Him
- The Last Supper
- The trial and crucifixion.
- The resurrection and transfiguration.
- The disciples
- The reform of religion
- The church.

It is hardly surprising that Q has never been found and that the Gospel of Thomas, which is of similar content, was lost for nearly 2000 years.

Early Christians held several views about the nature of Jesus and whether or not he was divine. These ranged from his being a very holy and wise man to (at the other end of the spectrum) divine and not a creature in the sense that people and animals are, His nature proceeding directly from God and equatable with God. The Jewish and Hellenistic cultures looked for more images to express their own ideas about Jesus and they built this picture, this mythology for want of a better word, from themes familiar to them.

The mythology developed in the Gospels contains many striking similarities or parallels with more ancient texts such as:

- The virgin birth of a god
- His astrological associations
- His birth among cattle

- His imprisonment
- His death
- His disappearance for 3 days
- His resurrection
- His exaltation to Heaven.

The Gospels then came to bear a striking resemblance to the life and death cycles of Tammug, Adonis, Artis, Osiris, etc, which had been around for several thousand years before Jesus. Thus we return to the spread of a religion through the cultural beliefs of the various races.

Did Jesus ever claim Christological powers and authority for himself? The answer is no, but he was unique in his time for his ability to overcome all authority thinking. He did not expect his audience to rely upon any authority that of his own or of others. There is a major difference between what Jesus was like as a figure of history, and how he is spoken of by others in the Gospels and later Christian tradition. In the Gospels it is difficult to isolate the voice of Jesus from the added voice of the Church, as much of the content of the Gospels is added material, as has been proven so many times by so many eminent scholars.

Let us not forget that history is written by the winners and the content or canon of the New Testament was chosen by the historical winners. But the debates which surrounded the choices available demonstrate the wide range of choices that were available. Because the orthodox majority chose the canon of scriptures, all books which gave reference to a feminine divine were omitted, as were those where women played a prominent ecclesiastical role.

Essentially these books which represented the orthodox view and power of the 'institution' were kept and those that did not were rejected. Not only were they rejected but they were collected, destroyed, their ideas vilified and their proponents driven away and persecuted.

So successful were the efforts of the orthodox majority to destroy every trace of heretical blasphemy (ie those who did not conform to or toe the party line) that (apart from some small oddments found) it was not until the middle of the 20th century that copies of these books were discovered. Before then the only information available came from orthodox records of attacks against them. Thus we were denied a full picture of early Christian belief and tradition we were left with the tip of the iceberg and the loss of a rich heritage. In terms of organisation the Gnostic Groups, Pagans etc were no match for the large and efficient system of the Orthodox Church in real terms the Roman Empire.

CHRISTO-PAGANISM

As the latest generation of humans, we are increasingly insistent on simple black and white views of the world. There is not a lot of time in our lives to consider the existence of a God or of a supreme being. We are unaware of the cosmos, the black hole, the beginnings of civilisation. Archaeology is constantly providing examples of animals, insects, flora and fauna from millions of years ago. The humanoid form has been shown to have existed for millions of years, albeit in a very primitive state at first. We are constantly bombarded with the theory of development of species by natural selection, and while many are not prepared to accept this, there is no rational, sensible alternative. The belief in a god or supreme being, a supernatural force, is to the modern mind unproven. All the different religions with their own individual creeds just throw confusion into the argument. How is it possible for a creed or institutional set of rules to state categorically that this is the only way to find God etc, and say that unless you do it this way or believe this story then you will not find everlasting peace?

Ever since the day the first human saw lightning come from the sky and set fire to a tree, mankind was introduced to a previously unknown quantity. It was to them a miracle, and at some time people will have discussed its source and implications. From these humble beginnings we humans experienced an inexplicable phenomenon. Since that day it has developed through localised ceremonies and rituals into organised paganism with many interpretations of the events until organised religion became the method of controlling races and their behaviour, usually through fear. So races fought and conquered and original beliefs were interwoven until some religions or cults became large enough to eradicate others by force and whatever other means deemed necessary to arrive at one controlling faction.

Thus, for example, was born Roman Catholicism. Nothing was allowed to stand in its way; whatever the Pope said had happened became fact. This creed prevailed until the 20th century, when great discoveries were made which have shaken the foundations of the Church. Instead of standing up and saying yes, we were wrong in many things, but let us now go back to our roots - the message of Jesus - let us start anew from there. No way, the Church cannot admit to crimes it has committed to promulgate Christianity. True, in 1969 it had to admit that Mary Magdalene was not a prostitute as was declared true by Pope Gregory in 591 AD, but that is the smallest tip of the iceberg. We will never get all of mankind together in one belief in one God or Supreme Being until all the various religions agree on a NEW CREED, not enforceable but freely agreed, and what better way to start than 'I believe in God'.

I believe that God is the force of life and that the force of life is around us and within us, exactly as Jesus said, in the world and in the universe, always, everywhere. We have to recognise the fact that there is a divine source which is present in all things and is there for us to find and interact with it.

I do not see that Jesus' death is as significant in my personal relationship with the divine spirit which is known to me as God. Jesus tried to teach his disciples and all of us how to make that connection so that ultimately we might return to the state in which we entered this world. I do not accept that we came into this world bearing sin and he was sent to atone for our sins. I do believe, as the Celtic Christianity did and does, that we came into this world without sin. Our mission is to try to regain that state so that we might return to whence we came. That is the core of Jesus' teaching as I understand it.

I now believe that every individual has a unique path to God, and we as a race need to revaluate our thoughts. Until we learn to accept that every person has a right to tread their own path in their own time, we will not find a collective way forward which in turn will bring everlasting peace.

CELTIC CHRISTIANITY IN BRITAIN

It is on record that three British clerics had attended Emperor

Constantine's very first Council of Arles in AD 324; they were Eborius of York, Restitutus of London and Adelfius of Caerleon. It is clear, therefore, that despite all Church propaganda to the effect that St. Augustine brought Christianity into Britain from Rome in the early 600s, what he actually brought was Catholicism. The Celtic Christian movement, based on the Nazarene tradition of the Ebionites of Qumran, was flourishing for nearly six centuries before Augustine made his appearance and, moreover, had a far more legitimate apostolic claim than the Roman foundation. The monk Gildas III Badonicus (born 516) wrote that Christian Britons were traceable back to 'the latter part of the reign of Tiberius Caesar' who died in AD 37, just four years after the crucifixion of Jesus.

In confirmation of the Glastonbury heritage, we have the words of St Augustine himself. After taking stock of the situation in England, he sent in his report to Pope Gregory in the year 600. Known as the *Epistolae and Gregorium Papam*, it states: 'In the western confines of Britain there is a certain royal island of large extent, surrounded by water, abounding in all the beauties of nature and necessaries. In it the first neophytes, God beforehand acquainting them, found a church constructed by no human art, but by the hands of Christ himself for the salvation of his people.'

Plainly the chapel of Glastonbury was not built by the hands of Christ himself, but Augustine was sufficiently impressed, and there was indeed a tradition that Jesus had been to the place in AD 64 and consecrated it to his mother. How then did the Catholic churchman Augustine of Rome go along with this presumption when it was known that the chapel had been built and consecrated three decades after the crucifixion of Jesus? And why would the famous Domesday Book of 1086 refer to an aspect of the

Glastonbury chapel as the *Secretum Domini* - the Secret of the Lord?

The Chronica Majora held at Corpus Christi College, Cambridge, explains that AD 63, the year when William of Malmesbury states that Joseph's chapel was built at Glastonbury, was the very year in which Mary Magdalene died in Aix–en–Provence.

Who then was the son who had dedicated the foundation to his mother Mary in AD 64, as claimed in the ancient records? Although there are no indications in any archive which suggests that Jesus Christ ever came to Britain, there are a number of instances where a younger Jesus is recorded in England's West Country, to where he was said to have travelled with his uncle, Joseph of Arimathea. These were the traditions that gave rise to William Blake's famous 18th-century poem, *Jerusalem*.

> *And did those feet in ancient time*
> *Walk upon England's mountains green?*
> *And was the holy Lamb of God*
> *On England's pleasant pastures seen?*

The accounts of Joseph of Arimathea and a young Jesus in south-western Britain focus on three separate occasions. The first relates to a time when Joseph and Jesus voyaged to Marazion in Cornwall. The second recounts a time when they were at the Mendip village of Priddy in Somerset. Thirdly is the account of a young Jesus dedicating the Ealde Church of Glastonbury to his mother in AD 64. Clearly this could not have related to Jesus Christ and his mother Mary, but more likely to a younger Jesus and his mother, Mary Magdalene, as referred to by St Bridget.

What we need to ascertain, however, is who precisely was Joseph of Arimathea. Joseph makes his first and only New Testament appearance at the time of Jesus' crucifixion. He negotiated with the Roman governor, Pontius Pilate, to have Jesus' body removed from the cross before the Sabbath and placed in his own garden sepulchre. He is described in Mark as an honourable counsellor who waited for the Kingdom of God. Joseph made all the arrangements for the burial and all of the family accepted his authority without question, which may of course suggest that he was a relative, especially as both Roman and Jewish law had provisions for nearest relatives to take charge of the bodies if they so wished.

BUDDHISM

Buddhism is a path of practice and spiritual development leading to insight into the true nature of life. Buddhist practices such as meditation are means of changing oneself in order to develop the qualities of awareness, kindness, and wisdom. The experience developed within the Buddhist tradition over thousands of years has created an incomparable resource for those people who wish to follow a path - a path which ultimately culminates in enlightenment or Buddhahood.

Because Buddhism does not include the idea of worshipping a creator God, some people do not see it as a religion in the normal, Western sense. The basic tenets of Buddhist teaching are straightforward and practical: nothing is fixed or permanent; actions have consequences; change is possible. Thus Buddhism addresses itself to all people irrespective of race, nationality, or gender. It teaches practical methods (such as meditation) which enable people to realise and utilise its teachings in order to transform their existence, to be fully responsible for their lives and to develop the qualities of wisdom and compassion.

There are around 350 million Buddhists and a growing number of them are Westerners. They follow many different forms of Buddhism, but all traditions are characterised by non-violence, lack of dogma, tolerance of differences, and, usually, by the practice of meditation.

A BUDDHIST CONCEPT OF LIFE

The world as it stands today is running on desire. Every time you wake up you have a desire, whether it be for a shower, a shave, a cup of coffee; they are all desire led.

Our desires are fed by what we are surrounded by and whatever influences us. In this modern age these influences are multifaceted, from the TV to the Internet and from books to preachers.

All these things influence us, and over the course of our lives they make us who we are and what we do. As we grow up and leave home we look outwards towards these mental and physical foods.

But we are not really inwardly conscious that we desire at all. Our mind simply blots this out all we know is that we are hungry, thirsty, lonely, bored or any number of other things. Because we are not aware of our desires it is difficult to control them or balance them.

As we leave the parental nest we look around for help and influence, but most of the time what we find are bad desires. We are brainwashed by the media and the advertising man, by the availability of goods and the easy availability of purchasing power, in either cash or credit. The marketing man has had a heyday as far as religion is concerned, providing a spiritual cure-all.

No amount of TV or internet can teach us what we can learn ourselves in practice. Desires are twofold; there are good desires and bad ones. A good desire is to love; a bad desire is to love to extreme, to be jealous or overbearing. A good desire is to be hungry; a bad desire is to be gluttonous and greedy. A good desire is to succeed; a bad desire is to want to succeed so much that you hurt other people in the process.

It is easy to tip the balance and veer off into the world of extremes. The way to deal with these issues is to be conscious and aware of them. If we keep our thoughts within our minds concentrated on the good desire we should know that we are walking along the path of ancient wisdom. If we continually succeed in doing this then we will get better and better. We will become more confident and more enlightened and we will lose all the bad parts of us that are not truly us. Only then will we wake up and be resurrected, as the ancient people would say.

History provides us with avatars (higher entities existing for the benefit of mankind), Christ, Buddha, Zoroaster, Mohammed and many more. The teachings of avatars expand our understanding of ourselves, of humanity and the evolution of mankind on a spiritual level. The evolution of the spirit is said to affect the physical evolution of mankind and is thought to be a way back to divinity. The avatar has reached a higher state of enlightenment and possesses great comparison, which is one of the lessons we must learn to be able to reach any stage of enlightenment. If more of us could learn to control our own bad desires and grasp the art of comparison then we would live in a much better world.

THE EBIONITES AND NAZARENES

The Ebionites were an early Jewish sect and its followers were among the earliest supporters of Jesus. The term itself is Hebrew for 'the poor ones'. Though they upheld the teachings of the Jewish Torah they were also followers of John the Baptizer, James the Just and Jesus himself.

The Ebionites flourished during the years 30-80 AD, and in fact many associate them with the Nazarenes in the same period. Together they were called the Ebionite Nazarene movement of Yachad, a Hebrew word meaning together.

According to the Romans the Ebionites were heretics who rejected Paul as well as Jesus' divinity including the virgin birth. Indeed, because their views were held to be in conflict with orthodox Christianity, we must accept that historical information about them may have been compromised by the historians recording it at the time.

According to what we know about the Ebionites their central beliefs regarding the life of Jesus consisted of the following:

- Jesus was not divine, nor was he the Messiah, although he did undertake a Messianic mission meant to bring the Messianic age through kindness and righteousness.

- He was a devout Jew.

- He was liberal in his practice of the Jewish law.

- Although his teachings may have been in conflict with certain sects of Judaism they were within the general framework.

- Though not a Pharisee or an Essene, Jesus did uphold some of their beliefs.

- Jesus may have performed miracles but Christian documentation of them may not be accurate.

Since the establishment of the Christian Church and its persecution of the Ebionites as heretics and Judaizers, information about them has been fragmented and compromised. The most complete account available comes from the 4th century, from Epiphinius, who recorded a list of heretics which was aimed to denounce 80 so-called heretical sects, including the Ebionites.

What eventually became of them remains a point of contention among historians. Some say they were eliminated by the Romans in 135 AD while others believe they survived until at least 1000 AD.

In the late 20th century the movement was revived. However, to what degree the beliefs currently upheld by members of this community are in keeping with those of the original Ebionites cannot be verified except, that the following are extracts from the Ebionites web page:

The only question that every person must ask themselves is whether they want to seek and know the Truth now, while they still have the opportunity to make meaningful spiritual change in their lives? Or do they want to find out the Truth when they pass from this life, and they no longer have the same opportunity they do while in the body-vessel? When you build upon the original spiritual foundation that Yeshua taught, you are no longer shackled by faith and blind belief in manmade Church doctrines, because as the prodigal sons and daughters of your Heavenly Father, it is within your ability to inherit the Promise - and know all things as they truly are.

Why did Yeshua have compassion on the common people?
People who were condemned as sinners by the religious leaders

While the teachings of Yeshua/Jesus are the truth
The way of the churches bring spiritual death

Nothing has changed - history repeats itself
Your choice is to follow the doctrines of men
Doctrines which were/are openly condemned in the Bible
Or walk in the way that Yeshua ordained and taught

You can't serve two masters
You can't be faithful to manmade Church doctrines
And be faithful to Yeshua/Jesus

Yeshua/Jesus came to all those who would follow in the way
But few are willing to make the journey.

THE CATHARS

The Cathars were a religious sect whose heartland was the Languedoc in the deep southern coastal region of France. They used the ancient stone citadel on top of a mountain at Montsegur as a meditation site (and, some say, a protective haven to house the sacred Grail). Later, they reconfigured and fortified the citadel for protection against assaults by Crusaders, to whom it fell in 1244. Here are some other interesting facts about this medieval sect:

- They were Gnostics and called the Pure Ones because their name derives from the Greek word *kathiaros* meaning 'pure'.

- The Cathars were vegetarians and pacifists who advocated resisting all forms of tyranny, religious or secular.

- They believed that humans have a body, soul, and spirit. The soul lives in the body and the spirit (which is a spark of the divine) dwells in the soul.

- They felt spiritual purity was of paramount importance if their spirit's divine spark was to return to its source, the Light (God).

- They established prosperous communities focused on the spirit of cooperation and self-sufficiency, and abhorred the Church's excesses.

- Their most spiritually advanced masters were known as Perfects or Parfaits (and included women).

- They worshipped on mountain tops or in forests.

- They shunned the material world and the veneration of material objects, including the relics of saints and the icon of the cross.

- They believed in reincarnation.

- To them, Jesus was cosmic and therefore could not have died on the cross.

- They felt the Roman Catholic Church had altered many of the early Christian teachings for its own gain.

- They believed the spirit grew stronger through prayer and spiritual purity.

The Cathars were branded as heretics by the Roman Catholic Church because they believed in two Gods, one spiritual and good and the other earthly and evil. They denied the physical reality of the crucifixion.

For many years Catharism was the prevalent form of Christianity in large areas of France, Spain and Italy. They called themselves the friends of God and condemned the literalist church as anti-Christ.

They claimed to be the living inheritors of the true Christian heritage that had persisted in secret. Like the original Christians they were vegetarians and believed in reincarnation. They were respected for their goodness even by their opponents.

Despite this the infamous Inquisition was set up by the Roman Catholic Literalist Church especially to eradicate the Cathars, which it did with ferocious enthusiasm, burning men, women and children alive. From 1139 onwards the Roman Church began calling councils specifically to condemn heretics.

Pope Innocent III declared that 'anyone who attempted to construct a personal view of God which conflicted with Church dogma must be burned without pity'. Over two centuries it is estimated that up to one million Cathars were eliminated.

Cathars were perceived as a threat to Roman Catholicism because of their claim to be the living inheritors of the true Christian heritage. Looking at the main points of their beliefs it is easy to see their link with the original teachings of Jesus, particularly in respect of the spirit and the soul and the return to the source (ie God). They were totally against what they considered to be the excesses of the church which again is reminiscent of Jesus' teachings and warnings to the Jews.

For further information read accounts of the Albigensian Crusade.

CHAPTER TWENTY TWO

KABBALAH

Kabbalah is a philosophical system of Jewish thought said to predate any religion. In essence it is thought to be a set of precepts that were provided by the Good Creator God so that people could improve their lives and achieve fulfilment.

It is specifically the complication of traditional Jewish mysticism and attempts to go behind the traditional dogma in order to satisfy the needs which certain individuals have, to experience the divine directly without the enlivenment of an appointed body of 'fathers'.

A traditional Kabbalistic view is that a Kabbalist by virtue of his or her state of consciousness can bring about a real healing. When Moses received the written law he also received certain laws orally which were handed down by word of mouth, but only to the initiated. This oral law is sometimes referred to as Kabbalah.

Kabbalah does not attempt to define God nor does it tell the individual what to believe. It assumes that some level of direct experience of God is feasible and gives practical methods for achieving this. Ritual has always been an integral part of Kabbalah.

HERMETICISM

Hermeticism is very diverse and draws its material from many sources within the mystery 'traditions'. It considers that the whole of mankind is on a spiritual journey that is designed to return to a state of unity with the Mind of God. This state of unity is the prime purpose of Hermeticism; spiritual growth cannot be achieved without human effort. If humanity is to reach the divine, we must aspire to be divine. It is a collection of writings of scholars and sages going back before Christ. Its main tenets are:

- The Divine Creation of the Universe is ultimately good.
- Spiritual and magical practices include the use of meditation and ritual in order to attain access to the higher realms of knowledge.
- The Divine is both within and yet beyond everything.
- In coming to terms with all things a natural balance can be sought.
- It upholds the search for spiritual meaning.
- The divine can be found in the mysteries of nature.
- There is a natural rhythm to life and no necessity for self denial.
- It is not restricted to one God, arising from many expressions of the divine yet it ultimately comes from one source.

Hermeticism and Kabbalah appear to the uninitiated be systems of magic. Each system works on the assumption that spiritual awareness is more important than power over the mundane so they highlight the influence of their non Christian beginnings.

GNOSTICS AND GNOSTICISM

The idea of so called Gnosis and Gnosticism is revealed in the study of Egyptology. The sophisticated and incredibly high levels of sacred knowledge, or gnosis, preserved and enhanced by the Egyptian priesthood, were passed down through successive generations from master to pupil by the process of initiation into the Temple mysteries. They were not used for personal gain by the priestly and royal initiates, for while rank and royal birth undoubtedly carried enormous levels of privilege, sacred knowledge of subjects such as astronomy, agriculture, architecture, building, medicine, mathematics, navigation, and metallurgy was used for the benefit of the entire community served by the priests, the pharaohs and the aristocracy.

Sustained by divinely inspired gnosis and protected by the deserts that surrounded it, Egyptian civilisation developed a degree of sophistication, stability and complexity that has yet to be equalled, much less exceeded. A vast body of esoteric knowledge was recorded within the Pyramid Texts, the Edfu Texts and the *Book of the Dead* as well as being encoded on temple walls and elsewhere. The Edfu Texts in particular refer repeatedly to the 'wisdom of the Sages' and constantly emphasise that, to the Egyptian elite, their most valued gift was knowledge.

The ancient Egyptians had their own unique and effective way of understanding the universe and man's place within it, in a completely different knowledge system from that revered by modern man. This sacred 'way of knowing' could not be adequately transmitted by the normal vehicle of language but could only be taught or shown in myth and symbolism.

Gnosis came to be used generally in the second century BC to refer to a mode of religious thought that claimed to have exclusive information about the origin of the universe and its inhabitants

It taught that the material world was the work of evil powers which had operated in the defiance of the God of Light who was the true and beneficent Sovereign of the Universe.

One of the main things that separated Gnostics from orthodox

Christians was their mysticism, communion with what was considered to be sacred. It began with their views of God and creation. Gnostics perceived the one which they called the true or unknown God as also having a feminine part which was the spirit. Their duality was central to their creation myths and incorporates echoes of Taoism and the principle of Yin and Yang. More importantly, this idea also has links with other pre-Christian-era religions. The core of Gnostic myth rests on the belief that there is a spark of divinity in Humans put there by a supreme divinity. The divinity within each can be awakened and discovered only through the process of contemplation and self-knowledge. The process of internal enlightenment or illumination can best be accomplished with the assistance of a divine mediator or redemption figure. A human instructor can sometimes help, but by and large Gnostics seem to be anti-clerical. Salvation is primarily each individuals own responsibility.

Many Gnostics believed in the existence of a pure spirit world and a corrupt material world from which man, though originally divine, had become separated. Gnostic Christians believed that Jesus has been sent from the Spirit world to impart the knowledge (gnosis) which would enable them to return to their Spiritual world.

Many Christian scholars consider the Gospel of Thomas to be Gnostic insomuch as the majority of the Logos refer to the special knowledge we must learn to be able to reach within ourselves and find our true self.

There is also a school of thought which considers Christ to be a Gnostic, in the Gospel of Mark Ch.4 v.33-34. 'Jesus talked to them with parables, like these, such parables as they were able to hear. And without parables he did not speak to them, but to his disciples among themselves he explained everything.' This is a clear indication that there was some special knowledge (gnosis) which he explained only to his disciples.

In the Gospel of Thomas Logo 17 Jesus says to his disciples:

I will give you what no eye has seen
And what no ear has heard
And what no hand has touched
And what has not arisen in the heart of a man.

And again in Logo 108 Jesus said:

He who drinks from my mouth
Shall become as me
And I myself will become him
And the hidden things shall be manifested.

And finally in Logo 114 Jesus talks of duality

Simon Peter said to them
Let Mary go out from amongst us
Because women are not worthy of the life
Jesus said
Behold I will guide her being
In order that I make her whole
That she shall become a living spirit
Like you males
For every woman who makes herself male
Shall enter the kingdom of the heavens.

This logo needs some common-sense treatment to put it in perspective. Peter wants Mary to leave the group, as only men are worthy of the life Jesus talks about.

Jesus puts duality in place, stating that there is a state in oneness beyond being a woman or a man, and only when that transcended state has been reached will the real self be found. Once again you have to rise above duality so that spiritual truth replaces worldly truth and is independent of time and all things.

In the late second century AD certain Christian theologians decided that the Gnostics were heretics. From their perspective the Gnostics were, but due to the rich and diverse tradition of Christianity which found expression during this century the terms heresy and orthodoxy have no meaning - this had to wait a few centuries until orthodoxy had consolidated.

In 1945 a large number of Gnostic codices were discovered. It was interesting that these writings contained a wide variety of texts revealing a wide variety of traditions - Christian, Platonic, and Hermetic. These texts were finally edited and published in 1978.

It was the sacred knowledge these texts expressed which was important, not the tradition they might have come from. There was an emphasis on *experience* in order to acquire this knowledge.

This brings us to the important difference between knowledge and belief: it can be shown that belief is not an end in itself but a stepping stone towards knowledge. A Sufi story explains this: you can be told not to put your hand into fire because you will get burned and feel pain. You can believe this to be true and during your life never act in this way. But while it affects your actions you can never say that you *know* the effect, that you feel the pain; you simply believe this to be true.

If however, you actually place your hand into the fire you experience the pain directly, you *know* it, and avoid doing it again. So, while the actions of the two people might look the same, one is done from a point of view of knowledge and one is done from a point of view of belief. The Gnostics held that to *know* matters spiritual through *experience* is better than to simply believe.

HINDUISM

Hinduism is a religious tradition which originated in the Indian subcontinent. In contemporary usage Hinduism is also sometimes referred to as Sanatana Dharma, a Sanskrit phrase meaning 'eternal law'. Hinduism, many of whose origins can be traced to the ancient Vedic civilization, is the world's oldest extant religion. A conglomerate of diverse beliefs and traditions, Hinduism has no single founder. It is also the world's third largest religion following Christianity and Islam, with approximately a billion adherents, most of whom live in India and Nepal. Other countries with large Hindu populations include Bangladesh, Sri Lanka, Pakistan, Indonesia, Malaysia, Singapore, Mauritius, Fiji, Suriname, Guyana and Trinidad and Tobago.

Hinduism contains a vast body of scriptures. Divided as revealed and remembered and developed over millennia, these scriptures expound on theology, philosophy and mythology, providing spiritual insights and guidance on the practice of religious living.

Hinduism is based on the accumulated treasury of spiritual laws discovered by different persons in different times. The scriptures were transmitted orally in verse form to aid memorization for many centuries before they were written down. Over the centuries, sages refined the teachings and expanded the canon. In post-Vedic and current Hindu belief, most Hindu scriptures are not typically interpreted literally. More importance is attached to the ethics and metaphorical meanings derived from them.

Hinduism is a diverse system of thought with varied beliefs but devotion to a single God while accepting the existence of other gods, but any such term is an oversimplification of the complexities and variations of belief.

Most Hindus believe that the spirit or soul - the true 'self' of every person is eternal.

Hindu practices generally involve seeking awareness of God and sometimes also seeking blessings. Therefore, Hinduism has developed numerous practices meant to help one think of divinity in the midst of everyday life. Hindus can engage in worship or veneration, either at home or at a temple. At home, Hindus often create a shrine with icons dedicated to the individual's chosen form(s) of God. Temples are usually dedicated to a primary deity along with associated subordinate deities, though some commemorate multiple deities. Visiting temples is not obligatory. In fact, many visit them only during religious festivals. Hindus perform their worship through icons. The icon serves as a tangible link between the worshipper and God. The image is often considered a manifestation of God.

The vast majority of Hindus engage in religious rituals on a daily basis. However, observation of rituals greatly vary among regions, villages, and individuals. Devout Hindus perform daily chores such as worshipping at dawn after bathing (usually at a family shrine, and typically lighting a lamp and offering foodstuffs before the images of deities), recitation from religious scripts, singing devotional hymns, meditation, chanting mantras, reciting scriptures etc.

A notable feature in religious ritual is the division between purity and pollution. Religious acts presuppose some degree of impurity or defilement for the practitioner, which must be overcome or neutralised before or during ritual procedures. Purification, usually with water, is thus a typical feature of most religious action. Other characteristics include a belief in the effectiveness of sacrifice and a concept of merit, gained through the performance of charity or good works that will accumulate over time and reduce sufferings in the next world.

ISLAM

The rise of Islam begins with the Prophet Muhammad, who was born in the city of Mecca in about 570 AD and orphaned at the age of six. In the year 610 Muhammad received the first of a series of revelations from Allah (God). These occurred over a period of twenty-three years, and were memorised and dictated by Muhammad to his companions. These revelations are known as the Qur'an or Koran (which means 'reading'), the sacred book of Islam.

Through the visionary experiences of prophet Mohammed the Islamic tradition affirmed the creation stories of Genesis and added stories found in early Jewish folklore.

In addition Islam contains another creation tradition not encountered before. Allah offered the divine image to the living beings who had preceded humanity, but they declined it. So humanity took on board the divine image found at creation.

The Koran describes the human journey as a return to the

original condition of the divine image found at creation. It clearly states that this is not a new religious message but just a revival of an ancient religion of submission to the divine who had no name.

Almost in reverse of what happened in Judaism and Christianity, individual mystics and ascetics took up the spiritual practices associated with the creation story as they sought to bring an inner dimension back to faith.

An early saying of Mohammed indicates that this primordial religion is simply the recovering of one's original divine image. Every child is born according to primordial nature, and then their parents make them into a Jew, Christian, a Muslim or any other so-called religion.

Muhammad's message was not favourably accepted by all people of Mecca. Subjected to economic social and economic boycott by the powerful merchants of Mecca, Muhammad, his family and followers emigrated to the town of Yathrib (which later acquired the name Medina, 'the city of the prophet') in the year 622. This event (known as the Hira, 'emigration') is regarded by Muslims as the starting point of Islamic history. From this point Muhammad gradually consolidated his power in the region. After repelling a Meccan attack on Medina in 627, he was able to take control of Mecca itself in 629. By the time of his death in 632 all but a few isolated pockets of Arabia were under Muhammad's control.

Islam is an Arabic word which means 'peace' and the act of resignation to God. Muslims believed that Muhammad was the last of a line of prophets which began with Adam. Each prophet was sent to remind people of the will of God. Islam holds that the messages of all prophets has but one essence and a core composed of two elements. First is *tawhid*, the acknowledgement that there is only one God and that all worship, service and obedience are due to Him alone. The second is morality, which the Koran defines as service to God, doing good and avoiding evil. Muslims attribute particular importance to social service, alleviating other people's suffering and helping the needy.

Islam assumes that all people are born innocent and capable through their reason and conscience of discerning good and evil. Adam's disobedience was his own personal error, for which he was forgiven by God when he repented. Since Muslims do not believe in original sin they do not believe in the need to be saved from sin. Salvation is acquired through performing good deeds, not through the mediation of a saviour.

Another feature of Islam is the absence of clergy. The preacher does not have a different sacramental status from the laity. Jews, Christians and Sabaeans are referred to as 'People of the Book'; this means that they are tolerated and protected when under Islamic jurisdiction. Islamic teaching believes in a Last Day when the world will come to an end, the dead will be resurrected and everyone will be judged according to their deeds. According to the Torah there is no intercession, although God, in his mercy, may forgive sinners. Those who are condemned will go to hellfire; those who are saved will enjoy the pleasures of Paradise.

Islamic practice is based on what are called the five pillars of faith. The first is the *shahadah* (the confession of faith): 'there is no God but Allah and Muhammad is his messenger'.

The second is *salat* (the performance of five daily prayers). These prayers occur before sunrise, between mid-day and mid-afternoon, between mid-afternoon and sunset, immediately after sunset and between twilight and dawn. Before worshipping it is necessary to wash the hands, mouth and teeth, arms, face, nose and feet. When Muslims pray they always face the Ka'ba in Mecca. Congregational prayers are held on Friday; otherwise, Muslims can pray on their own or with others.

Zakat, the third pillar, is the payment of 2.5% of one's total income to the state for distribution to the poor and less fortunate. The term zakat literally means 'purification', suggesting that wealth is defiling unless shared with others.

Sawm, the fourth pillar, is the practice of fasting. During the month of Ramadan Muslims are required to abstain from food, drink and sex each day from dawn to sunset (children, the sick and those journeying are exempt from the requirement to fast). The purpose of the fast is to cultivate spiritual, moral and physical self-discipline. The end of Ramadan is marked by a festival called Eid al-Fitr, which Muslims celebrate with congregational prayer that first morning after Ramadan with gifts and visits to relatives and friends.

The fifth pillar is the *Hadj*, a pilgrimage to the shrine called the Ka'ba in Mecca which is incumbent once in the life of all Muslims whose health and financial resources enable them to make the journey.

Muslims believe that the Ka'ba was the first house of God on earth built by the Prophet Ibrahim, and this is commemorated by the Hadj. Another event that is commemorated by Muslims is Muhammad's ascent into heaven from Jerusalem. The mosque known as the Dome on the Rock in Jerusalem is believed to have been built on the spot where Muhammad ascended into heaven.

SUFISM

Sufism, or *Tasawwuf* as it is known in the Muslim world, is Islamic mysticism. Non-Muslims often mistake it for a sect of Islam, but it is more accurately described as an aspect or dimension of Islam. Sufi orders (Tariqas) can be found in Sunni, Shia and other Islamic groups, Ibn Khaldun, the 14th century Arab historian, described Sufism as 'dedication to worship, total dedication to Allah most high, disregard for the finery and ornament of the world, abstinence from the pleasure, wealth, and prestige sought by most men, and retiring from others to worship alone'.

Ibn Khaldun's words are an accurate description of Sufis today. Sufis are, among other things, sagacious, cheerful and disarming. Sufis share these personality traits because they are emphatic that Islamic knowledge should be learned from teachers and not exclusively from books. Tariqas can trace their teachers back through the generations to the Prophet himself. Modelling themselves on their teachers, students hope that they too will glean something of the Prophetic character.

Although Sufis are relatively few in number they have shaped Islamic thought and history. Through the centuries Sufis have contributed hugely to Islamic literature for example Rumi, Omar Khayyam and Al-Ghazzali's influence extended beyond Muslim lands to be quoted by Western philosophers, writers and theologians. Sufis were influential in spreading Islam, particularly to the furthest outposts of the Muslim world in Africa, India and the Far East. Today Sufism remains part of Muslim culture and many Muslims critical of Sufism eventually laud it or even join its ranks.

Sufism is called 'the way to the heart', which of course means the centre. The name Sufi may have been developed or derived from Sophia, which is the concept of wisdom spoken of again and again in esoteric literature and which has come down today through many faiths.

Sufism is a mystic tradition of Islam similar to the Albigensians or Cathars of the Christians, who were known as the pure ones. However no one is sure of the origin of the movement, although it probably predates Islam.

Sufism then is the mystical side of Islam. To be a true mystic one must know oneself and one's own unconscious world. Not everybody has the time and will to do this, while some seem to be able to do it almost by accident.

The Sufi message is a message of 'spiritual liberty', revealing in its essence the true nature of spirituality as being the liberation from dogmas and preconceived ideas. And in its call for unity of spiritual ideals, the Sufi message offers a source of inspiration, reaching far beyond such feelings as 'my religion' as opposed to 'your religion', because there is only one religion and several interpretations of the one truth.

The unity of religious ideals is followed unconditionally in search of truth, without going astray in following the followers of the followers of the great religious reformers, whose messages have been altered beyond recognition through the centuries by those who confuse mysticism with fanaticism.

The Sufis see themselves as moving through his world as if they are part of it and always knowing that there is much more. They feel at all times the Divine presence.

The present-day Sufi movement is a movement of members of different nations and races united together in the ideal of wisdom;

they believe that wisdom does not belong to any particular religion or race, but to the human race as a whole. It is a divine property which mankind has inherited, and it is in this realization that the Sufis, in spite of belonging to different nationalities, races, beliefs, and faiths, still unite and work for humanity in the ideal of wisdom.

In short, Sufism means to know one's true being, to know the purpose of one's life, and to know how to accomplish that purpose. Through disappointment many say 'I shall probably never be successful in my life', not realising that man is born to do what he longs to do, and that success is natural, while failure is unnatural. When man is himself, the whole world is his own; when he is not himself, then even this self does not belong to him. Then he does not know what he is, where he is, nor why he is here on earth; then he is less useful to himself and to others than a rock.

It is in self-realization that the mystery of the whole of life is centred. It is the remedy of all maladies; it is the secret of success in all walks of life; it is a religion and more than a religion. And at this time when the whole world is upset, the Sufi message conveys to the world the divine message. What is wrong with humanity today is that it is not itself, and all the misery of the world is caused by this. Therefore nothing can answer the need of humanity save this process of the sages and the wise of all ages which leads souls to self-realization.

The Sufi sees the divine presence reflected in all names and forms, and is limited by none. Knowing that no man-made distinction can contain the One Being, the Sufi offers sincere respect to all forms of worship, while ever striving to be free of dogmatic limitation.

The shrine of Nizam–ud-din was featured in a Channel 4

documentary in 2008 entitled Sufi Soul. At this shrine, which is widely renowned as a meeting place for those of all faiths, one worshipper remarked 'What is nice about this place is that no one is Hindu, Muslim, Sikh or Christian, all faiths pray together. I've found a lamp of love here for all religions, it's like a beacon.'

The Great Sufi mystic poet Jelalludin Rumi, also known as Mevlana, states in one of his poems that the love of God lifts us above all the divisions of religion: 'I enter the Mosque, the Synagogue, the Church and the Temple and I see but one God.'

PURITANISM

The Puritans were a group of people who grew discontented with the Church of England and worked towards religious, moral, and societal reforms. The writings and ideas of John Calvin, a leader in the Reformation, gave rise to Protestantism and were pivotal to the Christian revolt. They contended that the Church of England had become a product of political struggles and man-made doctrines. The Puritans were one branch of dissenters who decided that the Church of England was beyond reform. Escaping persecution from Church leadership and the King, they went eventually to America.

The Puritans believed that the Bible was God's true law, and that it provided a plan for living. The established Church of the day described access to God as monastic and possible only within the confines of Church authority. Puritans stripped away the traditional trappings and formalities of the Christianity which had been slowly building throughout the previous 1500 years. Theirs was an attempt to purify the Church and their own lives.

What many of us remember about the Puritans is reflective of the modern definition of the term and not of the historical account. They were not a small group of people. In England many of their persuasion sat in Parliament. So great was the struggle that England's Civil War pitted the Puritans against the Crown Forces. Though the Puritans won the fight with Oliver Cromwell's leadership, their victory was short-lived; hence their displacement to America.

Most of the Puritans settled in the New England area. As they immigrated and formed individual colonies, their numbers rose from 17,800 in 1640 to 106,000 in 1700. Religious exclusiveness was the foremost principle of their society. The spiritual beliefs that they held were strong. This strength held over to include community laws and customs. Since God was at the forefront of their minds, He was to motivate all of their actions. This premise worked both for them and against them.

The common unity strengthened the community. In a foreign land surrounded by the hardships of pioneer life, their spiritual bond made them sympathetic to each other's needs. Their overall survival techniques permeated the colonies and on the whole made them more successful in several areas beyond that of the colonies established to their south.

Each Church congregation was to be individually responsible to God, as was each person. The New Testament was their model and their devotion so great that it permeated their entire society. People of opposing theological views were asked to leave the community or to be converted.

Their interpretation of scriptures was a harsh one. In principle, they emphasized conversion and not repression. Conversion was a rejection of the 'worldliness' of society and a strict adherence to

Biblical principles. While repression was not encouraged in principle, it was evident in their actions. God could forgive anything, but man could forgive only by seeing a change in behaviour. Actions spoke louder than words, so actions had to be constantly controlled.

The doctrine of predestination kept all Puritans constantly working to do good in this life to be chosen for the next eternal one. God had already chosen who would be in heaven or hell, and each believer had no way of knowing which group they were in. Those who were wealthy were obviously blessed by God and were in good standing with Him. The Protestant work ethic was the belief that hard work was an honour to God which would lead to a prosperous reward. Any deviations from the normal way of Puritan life met with strict disapproval and discipline. Since the Church elders were also political leaders, any Church infraction was also a social one. There was no margin for error.

The devil was behind every evil deed. Constant watch needed to be kept in order to stay away from his clutches. Words of hellfire and brimstone flowed from the mouths of eloquent ministers as they warned of the persuasiveness of the devil's power. The sermons of Jonathan Edwards, a Puritan minister, show that delivery of these sermons became an art form. They were elegant, well-formed, exegetical renditions of scriptures, with a healthy dose of fear woven throughout the fabric of the literary construction. Schoolchildren were quizzed on the material at school and at home. This constant subjection of the probability of an unseen danger led to a scandal of epidemic proportions.

Great pains were taken to warn members and especially their children of the dangers of the world. Religiously motivated, they were exceptional in their time for their interest in the education of their children. Reading of the Bible was necessary to living a pious life. The education of the next generation was important to further 'purify' the church and perfect social living.

Three English diversions were banned in the New England colonies, drama, religious music and erotic poetry. The first and last of these led to immorality. Music in worship created a 'dreamy' state which was not conducive in listening to God. Since the people were not spending their time idly indulged in trivialities, they were left with two godly diversions.

The Bible stimulated corporate intellect by promoting discussions of literature. Greek classics in the works of Cicero, Virgil, Terence and Ovid were taught, as well as poetry and Latin verse. They were encouraged to create their own poetry, always religious in content.

For the first time in history, free schooling was offered for all children. Puritans formed the first formal school in 1635, called the Roxbury Latin School. Four years later, the first American College was established, Harvard in Cambridge. Children aged 6-8 attended a 'Dame School' where the teacher, usually a widow, taught reading. 'Ciphering' (maths) and writing were low on the academic agenda.

In 1638, the first printing press arrived. By 1700, Boston had become the second largest publishing centre of the English Empire. The Puritans were the first to write books for children and to discuss the difficulties in communicating with them. At a time when other Americans were physically blazing trails through the forests, the Puritans' efforts in areas of study were advancing the country intellectually.

Religion provided a stimulus and prelude for scientific thought. Of those Americans who were admitted into the scientific Royal Society of London, the vast majority were New England Puritans.

The large number of people who subscribed to the lifestyle of the Puritans did much to establish a presence on American soil. Bound together, they established a community that maintained a healthy economy, established a school system, and focused an efficient eye on political concerns. The traditional moral character of England and America was shaped in part by the words and actions of this strong group of Christian believers.

THE SOCIETY OF FRIENDS - THE QUAKERS

In 1643 George Fox, a shoemaker from Fenny Drayton, Leicestershire, began touring the country giving sermons in which he argued that consecrated buildings and ordained ministers were irrelevant to the individual seeking God.

Fox formed a group called the Friends of Truth. Later they became known as the Society of Friends. Fox's central dogma was that of the inner light, communicated directly to the individual soul by Christ. Eventually members of the Society of Friends became known as the Quakers.

During the reign of Charles II, 13,562 Quakers were arrested and imprisoned in England and 198 were transported as slaves. 338 died in prison, or of wounds received in violent assaults on their meetings. The Society of Friends continued to grow and by 1660 Fox had made more than 20,000 converts. Missionaries were at work in Ireland, Scotland, Wales and the American colonies. After considerable debate, the Society of Friends evolved a form of organisation with regular monthly, quarterly, and annual meetings.

Quakers believe that there is something of God in everybody and that each human being is of unique worth. This is why Quakers value all people equally, and oppose anything that may harm or threaten them.

Quakers seek religious truth in inner experience, and place great reliance on conscience as the basis of morality.

They emphasise direct experience of God rather than ritual and ceremony. They believe that priests and rituals are an unnecessary obstruction between the believer and God.

Quakers integrate religion and everyday life. They believe God can be found in the middle of everyday life and human relationships, as much as during a meeting for worship.

Among key Quaker beliefs are:

- God is love
- The light of God is in every single person
- A person who lets their life be guided by that light will achieve a full relationship with God
- Everyone can have a direct, personal relationship with God without involving a priest or minister
- Redemption and the Kingdom of Heaven are to be experienced now, in this world

TAIZE

The influence of the Taize community on the Church in the UK and throughout the world has been pretty remarkable. A monastic community in a small village in Burgundy, it has never advertised, or recruited, or marketed its style of worship. But all over Britain, and throughout the world, there are churches running weekly Taize services, or which incorporate its style and approach into services.

This is simply because since Brother Roger Schutz founded the community during the Second World War, Christians have dropped in, been impressed and spread the good news abroad. Up to 5,000 people a week visit the brothers, who number only 100.

The emphasis of its style is on silence, light, and above all the meditative weaving together of prayer and music. Taize is also deeply committed to religious unity, and although its founders were all Protestants, it drew on various Christian traditions.

Brother Roger first started the community in 1940 as a sanctuary for wartime refugees, including Jews and later German POWs. He only prayed alone in his room or the nearby woods, not wanting to pressurise non-Christian guests.

BAHAI

The Bahai Faith is the youngest of the world's independent religions. From its obscure beginnings in Iran during the mid-nineteenth century, it has now spread to virtually every part of the world, established administrative institutions in over 200 independent states and major territories and embraced believers from virtually every cultural, racial, social and religious background.

Bahais believe that there is only one God, the Creator of the Universe. Throughout history, God has revealed Himself to humanity through a series of divine messengers, each of whom has founded a great religion. The messengers have included Abraham,

Krishna, Zoroaster, Moses, Buddha, Jesus, and Muhammad. This succession of divine teachers reflects a single historic 'plan of God' for educating humanity about the Creator and for cultivating the spiritual, intellectual, and moral capacities of the race. The goal has been to develop the innate noble characteristics of every human being and to prepare the way for an advancing global civilisation.

Knowledge of God's will for humanity in the modern age, Bahais believe, was revealed just over one hundred years ago by Bahaullah, who is the latest of these divine Messengers. In the Bahai view, the purpose of this life on earth is for each individual to develop the spiritual and moral qualities that are at the core of his or her nature. Bahaullah referred to the human being as a '*mine rich in gems of inestimable value*'. These 'gems' or qualities can be 'mined' or developed only when a person turns to God. But while this awesome task must remain the responsibility of the individual, humanity has received continual guidance from a loving Creator on how to accomplish it. The Bahai conceptions of human nature and the soul, then, are essentially positive, as are Bahai views on the purpose of life and life after death.

According to Bahai teachings human nature is fundamentally spiritual. Although human beings exist on earth in physical bodies, the essential identity of each person is defined by an invisible rational and everlasting soul.

The soul animates the body and distinguishes human beings from the animals. It grows and develops only through the individual's relationship with God.

Cultivation of life's spiritual side has several benefits. First, the individual increasingly develops those innate qualities which lie at the foundation of human happiness and social progress. Such qualities include faith, courage, compassion, trustworthiness and humility. As these qualities are increasingly manifest, society as a whole advances.

Another effect of spiritual development is alignment with God's will. This growing closer to God prepares the individual for the afterlife. The soul lives on after the body's death, embarking on a spiritual journey towards God through many 'worlds' or planes of existence. Progress on this journey, in traditional terms, is likened to 'Heaven'. If the soul fails to develop, one remains distant from God. This condition of remoteness from God can in some sense be understood as 'Hell'. Thus, heaven and hell are regarded not as literal places but descriptions of one's spiritual progress toward the light of God.

Bahaullah emphases the fundamental obligation of human beings to acquire knowledge with their 'open eyes and not through the eyes of others'. One of the main sources of conflict in the world today is the fact that many people blindly and uncritically follow various traditions, movements and opinions. God has given each human being a mind and the capacity to differentiate truth from falsehood. If individuals fail to use their reasoning capacities and choose instead to accept without question certain opinions and ideas, either out of admiration or from fear of those who hold them, then they are neglecting their basic moral responsibility as human beings. Moreover, when people act in his way, they often become attached to some particular opinion or tradition and thus intolerant of those who do not share it. Such attachments can, in turn, lead to conflict.

The fact that we imagine ourselves to be right and everybody else wrong is the greatest of all obstacles in the path towards unity, and unity is necessary if we would reach truth, for truth is one.

FREEMASONRY

Freemasonry has been described by its critics as a secret society. It is not and never has been a secret society, though as with many other societies, religions and organisations throughout the world, it *is* a society with secrets. Much has been written about Freemasonry and the information is widely available in bookshops and libraries.

Although many of its historians claim Freemasonry's origins to be in the 17th century in England there are many who claim that it has a much older pedigree. This is hard to substantiate, as there is a lack of tangible written evidence.

As with religion, much of its history is oral, which probably accounts for the lack of proof of early beginnings, but within its ritual (a common form of passing on oral information) is to be found the following passage:

'The usages and customs among Freemasons have ever borne a near affinity to those of the ancient Egyptians. Their philosophers unwilling to expose their mysteries to vulgar eyes couched their systems of learning and polity under signs and hieroglyphical figures which were communicated to their chief priests or MAGI alone, who were bound by solemn oath to conceal them. The system of Pythagoras was founded on a similar principle as are many others of more recent date. Masonry however is not only the most ancient but the most honourable society that ever existed, as there is not a character or emblem here depicted but serves to inculcate the principles of piety and virtue among all its genuine professors.'

This was written in the eighteenth century, being first published in 1772. Does any of it seem familiar? have we heard of some of these ideas and principles before?

Freemasonry offers the following description of itself in one of its Ritual Dramas. It is a peculiar system of morality, veiled in allegory and illustrated by symbols. The three grand principles on which the order was founded are cited as brotherly love, relief and truth. Are these 17th century inventions, or do they go back to the earliest teachings of Jesus, or even before?

During his introduction into Freemasonry a candidate is urged to study as much of the liberal arts and sciences as may lie within the compass of his attainment. Later he is permitted to extend his researches into the hidden mysteries of nature and science, in much the same way as our forefathers studied and understood the cosmos and Creation.

Even more important is an address delivered to an initiate at his initiation ceremony reminding him of the important duties he owes to God by never mentioning his name but with that awe and reverence due of the creature to his Creator and to his neighbour by rendering him every kind office which justice or mercy may require by relieving his necessities and by soothing his afflictions. This is fairly consistent with the first two great Commandments.

FREEMASONRY AND GNOSTICISM

There are those who would say that Freemasonry has a Gnostic centre; others would vehemently disagree. Yet, it is true that the spirituality of Freemasonry is drawn from many traditions and is concerned, through the type of ritual, with experience. That is not to say that performing the ritual correctly inevitably produces such an effect.

We need to look deeply into the key points of the ritual,

because it is there that we find the value of experience and knowledge over belief. Thus intellect can take you only so far. This is quite obvious if we remember for a moment that language - that which carries and communicates enquiry - has its limitations; it cannot deal with anything ineffable. Poetry is probably the closest it can get.

Freemasons are told to listen to the voice of nature. It is that which speaks from the silence and stillness. If the genuine secrets are to be found in the centre, and, if within the centre is found that point of silence and stillness, that source of the voice of nature, then 'a Master Mason cannot err'.

The Gnostics used the symbol of a spark of divinity being trapped within every person. Masonic ritual speaks of the rising of the 'bright morning star'. What is this star? Is it a hint that we wait for the discovery of the fragment of divinity within? In both Gnosticism and Christianity, this divinity - and any fragment - is termed 'the Word.'

Now, can we see the search for the lost word as the search for the spark of divinity hidden within each and every one of us - a treasure hidden but able to be found after a search? And is that the moment when 'time or circumstances' restores to us our heritage and allows us to move from belief to the certainty of knowledge?

Every Freemason has solemnly sworn never to reveal any of the secrets or mysteries of masonry - but what exactly is meant by that?

There is no doubt that in medieval times the secrets of the operative masons were very practical indeed. They included the methods of proving uprights and horizontals, the knowledge of tools and their uses, and - perhaps the most important - the ability to construct an angle of ninety degrees to ensure that a stone was square. These secrets took a considerable time to learn and involved a long apprenticeship, followed by years as a craftsman, before eventually perhaps becoming a Master of the Art.

Only in that way could the true mystery - or mastery - of an operative mason be preserved and passed on to future generations. But, of course, then as now, there were unscrupulous cowboy builders - they called them Cowans in those days - who would offer to build or repair a structure without possessing the genuine knowledge. Such men would sometimes endeavour to infiltrate lodges of operative masons and try to obtain the secrets the easy way, without being worthily recommended and properly prepared. It was to prevent such conduct that passwords and tokens were entrusted to a genuine mason so that they could identify themselves if, for instance, they moved to another town and sought work there. Is it so improbable that such practices were also observed by the ancient builders whose techniques were carried down from generation to generation, in much the same way that son once followed father followed grandfather, and so on?

Freemasons are not now all operative, but they are free and accepted or speculative. So what are the secrets they pledge to keep inviolate? Words, signs and tokens? Yes, of course, but these are a mere detail. The real secret of Freemasonry cannot be described at all; it is something that can only be learned by experience, by humanity and patience.

It is really as a test of trustworthiness that candidates are obligated to secrecy. If they keep the promise about little things, then it is easier to have confidence in them about greater things. To quote from the Bible: 'He that is faithful in that which is least, is faithful also in much'.

Freemasonry brings men into a more moral and more socially-responsible way of life. But it does more than this. Masonic rituals gently but methodically guide and initiate each man though the degrees until, symbolically, the limits of mortality are bought to the forefront of attention. Once there the mason is confronted with the question of who he really is, and he is asked to fix his thoughts upon the glimmering ray of light from above. Where have we seen the importance of light before in our studies? We have in Freemasonry, I believe, a distant but actual echo of those ancient mysteries; an echo of ancient Egypt.

But the resonance between the first degrees of Freemasonry is not restricted in their beginnings. If we view the whole of Freemasonry as an allegory of a journey, leading from birth through life to death and perfection, then within each of those degrees we find pilgrimages within the overall journey.

Freemasonry has an important spiritual significance. Though the rituals have been clouded by later additions, enough remains for us to see what our forefathers were trying to do. There is no dogma in Freemasonry- it is not a Religion. It says only that if you practise its tenets and principles you will become wiser. Its final goal is the wisdom and truth to which we dedicate our hearts. It is a system with philosophical principles which has psychological effects on those who practice it.

The truths of the Masonic system are communicated by allegorical two-part plays, much the same as the medieval mystery plays. These plays are three in number, each one referred to as a 'degree', or in other words a grade of achievement. Each degree is conferred on an aspirant, or candidate, by means of a ritual form of words, actions, movements, much as any stage play is conducted.

The aspirant has the degree conferred on him in the Lodge and the actual conferral is made by the Master of the Lodge.

Since Freemasonry works according to allegory, the first degree is concerned with birth - birth of the spirit, the emergence out of darkness, or unknowing, into the light of knowledge, the knowledge of the self. The second degree is concerned with light and life and, most importantly, the intellectual and moral growth each individual experiences on his journey. The third degree explores the transfiguration possible at the end of life, and suggests the death of the old, unregenerated person, to give way to the spirit seeking perfection and wholeness.

Initiation into mysteries has followed many different paths through history, and indeed from prehistoric times. In the first degree, that of initiation, the aspirant is first tested to see that he is free, or seeks to be free, of the attachments of the material world - wealth, power, doctrine and dogma, political or ideological considerations. After this, the Master questions him as to his motives for wishing to be initiated - are his motives free of selfish or self-centred notions? Does he sincerely wish to work for the betterment of himself and the society of which he forms a part? The aspirant undertakes three symbolic pilgrimages in the lodge during his testing. The allegorical light which he is then able to attain becomes, he learns, the light of knowledge and truth.

In the second degree, the aspirant learns of his responsibility to his fellow men. He symbolically follows the path of those in King Solomon's temple who ascended to the Middle Chamber of that Temple. They went there to make restitution for past transgressions and to receive their spiritual wages as a reward for making moral progress in themselves. In the process, the aspirant's intellect, the intellect of the heart, is engaged.

In the third, sublime degree, the aspirant learns that he must now renounce his former unregenerated self and seek perfection. Now he understands that the light of the first degree, and the understanding or intellect of the second degree, have been calling him to a pursuit of the path leading to perfection of his character, of his being, his true self: the same message that Jesus tried to convey to his Disciples.

Fundamentally, Freemasonry is a code for living based on the highest ethical and moral standards. Among its principal aims are:

- To promote the brotherhood of man under the Fatherhood of God;
- To render practical aid to the less fortunate members of the community;
- To develop such behaviour in daily life as will demonstrate that the teachings of the Order have a profound and beneficial effect on all who sincerely embrace its precepts;
- To encourage the practice of every moral and social virtue.

Membership is open to all men of good reputation and integrity, of any race or religion, who can fulfil the one essential qualification that the applicant believes in a supreme being. He is also required to acknowledge obedience to lawful authority and the laws of the land in which he resides.

The lessons of Freemasonry are based upon the Volume of the Sacred Law, while it is founded on the principles of the brotherhood of man under the Fatherhood of God, and the acknowledgement of a Supreme Being. It has preserved the right of each individual soul from all sects and creeds while requiring its members to tolerate, revere and respect, or at least regard with clarity, that which his fellows hold sacred.

Masonry does not divide men; it unites them, leaving every man free to think his own thought and fashion his own system of ultimate truth. All its emphasis rests upon two extremely simple and profound principles - love of God and love of man. Or in other words, the first two commandments.

At the end of the Masonic ritual journey, the true journey has only just begun. How many times has this same point been reached as we have travelled on through our quest?

CHAPTER 23

❦

Conclusion

THE EGO AND THE SOUL (THE TRUE SELF)

I have been trying to find the basis of what Jesus actually said. He is always trying to teach us to abandon the ego and find our true self which is within us all. And when we do find our true self, we will find God our divine creator.

So what is the difference between the ego and the soul?

The ego

- The ego believes that everything is separate from everything else that it perceives. In other words, you're split apart from the person sitting next to you, the house in which you live, the world that supports your existence, and the Universe that contains all life. Of course in the end, and most especially, you are separate from God.

- Because you're isolated and alone, you must find a way to defend your life from all the other things that may and probably will attack you. If you don't, then something - at one point or another - is going to come along and claim you. This is what the ego calls death.

- Since death is the only thing that the ego is completely sure of, it must live in fear. It's afraid of almost everything, because there's no way to know which part of the 'separate' universe will attempt to claim its life.

- One way for the ego to ward off death, at least for a little while, is to gather as many worldly possessions as possible. Anything that seems to have value will do, but the ego prefers the *big stuff*. The grander the house, the more comfortable the ego feels - until, of course, it realizes that nothing can secure its life. It keeps searching, hoping to find the next big thing that might keep it alive. But in the end, everything fails no matter how grandiose, and the ego dies as surely as everything else is created and perceives.

The soul, or true self

- The soul never seeks to *get* anything, because it knows that it already possesses everything of value. Why? Because the soul knows that everything flows easily and naturally in its direction when it is aligned with its Divine Source. God, abundance, ideal relationships and security aren't the goals but are achieved without effort.

- Where the ego seeks to *get*, believing that it then possesses whatever it needs, the soul seeks to *give*, knowing that its needs are already fulfilled.

- The soul understands that death isn't real because whatever is real can't be injured or threatened in any way. Fear, therefore, is overcome because the soul knows itself to be invulnerable, perfectly protected from any perceived threat or error.

It goes without saying that the ego, with all its defences and desire, isn't real, or at the very least, it is a shadow of reality. Yet we have built our entire existence on believing in this illusion, putting all our faith in its assertions and endowing it with its own world where it can conquer and rule.

Matthew 6:24: No man can serve two masters for either he will hate the one and like the other or he will honour one and despise the other. You cannot have good and mammon (i.e. wealth/ego).

CHAPTER 24

❧

What if?

Early in 2007 the UK national press carried a story that the remains of Jesus had been found. Apparently in 1980 in Talpiol, Jerusalem, a tomb was found during excavations. Between 30 BC and 70 AD a common burial practice in Jerusalem was to wrap the body in a shroud and place it in a tomb. A year later, when the flesh had decomposed, the bones would then be put in an ossuary and reburied. Six of the ten ossuaries in the Talpiol tomb had inscriptions which included the names of Jesus, Mary and Judah, son of Jesus. However the names were very common at that time. And it has been estimated that nearly a quarter of all Jewish 1st century women were called Miriam (Mary).

If we consider the consequences if it really were the body of Jesus Christ, where would that leave the Christian faith? St Paul said 'If Christ is not risen from the dead our preaching is useless and so is our faith'. Why, I ask, must this be true when our fundamental and basic belief is in God? What is resurrection? Is it the resurrection of the body or of the soul, the inner part of all of us which Jesus tried to teach us to find within ourselves? The very essence of his teachings is what the early so-called Christian Church tried to eradicate; it very nearly succeeded.

Why is the Resurrection story not mentioned in St Mark's

Gospel? Is it perhaps because Mark knew that the Resurrection meant the resurrection of the soul, that the only true path to God was through your own heart? As we are all made in God's likeness, if we wish to return whence we came we must divest ourselves from all our worldly possessions and seek the Kingdom of God through our own inner being. Surely this is what Jesus was teaching, what he was all about. Too often we are all too willing to deify Jesus and forget that what we are seeking is a reunification or a Resurrection with God.

I believe God's people can all worship Him without any religious obligations. Let us regard spirituality as the religion of the heart, wherein the unity of religious ideals is followed unconditionally in search of truth, without going astray. Instead we have been following the messages of the great religious reformers, whose text has been altered beyond recognition through the centuries by those who confuse mysticism with fanaticism.

There should be no place for comparisons or preferences. All messengers and prophets should be regarded with the same respect and their messages worshipped with the same veneration. Knowing that Buddha was not a Buddhist, Christ was not a Christian and Mohammed was not a Mohammedan is unimportant. They were bringers of new impulses of the Divine Message.

Through the ages there has been one religious belief after another, but each one came as a confirmation of the previous one. Now, in our century and with the development of science and communication, it has become clear that each religion had a special purpose to fulfil at a particular period of human development. One can only be really attuned to any religion if one's heart is open to all religious beliefs, with the same love and understanding for each.

It seems to me that the whole point of what Jesus was trying to tell us has been missed. All kinds of Christians, or to be exact, people who call themselves Christians, are inflexible in their own perception of what is meant by being a Christian. This is because of a systematic indoctrination by the Church of their choice or persuasion, usually in the form of a Creed.

If we believe in the first two commandments and live our lives practising truth, showing brotherly love and bestowing charity when we can, then these surely are the principles taught by Jesus. Why then is it necessary to have to accede or believe in any creed which introduces specific conditions to be observed in order to practise the basic belief contained in the first two commandments?

In a way it does not matter if the Gospels are part fact and part fiction or have been changed beyond recognition. What does matter is their basic story - truth, love and charity and a belief in one God. Why then must the teaching of the religious institutions be so dogmatic, implying that you must do it this way or believe these conditions and if you don't then you cannot call yourself a Christian, or whatever other faith you may follow? I feel very strongly that this kind of institutional indoctrination serves only to divide mankind instead of uniting it under one banner as the REAL Jesus taught.

We should all try to experience 'spiritual liberty', the liberation from dogmas, creeds and preconceived ideas. In a call for unity of spiritual ideals, let us offer a source of inspiration, reaching far beyond such feelings as 'my religion' as opposed to 'your religion', because there is only one religion and many interpretations of the one truth.

In many respects the Gospel of Thomas sends forth this

message, a message the Disciples failed to fully understand and one that was crushed, obliterated and almost wiped off the face of the earth by 'organised' religious institutions.

Jesus, in the Gospel of Thomas, explains the theory and Mark expands it. It is my considered opinion that we should all go forth in peace, love one another and try to grasp the message that Jesus tried so hard to pass on - that the real Kingdom of God is here now, within us. It is ours to seek and understand. Now it is time to go back to basics, time to understand Jesus' message. Who He was, where He came from, whether He was married, had children or whatever, are unimportant compared to His message. The fact is that His disciples found difficulty understanding it in simple terms - 'if you do what I tell you and learn and understand, then you will find God within yourself'.

Every one of us who has not recognised the image of God in himself, has not seen the artist who made us what we are, has deprived himself of a vision most sacred and holy, and an understanding of all of creation.

Mark 7:14 - Then Jesus called all the people and said to them

15 - Hear me all of you and understand
There is nothing outside of a man if it should enter him which can defile him but what goes out of him, that defiles man.

16 - He who has ears to hear let him hear

17 - When Jesus entered into the house his disciples asked him concerning that parable

18 - And he said to them 'So even you find it hard to understand. Do you not know that whatever enters into a man from outside cannot defile him?

19 - *Because it does not enter into his heart, but into his stomach, and then is thrown out through his intestines, thereby purifying the food.*

20 - *It is what goes out of man which defiles the man.*

21 - *For from within, from the hearts of men come evil thoughts, such as fornication, adultery, theft, murder,*

22 - *Extortion, wickedness, deceit, lust, an evil eye, blasphemy, pride, foolishness;*

23 - *All these faults come from within, and they defile the man.*

CHAPTER 25

Back to a new beginning

Every time a lost tribe is discovered as more Amazonian rainforest is destroyed to supply the demands of the world for wood, so history repeats itself. One by one they are sucked into the 'modern' way of life. It has happened a thousand times in many lands all over the world; Africans, Aborigines, Desert Nomads, jungle people, all have been embroiled in the march to modernisation, all have succumbed to the big organisations. Their culture, their oral legends, have been slowly eroded and will become changed as they are written down and recorded for posterity to suit the modern world. We have seen it happen before, all through the history of the world and nowhere is it more evident than in religion. What started as a basic and humble belief in Creation and the God of Creation has been changed and manipulated to preserve the organisations and societies who want to set down a creed for all, but it isn't the creed of the oral tradition, it is the creed decided upon by a group of people intent on perpetrating their own self interest. They have made a set of rules to suit themselves, irrespective of the oral tradition and truth, and anyone who deviated was branded a heretic or non-believer.

It is time to shift the focus from religion to spirituality, which may be defined as 'experiences of the sacred', while religion means 'orthodox concepts (often rigidly enforced) about the sacred'.

The original meaning of religion was 'that which binds together', and catholic supposedly means 'universal'. But we must question the value of bonds that have served to divide human beings from one another and also from the natural world.

We need to promote a new beginning in the relationship between Christians, Jews and Muslims, and indeed all faiths. We can find support for this in our shared story of beginnings rather than in the divisive and more recent interpretation concerning our endings which focus on who will be the most blessed at the end of time. For the people who first told the creation stories the' end of time' was the living beginning.

Judaism, Christianity and Islam all agree that 'In the beginning, God...' They disagree at the level of 'I believe'. Why therefore, in relations with each other, can we not return to the beginning instead of emphasising doctrinal differences? The latter only reinforce the egotistical side of human nature, against which all the traditions of these religions speak.

THE WAY AHEAD

I believe that all the emphasis should now be on spiritual or shared beginnings and the common Creation story. Let us remember that:

- Shared beginnings unite all religions.
- Ideas about endings and who was, is or will be the most blessed divide religions.

The misplaced focus on endings, or the end over the meaning, misappropriates the original story in which all of the Creation traditions stress that the final outcome is to reunite with the Holy One, who was responsible for the beginning.

I have discovered that the way forward for me is the way back, to relive the Creation story that is common to all religions; a recognition or realisation that there is something in the universe greater than human intellect and ego.

According to the original stories, looking ahead was looking to the beginning. Our ideal future is not something that we haven't seen before; it is the divine image that was with each one of us at the beginning of time.

METANOIA

Metanoia is a Greek word meaning a change of mind, a radical revision and transformation of our whole mental process. That change of mind is something whereby God takes a central place in our consciousness, in our awareness and in our minds. In this world we really need metanoia, to allow the grace of God to enter our lives and teach us how to see ourselves and how to come to the true self.

Gospel of Thomas Logo 5: Jesus said 'Know him who is before your face and what is hidden from you, shall be revealed to you, for there is nothing hidden that shall not be manifest'. In essence this means 'If you know what you are seeking, all will be revealed and nothing will be hidden'.

The revelation of spiritual truth comes about through seeking with the assurance of finding.

The disciples could see the Master with their bodily eyes, but would need to use their inner eyes to know him. We must strive to get the inner eye working to find the true self, spiritual truth in oneness.

FINALLY...

As I stated at the beginning of this quest, I have read many books and articles by a variety of authors ranging from archaeologists, historians, academics and researchers to fiction writers. They emanate from many different backgrounds and upbringings and include atheists, Christians, Jews, Muslims, Gnostics, Sufis, Buddhists, Hindus and other persuasions. Between them they have studied many of the ancient languages, Aramaic, Coptic, Hebrew and Greek, together with various regional dialects.

What you have read so far then has been extracts from many of these books and pamphlets, which I have selected and in many cases added to, or amended, to include my own thoughts in order to provide me with an insight to what Creation and belief in God is really all about. In many circumstances my selections are provocative; they will not be to everybody's liking. But then it is not meant to be, as this is my personal quest.

The simple and basic truths are relevant for us all today and always have been, ever since we became human. They have been discussed, developed, passed on, argued over. Finally, when we were able to do so, they were written down and recorded from oral traditions to become the basis of the books of our religions. These ancient views are fully on view in the Bible, the Koran, the Mahabharata, the Vedas, the Upanishads and any number of other ancient texts.

Times have changed from our original simple beliefs and truths. Language has changed. The huge, dominating, empire-building religious institutions have changed the scenario completely. In many ways they have stamped out and suppressed the original truths and replaced them with a narrow-minded literalism and doctrine which they have introduced along with a fear factor to control humanity.

They justify their own existence by their actions. They have deemed it acceptable to destroy millions of people who have not toed the party line. Nearly all wars are religious wars, fought in the name of differing religious beliefs and practices. The problem of religious conflict in the world continues; even now there are many in the Middle East who fear that the western world is still waging a crusade. When talking of the response to 9/11, President Bush spoke of waging a crusade against bombers and fanatics. All this did was to provide Osama Bin Laden with fuel to wage his hate campaign, using the original crusades as a theme.

Perhaps the quest has taught me that there are religious people and there are spiritual people, and sometimes we come across special people who are, or have been, both. To me the difference is simple:

Religious people believe that God is in Heaven; spiritual people believe that God is with us.

Religious people believe they will only enter heaven when they die; spiritual people know that the Kingdom of God is within them.

Religious people believe that God's love is conditional and that we must follow certain faiths and creeds to reach it; spiritual people know that God's love is with us now and that it is unconditional and eternal.

Through the religious institutions, the world has become religious at the expense of the spiritual. These institutions have introduced us to Hell as a literal place to go if we do not comply. The Pope will excommunicate us, a Holy was or Jihad will be waged against us if we do not agree. But where is the balance? Where is the compassion? This is certainly not spiritual.

Many of the religions and beliefs I have studied and read about still exist today; many have been lost through wars and persecution. It is not difficult now for me to accept that many of these have a similar basic belief in God. Those that no longer exist have been victims of history. The strongest calls the tune, the weakest are either enveloped or die. The Roman Empire was founded on this principle, for the lost religious persuasions were in essence spiritual in their belief, which ultimately caused their downfall.

MY CONCLUSION

History, as we all know, is written by the victors. It is not necessarily an expression of fact; it is a compilation of documented record. By its very nature, it does not amount to proof of anything but constitutes written accounts of past characters and events. The content of the Bible is not in itself a proof of its inherent fact, but it is documentary evidence of what its writers believed to be true at the time. The same can be said of all other chronicles, annals and books of historical record.

What we do know for a fact is that the currently accessible records of history are the only records we have. Whether or not we elect to believe them is a matter of personal choice. Only enforced dogmatism does not. Whether presented as hard or circumstantial evidence, history is always open to interpretation, and clearly its authors are not consistently objective. Just as in modern news reporting, there have always been personal, national, social, political or religious opinions to consider.

I cannot accept the views of that well-known atheist Sir David Attenborough and believe that all life on Earth has evolved over millions of years and in millions of forms and that what we human beings are today is the result of natural selection. I do believe in some form of evolution among species but feel that we, the human race, have had some guidance, assistance or whatever from some unseen indeterminable force which has guided our development into what we are today. It is that force, that unknown intelligence or being that is represented by one word - GOD. God created man as we know him.

So at long last, my quest is finally over. So what have I learned? What do I really believe in? Where do I stand?

One thing then is absolutely certain - my belief in God and Creation has been greatly strengthened. If it was ever in doubt it certainly is not now that my quest has been fulfilled.

There is wisdom in the original oral traditions and texts. We must ignore the literal interpretations of the large religious institutions and listen to our own selves. The old texts were written at different times and by different people, who had their own desires and compassions. They developed ways of dealing with desire and compassion and had a better, more enlightened way to exist.

As we study the teachings of the prophets we seek to achieve the enlightenment they say we can share with them - the inner belief, the perfect state - we will realise that there is much more to life than material goods. We will understand that we are at one with the universe around us, we are part of that greater whole. This is the truth that our ancestors realised and passed on. We must not allow hatred and intolerance to take it away from us. We must become enlightened.

God is in every detail of our lives, guiding us into the infinite reality in which we were created and still remain. What better way to explain this than by quoting Ecclesiastes 3.

1. *To everything there is a season, and a time for every purpose under the sun:*
2. *A time to be born and a time to die; a time to plant and a time to pluck up that which is planted;*
3. *A time to kill and a time to heal; a time to tear down and a time to build up;*
4. *A time to weep and a time to laugh; a time to mourn and a time to dance;*
5. *A time to cast away stones and a time to gather stones together; a time to embrace and a time to refrain from embracing;*
6. *A time to lose and time to seek; a time to tie up and a time to untie;*
7. *A time to rend and a time to sew; a time to keep silent and a time to speak*
8. *A time to love and a time to hate; a time for war and a time for peace;*
9. *What profit has the worker in his labour?*
10. *I have seen the toil which the Lord has given to the sons of men to be engaged therewith.*
11. *He has made everything beautiful in his time; also he has made the world dear to man's heart. So that no man can find out the works which the Lord has done from the beginning to the end.*
12. *I know that there is no good in worldly things, but for men to rejoice and to do good in their lives.*
13. *And also that every man should eat, drink and enjoy the good of all his labour; it is the gift of the Lord.*

14. *I know that whatsoever the Lord does, it shall be for ever; nothing can be added to it and nothing taken from it; and the Lord has so made it that man should reverence him.*

In his book *Christian Beginnings* Gezar Vermes observes:

It is impossible to ignore the colossal difference between the Christ concept Nicaea and the Christology that preceded the council. The idea of consubstantiality never occurred to any of the leading representatives of Christianity prior to 325AD; it would have indeed sounded anathema. By contrast, after 325AD the claim of inequality before Father and Son amounted to heresy. After that surprising doctrinal volte-face, membership of the church primarily depended on adherence to the Nicene Creed. Intellectual assent to dogma gained precedence over the heart's openness to charisma urged by the historical Jesus.

At the end of this journey those readers who wonder where they now stand should remember that in the 16th century the rediscovery by Renaissance scholars of the ancient sources of classical civilisation forced Christians to return to the Bible for a revitalisation and purification of their faith. This revolution first created Protestantism, but subsequently spread over the whole spectrum of the churches. It would seem that by now it has reached, or will soon reach, a stage when a fresh revival will be called for, a new reformation, zealous to reach back to the pure religious vision and enthusiasm of Jesus, the Jewish charismatic messenger of God, and not to the deifying message, Paul, John and the church attributed to him.

WHAT NEXT?

There are many paths to God and our forefathers knew this; Jesus taught it. It is up to each and every one of us to find our own path to God, and this can be achieved by finding and recognising the true selves within us. It is through God and by God that we came into this world and it is by God and through God that we will return whence we came.

At last my quest is over. My mind is at rest. My faith is secure. At some time in the future I will return to God my Creator. What has become extremely important to me is that 'religion' must not interfere with my belief in the historical Jesus. For me Jesus is my guide on that journey of enlightenment; not the Jesus (Christ) as proclaimed by the Church but the Jesus of history that I know, who had communion with God and who tried to teach us all how to make that connection.

I am what I am.
I believe in God and the creation.

A PERSONAL CREED

I believe in one God
Our Father, the Almighty
Who made this earth we live on
And is the creator of all things
Both visible and invisible.

I give thanks to Him for my birth

That I was made in His likeness
That He, the giver and maker of all life
Is with me and within me now and always
That His creation is ongoing.

Through Jesus I search for the knowledge,
Faith and ability to communicate with God
Who is both my Creator and Father
To find the true self which is part of me
Now and shall be ever more.

I pray to God to banish all ego within me
So that finally I may return to that state of creation
From which I arrived on earth
Free from sin and all other and all forms of temptation
Pure and unsullied.

In the name of Our Father and Creator
Amen.

BIBLIOGRAPHY

Acharra S	The Christ Conspiracy
Alford Alan	When the Gods came down
Al-Khalili Jim	The Path Finders
Anderson J N	The Evidence for the Resurrection
Andrews Richard /Schellenberger Paul	The Tomb of God
Armstrong Karen	Then Great Transformation
Armstrong Karen	The Bible. The Biography
Armstrong Karen	A History of God
Armstrong Karen	Muhammad
Armstrong Karen	The Case for God
Bach Richard	Illusions
Bach Richard	Jonathan Livingston Seagull
Baigent Michael	Ancient Traces
Baigent Michael	The Jesus Papers
Baigent Michael Leigh Richard	The Dead Sea Scrolls Deception
Baigent Michael Leigh Richard Lincoln Henry	The Holy Blood and The Holy Grail
Baigent Michael Leigh Richard Lincoln Henry	The Messianic Legacy
Barber Malcolm	The Trial of the Templars
Barclay William	The Gospels and Acts
Barnes Ian	Mapping History of World Religions
Bauval Robert	The Egypt Code
Bauval Robert Adrian Gilbert	The Orion Mystery
Bauval Robert/ Hancock Graham	Keeper of Genesis

Berry Adrian	Gallileo and the Dolphins
Black Jonathan	The Secret History of the World
Blake Peter/Blezard Paul	The Arcadian Cypher
Blake Timothy/Gandy Peter	Jesus and the Goddess
Blake Timothy/Gandy Peter	The Jesus Mysteries
Blanchard John	Is God past His sell-by date?
Bloom Harold	Jesus and Yahweh
Bowden J	Christianity - The Complete Guide
Boyers J	Beyond the Final Whistle
Bradley Michael	The Secret Societies Handbook
Brown Dan	Angels and Demons
Brown Dan	The Lost Symbol
Brown Dan	The Davinci Code
Bruce F F	The Books and the Parchments
Bruce F F	The New Testament Documents
Burr Aubrey	Gods Heretics
Burstein Dan	Secrets of the Code
Butler Alan	The Goddess The Grail and The Lodge
Cadbury Deborah	The Dinosaur Hunters
Chaplin Patrice	The City of Secrets
Churton Tobias	Invisibles - The History of the Rosicrucians
Churton Tobias	Kiss of Death - The Gospel of Judas
Churton Tobias	The Missing Family of Jesus
Collins Andrew	From The Ashes of Angels
Copenhaver Brian. P.	Hermetica
Cotterell Arthur	The Encyclopoedia of Mythology
Cox Simon	Cracking the Davinci Code
Crotty Robert	The Good News in Mark
Dart John	Decoding Mark
Davies Stevan	The Gospel of Thomas

Davis Claire Henderson	After the Church
De Belzac Honore	The Gospel of the Holy Twelve
Delmar Duane Darrah	The History and Evolution of Freemasonry
Deviar Jamie	The Secret Unlocked
Douzet Andre	Saunieres Model and the Secret of Rennes-Le-Chateau
Ehrman Bart	Loist Christianities
Ehrman Bart	Jesus, Interrupted
Einhorn Lena	The Jesus Mystery
Eisenman Robert	The New Testament Code
Fanthorpe Lionel & Patricia	Mysteries of Templar and Treasure & The Holy Grail
Faulkner Neil	Apocalypse
Feather Robert	The Secret Initiation of Jesus at Qumran
Freke Timothy/Gandy Peter	Jesus and the Goddess
Freke Timothy/Gandy Peter	The Jesus Mysteries
Frye Northrop	The Great Code
Gardner Laurence	The Shadow of Solomon
Gardner Laurence	Genesis of the Grail Kings
Gardner Laurence	The Magdalene Legacy
Gardner Laurence	The Grail Enigma
Gardner Laurence	Lost Secrets of the Sacred Ark
Gardiner Philip	The Ark The Shroud and Mary
Gardiner Philip	The Shining Ones
Gardiner Philip	Gnosis
Gest Kevin	The Secrets of Solomon's Temple
Gest Kevin	The Secrets of the Holy Grail
Gibran Khalil	The Prophet
Haag Michael & Veronica	The Rough Guide to The Davinci Code
Hancock Graham	The Sign of the Seal
Hancock Graham	Finger Prints of the Gods

Hanson Kenneth	Secrets from the Lost Bible
Hancock Graham/Bauval Robert	Talisman
Hargreaves Cecil	The Gospels in a Word Context
Harvey Andrew/Baring Anne	The Mystic Vision
Hassnain Fida/Levi Dahan	The Fifth Gospel
Higginbotham Joyce & River	Christo Paganism
Hill J Hamlyn	The Earliest Life of Christ
Holmes Marjorie	I've got to talk to somebody God
Hyslop & others	The Resurrection Historical & True
Ind Right Rev Bill	With God we can
The Israel Museum Jerusalem	Cradle of Christianity
Jackson Keven & Stamp Jonathan	Pyramid
Jacobs Alan	The Essentual Gnostic Gospels
Kasser Meyer and Wurst	The Gospel of Judas
Kenyon J. Douglas	Forbidden History
Khan Hazrat Inayat	The Sufi Message
Khayyam Omar	The Rubaiyat
Khoury Raymond	The Last Templar
Kingsley Sean	God's Gold
Kinsler Clysta	Mary Magdalene Beloved Disciple
Klotz Neil Douglas	Desert Wisdom
Klotz Neil Douglas	The Hidden Gospel
Klotz Neil Douglas	Prayers of the Cosmos
Klotz Neil Douglas	The Genesis Meditations
Knight Christopher/Lomas Robert	The Hiram Key Revisited
Knight Christopher/Lomas Robert	Uriels Machine
Knight Christopher/Lomas Robert	The Second Messiah
Knight Christopher/Butler Alan	Solomon's Power Brokers
Knight Christopher/Lomas Robert	The Book of Hiram
Krosney Herbert	The Lost Gospel(of Judas Iscariot)

Ladurie Emmanuel/Le Roy	Montaillou
Laird Martin	Into the Silent Land
Lawton Ian	Genesis unveiled
Lawton Ian/Ogilvie/Herald Chris	Giza the Truth
Leloup Jean-Yves	The Gospel of Mary Magdalene
Leloup Jean-Yves	The Gospel of Philip
Lester Meera	Mary Magdalene
Lincoln Henry	The Holy Place
Lomas Robert	Turning the Templar Key
Lomas Robert	Turning the Hiram Key
Lomas Robert	The Secrets of Freemasonry
Lomas Robert	The Invisible College
Ludeman Gerd	The Great Deception
Lunn Martin	Davinci Code Decoded
Macculloch Diarmaid	Groundwork of Christian History
Magness Jodi	The Archaeology of Qumran and The Dead Sea Scrolls
McKnight Scott	The Story of the Christ
Meyer Marvin	The Gnostic Discoveries
Meyer Marvin	The Secret Gospel of Jesus
Michell John	The Temple of Jerusalem
Middleton J.R./Walsh B.J.	Truth is stranger than it used to be
Miller Hamish/Paul Broadhurst	The Sun and the Serpent
Mitton C Leslie	Jesus the fact behind the faith
Morison Frank	Who moved the Stone
Morton Chris/Thomas Ceri Louise	The Mystery of the Crystal Skulls
Newman Sharran	The Real History behind the Davinci Code
Oxbrow Mara/Ian Robertson	Rosslyn and the Grail
Pagels Elaine	Beyond Belief
Pagels Elaine	The Gnostic Gospels

Perrin Norman	The Resurrection Narratives
Peters F E	The Voice, the Word, the Books
Phillips Graham	The End of Eden
Phillips Graham	Act of God
Phillips Graham	The Marian Conspiracy
Phillips Graham	The Templars and the Ark of the Covenant
Phillips Graham/ Picknett Lynn/Prince Clive	The Templar Revelation
Picknett Lynn	Mary Magdalene
Picknett Lynn/Prince Clive	The Templar Revelation
Picknett Lynn/Prince Clive	The Sion Revelation
Picknett Lynn/Prince Clive	The Masks of Christ
Picknett Lynn/Prince Clive	Revelation
Polkinhorne John	Belief in God in a Age of Science
Porter J R	The Forgotten Bible
Prabhupada Swami	The Journey of Self Discovery
Puttnam Bill/ Wood John Edwin	The Treasure of Rennes le Chateau
Ridge Milan	Jesus The Unauthorised version
Robinson James M	The Secrets of Judas
Rohl David	The Lost Testament
Rohl David	Legend
Ross Hugh McGregor	Thirty Essays on the Gospel of Thomas
Ross Hugh McGregor	The Gospel of Thomas
Seward Desmond	The Monks of War
Shugarts David	Secrets of the Widows Son
Silverman David	Ancient Egypt
Simmans Graham	Jeus after the Crucifixion
Simon Bernard	The Essence of the Gnostics
Sinclair Andrew	The Sword and the Grail

Sinclair Andrew	The Secret Scroll
Smart Ninian & Alcht Richard	The Sacred Texts of the World
Smith Morton	The Secret Gospel
Smoot George Keay Davidson	Wrinkles in Time
Stanford Peter	Religion
Stark Rodney	One True God
Stevenson David	The Origins of Freemasonry
Stewart Bob/John Matthews	Legendary Britain
Strauss D F	The Life of Jesus critically examined
Tabor James D	The Jesus Dynasty
Thiede Carsten/ Matthew D'Ancona	The Jesus Papyrus
Thomas Ceri Lovisc	The Mystery of the Crystal Skulls
Tywman James E	The Moses Code
Valantasis Richard	The New Q
Vermes Geza	Christian Beginnings
Vermes Geza	The Dead Sea Scrolls
Vermes Geza	The Changing Faces of Jesus
Vermes Geza	The Authentic Gospel of Jesus
Wallace/Murphy Tim	Cracking the Symbol Code
Welburn Andrew	The Beginning of Christianity
Whyte Jack	Knights of the Black & White
Wilkerson David	The Cross & The Switchblade
Williams Archbishop Rowan & Sister Wendy Beckett	Living the Lords Prayer
Wills Garry	What Paul Meant
Wilson Ian	The Turin Shroud
Wilson Ian	The Evidence of the Shroud
Wilson Ian	Jesus the Evidence

Wippler Migene Gonzalez	Jesus and the mystic Kabbalah
Wippler Migene Gonzalez	The keys to the Kingdom
Wood David	Genesis the First book of Revelations
Periodical magazine	Freemasonry Today
Christianity the Complete Guide	
The Bible	
The Book of Kells	
The Diatessaron of Tatian???	
The Gnostic Gospels	
The Good News of Mark	
The Koran	
The Peshitta Bible	
The Treasure of Tutankhamun	